Frommer's

Best Day Trips from London

25 Great Escapes by Train, Bus, or Car

1st Edition

by Stephen Brewer & Donald Olson

Wiley Publishing, Inc.

Published by:

Wiley Publishing, Inc.
111 River St.
Hoboken, NJ 07030-5774

ISBN 0-7645-4321-0

Interior design contributed to by Melissa Auciello-Brogan

Editor: Christine Ryan
Production Editor: Suzanna R. Thompson
Cartographer: John Decamillis
Photo Editor: Richard Fox
Production by Wiley Indianapolis Composition Services

Front cover photo: Punting along the River Cam, Cambridge. Inset: Stonehenge.

For information on our other products and services or to obtain technical support, please contact our Customer Care Department within the U.S. at 800/762-2974, outside the U.S. at 317/572-3993 or fax 317/572-4002.

Wiley also publishes its books in a variety of electronic formats. Some content that appears in print may not be available in electronic formats.

Manufactured in the United States of America

5 4 3 2 1

Contents

List of Maps

An Invitation to the Reader

In researching this book, we discovered many wonderful places—hotels, restaurants, shops, and more. We're sure you'll find others. Please tell us about them, so we can share the information with your fellow travelers in upcoming editions. If you were disappointed with a recommendation, we'd love to know that, too. Please write to:

Best Day Trips from London, 1st Edition
Wiley Publishing, Inc. • 111 River St. • Hoboken, NJ 07030-5774

An Additional Note

Please be advised that travel information is subject to change at any time—and this is especially true of prices. We therefore suggest that you write or call ahead for confirmation when making your travel plans. The authors, editors, and publisher cannot be held responsible for the experiences of readers while traveling. Your safety is important to us, however, so we encourage you to stay alert and be aware of your surroundings. Keep a close eye on cameras, purses, and wallets, all favorite targets of thieves and pickpockets.

About the Authors

Stephen Brewer (trips 1, 4, 6, 10, 12–17, 20, and 21) is the author of *The Unofficial Guide to England,* soon to be published by Wiley. He has written about Italy, Greece, and other parts of the world for Frommer's and many other guidebooks and magazines, and he has never failed to be amazed by all the wonderful places to enjoy on easy day trips from London.

Donald Olson ("The Best Day Trip Experiences," "Planning Your Day Trips," and trips 2, 3, 5, 7–9, 11, 18, 19, and 22–25) is a novelist, playwright, and travel writer. His sixth novel, *My Three Husbands* (written under the nom de plume Swan Adamson), was published in 2003. *Oregon Ghosts,* his play based on Oregon's legendary spirits, premiered in Portland in 2003. His plays have also been produced in London, New York, Amsterdam, and Rotterdam. Donald Olson's travel stories have appeared in the *New York Times, Travel & Leisure, Sunset,* National Geographic guides, and many other national publications. He is the author of *London For Dummies, Germany For Dummies,* and *England For Dummies,* which won the 2002 Lowell Thomas Travel Writing Award for "Best Guidebook."

Frommer's Icons & Abbreviations

In this guidebook, we use **five feature icons** that point you to the in-the-know advice and unique experiences that separate travelers from tourists. Throughout the book, look for:

Finds	Special finds—those places only insiders know about
Fun Fact	Fun facts—details that make travelers more informed and their trips more fun
Kids	Best bets for kids, and advice for the whole family
Moments	Special moments—those experiences that memories are made of
Tips	Insider tips—great ways to save time and money

The following **abbreviations** are used for credit cards:

AE	American Express	DISC	Discover	V	Visa
DC	Diners Club	MC	MasterCard		

Frommers.com

Now that you have the guidebook to a great trip, visit our website at **www.frommers.com** for travel information on more than 3,000 destinations. With features updated regularly, we give you instant access to the most current trip-planning information available. At Frommers.com, you'll also find the best prices on airfares, accommodations, and car rentals—and you can even book travel online through our travel booking partners. At Frommers.com, you'll also find the following:

- Online updates to our most popular guidebooks
- Vacation sweepstakes and contest giveaways
- Newsletter highlighting the hottest travel trends
- Online travel message boards with featured travel discussions

The Best Day-Trip Experiences

Excuse us while we drag out those wise and oft-quoted words from Samuel Johnson yet again. You know the ones: When you grow tired of London you've grown tired of life.

Well, they're true. In all our years of traveling, we've never grown tired of London, and we doubt that you will ever tire of it, either. On the contrary, London rewards the repeat visitor with an inexhaustible array of things to see and do. The countless treasures in its museums, the centuries of history in its landmarks, the energy and innovativeness of its arts and culture scene, and the slices of British life glimpsed on the streets all increase your yearning to return and explore more of this fascinating city.

But we're here to tell you that a trip to London can include more diverse sights and scenery than you ever thought possible. In a small country like England, historic castles, picture-perfect villages, ancient cathedrals, and unforgettable landscapes are often no more than an hour away—close enough for you to easily visit as part of your London itinerary.

You may be surprised to discover just how much of England you can explore using London as a base. That is what this book is all about. We've rounded up our 25 favorite places in England that you can visit on easy day trips from London. Quite simply, these are some of the most remarkable palaces, towns, gardens, cathedrals, and other sights in all the land. You can reach them all by train, bus, or car; enjoy a day's outing in a fascinating place; and be back in the capital in time for dinner and a play. Some of our day trips are only 20 minutes away from central London and can be reached by the London Underground. The farthest, York, is 195 miles (314km) to the north but you can get there in 2 hours on a fast intercity train.

DAY TRIPS MADE EASY

When time is limited, it's more important than ever to have accurate, reliable travel information, so we've provided you with all the details you need to venture forth on some wonderful adventures.

For each day-trip destination, we tell you how to get there, how long the journey takes, and what it costs. We provide you with all the practical information you need to know, such as admission fees and opening hours. We suggest a day's itinerary and plot it all out on a map for you. In addition, we give you tips on dining and shopping and other "insider" details to help you get the most out of your day away from London. We want to make sure that you don't miss the Tiepolo painting in Leeds Castle, that you visit Sissinghurst Gardens at a time when you can enjoy them without a crowd, that you follow the best walking route when exploring the ancient town of Rye.

In "Planning Your Day Trips," you'll find general information on traveling in and out of London by train, bus, or car, including special bargain passes that will bring down the cost of your day trips. Following that, we devote a short chapter to each of our 25 recommended day-trip destinations.

There are a lot of trips to choose from, and each one is intriguing in its own way. All of them are worth a day of your time. What are your interests? Would you like to visit Monk's House, Virginia Woolf's

England

0 50 mi
0 50 km
N
Inverness
Peterhead
Loch Ness
Spey
Don
Mallaig
Aviemore
Dee
Aberdeen
Ben Nevis
GRAMPIAN MTS.
Montrose
Tay
Dundee
Oban
Perth
Firth of Forth
Forth
Edinburgh
Berwick-upon-Tweed
Glasgow
SCOTLAND
NORTH SEA
Clyde
Tweed
Ayr
The Cheviot
Arran
Moffat
Nith
CHEVIOT HILLS
Alnwick
Newton Stewart
Gatehouse of Fleet
Tyne
Carlisle
Durham
Stranraer
Kirkcudbright
Belfast
Penrith
LAKE DISTRICT
Middlesbrough
NORTHERN IRELAND
Isle of Man
Swale
Ambleside
Douglas
York
Leeds
Kingston upon Hull
Preston
Irish Sea
Liverpool
Manchester
Bakewell
Bangor
ENGLAND
Caernarfon Bay
Snowdon
Trent
Derby
Nottingham
Caernarfon
Norwich
Wolverhampton
Cardigan Bay
WALES
Birmingham
Stratford-upon-Avon
Aberystwyth
Severn
Cambridge
Northampton
Wye
COTSWOLD HILLS
Ipswich
Cardigan
St. Alban's
Cheltenham
Moreton-in-Marsh
Colchester
Gloucester
Oxford
Hampstead
Swansea
Cardiff
London
Reading
Windsor
Thames
Bristol Channel
Bristol
Bath
Sevenoaks
Canterbury
Ilfracombe
Staplehurst
Dover
Salisbury
Lewes
Rye
Southampton
Bude
Brighton
Battle
Exeter
Bournemouth
Isle of Wight
DARTMOOR
Plymouth
Lyme Bay
English Channel
CHANNEL ISLANDS
Guernsey
Jersey
FRANCE

country retreat near the Sussex Downs? Walk down the time-hallowed nave of 800-year-old Canterbury Cathedral? Stroll through a charming Cotswolds village where the cottages are built of honey-colored stone? Explore enormous Windsor Castle, the queen's favorite royal residence?

To get you started, we've listed below the many surprising places you can discover on day trips from London. Your biggest difficulty will be narrowing down the list and coming to terms with the fact that you don't have time to visit each and every one of these places. Take heart, though: You'll have more opportunities to visit these places on your many return trips to London. As another saying goes, "There will always be an England."

1 The Best Castles & Palaces

- **Brighton Royal Pavilion:** The Royal Pavilion in Brighton is one of the most flamboyant royal residences you'll ever see. Designed for the fun-loving prince regent (later George IV), who lived here with his mistress until 1827, it's an extravagant fantasy of turrets, minarets, and Chinese motifs. See p. 54.
- **Dover Castle:** The so-called "Key to England" has stood guard over the English Channel since Roman times. The 70-acre (28-hectare) fortification atop the famous White Cliffs has an ancient lighthouse, medieval tunnels, and even a secret underground compound to show for its important role in British history. See trip 6.
- **Hampton Court:** Henry VIII nabbed Hampton Court from its builder, Cardinal Wolsey, and turned it into a royal residence, which it remained until 1737. This enormous palace is glorious fun to explore, with rooms and kitchens dating back to Henry's Tudor times and separate suites designed by Christopher Wren for William and Mary in the early 18th century. See trip 9.
- **Hever Castle:** This vision of crenellations and turrets, surrounded by a moat, fits anyone's notion of what a medieval castle should look like. The fact that Anne Boleyn, wife of Henry VIII, grew up at Hever gives the place historical clout, and former tenant William Waldorf Astor, the American millionaire, added acres of luxurious gardens. See trip 10.
- **Knole:** Knole is officially a "house" rather than a "palace," but with 365 rooms and a courtyard for every day of the week, we think this perfectly intact 15th-century treasure qualifies as the latter. As you explore room after room filled with rare furnishings

and textiles and fine paintings, you'll see why Virginia Woolf, who set her novel *Orlando* here, described Knole as a "town rather than a house." See trip 12.

- **Warwick Castle:** Thousand-year-old Warwick Castle, easily accessible from Stratford-upon-Avon (and described in our Stratford day trip), is one of the most popular tourist attractions in England. It features lavishly furnished rooms peopled with historic figures created by the wax experts at Madame Tussaud's, plus a real dungeon and lots of intriguing side attractions. See p. 203.
- **Windsor Castle:** You've no doubt heard of Windsor Castle—it's one of the queen's three royal residences. Now about 900 years old, Windsor is the largest inhabited castle in the world and has its own Changing of the Guard ceremony. On a self-guided tour of the State Apartments you can visit the intimate chambers of Charles II and the enormous Waterloo Chamber, built to commemorate the victory over Napoleon in 1815. See p. 219.

2 The Best Cathedrals & Churches

- **Canterbury:** The first Gothic cathedral in England, Canterbury traces its history back to the arrival of St. Augustine in the 6th century. It became such a famous place of pilgrimage in the Middle Ages that Geoffrey Chaucer was inspired to write *The Canterbury Tales* about a group of Canterbury-bound pilgrims. It's an awe-inspiring sight inside and out. See p. 73.
- **King's College Chapel, Cambridge:** When you visit the most beautiful of the university's many churches and chapels, you may be lucky enough to hear the acclaimed King's Chapel Choir sing in a stunning setting embellished with a magnificent ceiling of carved stone and an altarpiece by Peter Paul Rubens. See p. 63.
- **St. Albans:** St. Albans wasn't officially made a cathedral until 1877, but it had been in existence hundreds of years before that. This venerable church has its roots in Anglo-Roman history, for it was built near the site where Roman soldiers executed Alban, considered the first English martyr. Like Canterbury, St. Albans was a medieval mecca, drawing pilgrims to the shrine of St. Alban, which you can still see. See p. 178.
- **Salisbury:** Built in the 13th century in record time, just 38 years, Salisbury Cathedral is a soaring masterpiece of Gothic architecture. The edifice is topped by England's tallest spire. In the Chapter House are two national treasures: a copy of the Magna Carta

and a beautifully preserved medieval stone frieze depicting stories from the Old Testament. See p. 187.

- **Winchester:** Before the Norman Conquest of 1066, Winchester was the capital of Anglo-Saxon Wessex and was more important than London. That importance is reflected in mighty Winchester Cathedral, one of the glories of England. Begun in 1079, it has the longest nave in Europe and is the repository of many historic treasures. See p. 211.

- **York:** York Minster is the largest Gothic structure north of the Alps, and one of the most beautiful cathedrals in the world. Over half of all the medieval stained glass in England is found in this cathedral, built between 1220 and 1472. Beneath the cathedral is a fascinating archaeological excavation of 2,000-year-old Roman remains. See p. 227.

3 The Best Literary Sites

- **Hampstead:** The poet John Keats lived for 2 years of his short life in a charming house in Hampstead, where he wrote "Ode to a Nightingale" and fell in love with his neighbor's daughter. Open to the public, the Keats House is one of several fascinating homes you can visit in Hampstead. See trip 8.

- **Monk's House:** The novelist Virginia Woolf and her husband Leonard Woolf often retreated from their home in London's Bloomsbury to this simple house and garden in Sussex, near the town of Lewes. Here they entertained the writers, artists, and intellectuals who formed the "Bloomsbury Group." Virginia drowned herself in the nearby River Ouse in 1941. See trip 14.

- **Rochester:** The literary aura of Charles Dickens hangs over the quaint town center, where many of the houses that line the appealing streets will be familiar to you—Eastgate House appears in *Pickwick Papers,* and Restoration House became Miss Havisham's home in *Great Expectations.* Dickens's final home, Gad's Hill Place, is nearby. See trip 17.

- **Rye:** The charms of Rye, with its ancient cobbled streets, have seduced many a writer. The great American writer Henry James became a British citizen and moved to Lamb House in Rye. After his death, Lamb House became the home of E. F. Benson, author of the brilliantly funny *Mapp and Lucia* novels. The house is now a National Trust property. See trip 18.

- **Stratford-upon-Avon:** England's greatest playwright was born, lived much of his life, and died in this Warwickshire village. William Shakespeare is a hot commodity in Stratford, but even the commercialization doesn't diminish the awe of visiting the house where he was born and other places associated with his Stratford life. See trip 22.
- **Winchester:** The ever-popular author, Jane Austen, died in Winchester and is buried in Winchester Cathedral. Her house in the nearby village of Chawton, 17 miles (27km) from Winchester, is filled with Austen memorabilia. See trip 23.

4 The Best Day Trips for Families

- **Dover Castle:** England's mightiest fortress has just about anything a connoisseur of castles can dream of—a ring of walkable walls, a huge keep (complete with multimedia shows), dank dungeons, miles of secret tunnels, great views over the English Channel, and even a Roman lighthouse. See trip 6.
- **Hampton Court:** Hampton Court is huge, and the littlest kids won't be much interested, but older kids may get a kick out of the costumed guides who lead tours of the staterooms. And have the young ones take a look at the Tudor Kitchens, set up in preparation for a 16th-century feast. There's nary a microwave in sight. See trip 9.
- **Leeds Castle:** An incredible maze of 2,400 yew trees, a creepy grotto, a well-stocked aviary, beautiful grounds and gardens and, oh yes, a castle to tour will make Leeds a big hit with all members of the family. See trip 13.
- **Windsor:** The castle will probably be of less interest to kids than Queen Mary's dollhouse, an enchanting miniature palace complete down to the tiniest detail. But most of all, kids will have a blast at nearby Legoland, an adventure park with lots and lots of rides. See trip 24.
- **York:** There's something *Harry Potter*–magical about York, with its medieval walls and ancient streets and snickleways (alleys). The kids will love Jorvik Viking Centre, an attraction where you sit in "time capsules" and ride back to the Viking age. The scenes of village life are based on archaeological research, and even the faces of the animatronic inhabitants are modeled on Viking skulls. Kids also love the National Railway Museum, filled with historic trains and climb-aboard locomotives. See trip 25.

5 The Best Historic Sites

- **Bath:** British history comes alive in this elegant city, which traces its origins to the Romans and became a fashionable watering hole in the 18th century. The Roman baths are remarkably intact, and lining leafy squares and crescents are Georgian town houses of golden stone that are so well preserved that UNESCO has designated the entire city a World Heritage Site. See trip 1.
- **Battle:** Battle was the site of a battle that changed the course of English history. It was here, in 1066, that William of Normandy defeated King Harold of England and became the new king of England. Today you can walk on the very battlefield and hear the story of what happened—it's a real thrill for history lovers. See trip 2.
- **Canterbury:** Canterbury Cathedral is one of the most venerable and venerated buildings in England. Throughout the Middle Ages pilgrims flocked to the cathedral to pray at the shrine of Thomas Becket, archbishop of Canterbury, who was slain by henchmen of King Henry II. Becket's shrine is gone, but the cathedral remains, every stone vibrating with history. St. Augustine's Abbey, a short walk from the cathedral, is one of the oldest monastic sites in England, set up by Augustine in A.D. 598 when he was sent from Rome to convert the natives. Today these ancient, evocative ruins have been designated a World Heritage Site by UNESCO, as has Canterbury Cathedral. See trip 5.
- **St. Albans:** Back in the 1st century A.D., the town that is now St. Albans was a thriving Roman community called Verulamium. Within the walled city were temples, official buildings, town houses, even an amphitheatre. On a day trip to St. Albans, you can visit the excavated remains of the amphitheatre, the largest such structure from Roman Britain, and see an array of Roman mosaics and implements in the Verulamium Museum. See trip 19.
- **Stonehenge:** This circle of monolithic stones erected more than 4,000 years ago is one of the world's most alluring ancient sites. The debate over what purpose this massive landmark could have once served has raged for generations, but what really matters is the eerie beauty of the place and its rich evocation of societies long vanished. See p. 189.
- **Winchester:** In post-Roman, pre-Conquest England, this lovely Hampshire town was the capital of the kingdom of Wessex. The remains of a dozen Anglo-Saxon kings rest in mighty Winchester Cathedral. The town has associations with the mysterious King

Arthur, too: Arthur's "Round Table" has been displayed in the Great Hall of Winchester Castle for some 600 years. See trip 23.

- **Runnymede:** In this meadow 3 miles (4.8km) from Windsor (described in our Windsor day trip), King John was forced in 1215 to affix his seal to a document called the Magna Carta. The Magna Carta established the principle of the constitutional monarchy and affirmed the individual's right to justice and liberty. The American Constitution is based on the Magna Carta. See p. 221.
- **York:** This beautiful Yorkshire city, the best-preserved medieval city in England, is girdled by high walls. On a visit to York, you can walk along the circuit of walls where sentries once stood watch and traitors' heads were placed on spikes. Going back further in time, you can discover the Viking side of York at Jorvik Viking Centre, an attraction that re-creates the city's Viking past. Stepping back even further, in the galleries of the Yorkshire Museum you can see a wealth of artifacts from York's Roman period, dating back almost 2,000 years. See trip 25.

6 The Best Gardens

- **Hampton Court:** Hampton Court is a wonderland both inside and out. The gardens that surround the palace are a delightful mix of 500 years of royal gardening history. Marvel at the formal gardens with their symmetrically clipped trees, get lost in the famous Maze, and have a look at the Great Vine, the oldest grape-producing vine in the world. See trip 9.
- **Kew Gardens:** The official name is the Royal Botanic Gardens, but everyone calls them Kew Gardens. These 300 acres (120 hectares) of superbly landscaped grounds are within Greater London and can be reached on the Underground. Visiting Kew is like escaping into a gardener's dream. You'll find rare plants and gorgeous landscaping in dozens of separate garden areas and in the giant glasshouse conservatories. See trip 11.
- **Sissinghurst Castle Garden:** Now among the most famous gardens in the world, this evocative series of "outdoor rooms" planted amid the partially restored remains of a medieval castle and manor house are the creation of the poet and novelist Vita Sackville-West and her husband, the diplomat and writer Harold Nicolson. See trip 21.

7 The Best Trips for Museum-Lovers

- **Cambridge:** The **Fitzwilliam Museum,** one of Britain's most important art collections, includes stunning collections of antiquities, medieval illuminated manuscripts, and a surprisingly large number of masterworks by artists from van Dyck to Picasso. See p. 65.

- **Greenwich:** Greenwich, designated a World Heritage Site by UNESCO, is full of beautiful buildings and unusual museums. Explore the 19th-century clipper ship *Cutty Sark,* then step into the **National Maritime Museum** (p. 90) for a fascinating look at England's seafaring past. Next door you can enjoy the architectural and artistic delights of the **Queen's House** (p. 90), the first neoclassical building in England and used as a model for the White House. Afterwards, climb the hill in Greenwich Great Park to the **Old Royal Observatory** (p. 91), where you can see the collection of gleaming chronometers that helped mariners establish longitude at sea; right outside the observatory is the Prime Meridian Line (longitude 0°), from which all time is measured.
- **Hampstead:** Palatial **Kenwood House** (p. 96) on Hampstead Heath contains a marvelous collection of paintings, including a Rembrandt self-portrait and Vermeer's *The Guitar Player.* **Fenton House** (p. 95), another Hampstead treasure trove, contains a priceless collection of early keyboard instruments.
- **Hampton Court:** The palace is filled with artwork, but the most important paintings are on view in the **Lower Orangery** (p. 105). This is where you'll find a series called *The Triumphs of Caesar* painted by Andrea Mantegna and completed in 1505. The series is considered one of the most important works of the Italian Renaissance. Hampton Court's **Renaissance Picture Gallery** (p. 103) contains 16th- and early-17th-century works by Lucas Cranach, Pieter Brueghel, Correggio, Bronzino, Titian, and others.
- **Kew:** The **Royal Botanic Gardens** at Kew (called Kew Gardens) is a living museum of plants from around the world. Now over 250 years old, this 300-acre (120-hectare) site is so botanically important that UNESCO designated it a World Heritage Site. Wander the beautifully landscaped grounds and visit the extraordinary Victorian glasshouse conservatories. See trip 11.
- **Oxford:** A visit to the world-class **Ashmolean Museum** is a highlight of a visit to one of the world's most famous universities. Casts of the Parthenon frieze and other antiquities, Islamic pottery and Chinese ceramics, and such masterpieces as Paolo Uccello's *Hunt in the Forest* are among the treasures. See p. 157.
- **York:** York is filled with museums, but pride of place goes to the **National Railway Museum** (p. 229), where you can view the

private train cars used by Queen Victoria in the 19th century and Queen Elizabeth II in the 20th. The **York Castle Museum** (p. 228) uses a trove of now-vanished everyday objects to re-create slices of life over the past 4 centuries. **York City Art Gallery** (p. 229) displays 7 centuries of western European painting. The **Yorkshire Museum** (p. 229) provides a solid overview of Yorkshire's history from the Roman era up to the 16th century.

8 The Best Restaurants

- **Popjoy's** (Bath): The former town house of Julia Popjoy, longtime mistress of 18th-century dandy Beau Nash, is the colorful setting for Popjoy's—a lovely place to enjoy excellent modern British cuisine. See p. 44.
- **Terre à Terre** (Brighton): For a new take on vegetarian cuisine, try Terre à Terre in Brighton. If you're curious about meatless cuisine but put off by the same old same old vegetarian choices, this hip and popular restaurant will awaken your taste buds to new possibilities. See p. 57.
- **The Wells** (Hampstead): A new restaurant in an old Hampstead house, The Wells is a great place for lunch, dinner, or a drink. The decor is sleekly contemporary but very comfortable, and the food is simple and satisfying without a lot of culinary frills. You can eat in the restaurant or choose from a bar menu. See p. 98.
- **Shelleys** (Lewes): At Shelleys you can enjoy a gracious meal after reliving the lives of the Bloomsbury Group at nearby Monk's House and Charleston. In a handsome old country-house hotel, chef Tim Early serves innovative dishes that use local lamb, fish, and produce. See p. 142.
- **The Monastery** (Rye): The Monastery is one of Rye's best restaurants and serves up delicious English and Italian dishes. Try pan-fried venison, chicken breast stuffed with prawns, or pasta. See p. 173.

9 The Best Charming Villages

- **Hampstead:** Though it's now part of Greater London, Hampstead was once a separate village, and it retains a village character to this day. Its old leafy streets and quiet lanes are filled with charming nooks and crannies and a medley of Regency and Victorian homes. You can visit several historic Hampstead homes on your day trip. Walk into the adjacent parkland of Hampstead Heath and you're in the country. See trip 8.

- **Moreton-in-Marsh:** If you've come to England with a preconceived notion that Brits wear tweeds and live in charming stone cottages surrounded by green meadows, you'll be pleased to find yourself in this typical Cotswolds village. Plus, other charming villages are nearby, and the beautiful countryside may well lure you out for a long ramble. See trip 15.
- **Rye:** The spell of Rye is hard to resist. This ancient town in East Sussex, perched on a hilltop near the sea, is a delight to explore. With its cobblestone streets and amazing assemblage of historic buildings, it immediately wafts you back to an earlier age. See trip 18.

10 The Best Places to Spend More than a Day

- **Bath:** Let your imagination run wild in this perfectly preserved 18th-century city. Consider what it was like to be a Roman legionnaire soaking in the Roman Baths; pretend that Number 1, Royal Crescent, a Regency-era town house-cum-museum, is your address; picture yourself attending a ball in the Assembly Rooms. Come evening, you can dine well in any number of excellent restaurants and attend a performance at the 300-year-old Theater Royal, one of Britain's oldest working stages. See trip 1.
- **Brighton:** If you fancy a short stay at the seaside, you might want to consider an overnight stay in Brighton on the Sussex coast. England's most popular seaside resort is filled with charming B&Bs and hotels (including The Grand, a handsome Victorian right on the seafront), fine restaurants, and up-to-the-groove nightlife. See trip 3.
- **Moreton-in-Marsh:** If London life has you craving a bit of bucolic R & R, you can do no better than this Cotswolds village in one of the most picturesque corners of England. You'll enjoy Moreton and other charming villages, quaint inns, and beautiful countryside that is a pleasure to explore on foot. See trip 15.
- **Rye:** Once you see Rye, you'll probably want to extend your stay. There are plenty of hotels and B&Bs in historic buildings, including the Mermaid Inn, one of the oldest inns in England. The town is noted for its fine restaurants, many of which specialize in seafood. For some scary fun, you can rent a "Ghost Walk" audio tour and explore the ancient streets at night. See trip 18.

- **Salisbury:** You'll probably feel right at home in this prosperous British cathedral city, where a lively market is spread around the medieval Poultry Cross. The cathedral spire, the tallest in England, pierces a sky that's often full of scudding clouds. If the scene looks familiar, it's probably because John Constable painted it so often. You can easily spend a day or more seeing such sights as 18th-century Mompesson House and nearby Stonehenge, and you can also nip over to nearby Winchester (trip 23) to experience another wonderful cathedral city. See trip 20.
- **York:** The Queen of the North, as York is called, has so much to see and do that you may want to prolong your stay. In this medieval walled city you'll find any number of fine hotels and excellent restaurants, plus good shopping and 2 days' worth of sightseeing. See trip 25.

Planning Your Day Trips

London is fun, but so is a good day trip away from the crowded capital. Within an hour or two you can leave the congested confines of London behind and be in the middle of a beautiful, bucolic countryside; in a charming country town; or visiting a world-famous palace, castle, or garden. Our nearest day trip is only 20 minutes from central London by Underground (Hampstead). The farthest, York, is about 2 hours away by fast train.

This chapter is about getting around London and getting to your day-trip destination. In each of our 25 day-trip chapters we give you specific information to help you get to your chosen destination by train, bus, or car. Below you'll find more general information about each of these transportation options. Also, to help you decide on a day trip, we've included a chart listing various attractions and activities available at each destination (see below).

Day Trips at a Glance

	Biking	Boating/River Excursions	Country Walks	Castle or Palace	Church or Cathedral	Historical/Archaeological Sites	Gardens	Charming Town or Village	Families	Literary Sites	Museums	Overnight Options	
Bath	✓	✓			✓	✓	✓	✓	✓	✓	✓	✓	p. 36
Battle					✓	✓			✓		✓		p. 45
Brighton				✓		✓		✓	✓		✓	✓	p. 50
Cambridge	✓	✓			✓	✓		✓	✓		✓	✓	p. 59
Canterbury	✓	✓			✓	✓				✓	✓	✓	p. 69
Dover Castle			✓	✓		✓			✓				p. 79
Greenwich		✓				✓			✓		✓		p. 87
Hampstead			✓					✓		✓	✓		p. 93
Hampton Court		✓	✓	✓		✓	✓		✓		✓		p. 99
Hever Castle			✓	✓		✓	✓	✓					p. 107
Kew Gardens		✓					✓		✓				p. 114
Knole			✓	✓			✓		✓				p. 121
Leeds Castle				✓			✓	✓	✓				p. 128
Monk's House & Charleston							✓	✓		✓		✓	p. 135
Moreton-in-Marsh/ Cotswolds	✓		✓				✓	✓	✓			✓	p. 143
Oxford		✓	✓				✓	✓	✓	✓	✓	✓	p. 151
Rochester				✓	✓	✓			✓	✓	✓		p. 161
Rye	✓		✓		✓	✓		✓		✓		✓	p. 167
St. Albans	✓		✓		✓	✓	✓				✓		p. 175
Salisbury & Stonehenge			✓		✓	✓		✓	✓			✓	p. 182
Sissinghurst Castle Garden							✓			✓			p. 192
Stratford-upon-Avon		✓		✓		✓	✓			✓		✓	p. 198
Winchester					✓	✓		✓		✓	✓		p. 208
Windsor & Eton	✓	✓	✓	✓		✓	✓		✓				p. 216
York		✓	✓		✓	✓		✓	✓		✓	✓	p. 224

1 Getting Around London

This guidebook is not about London; it's about day trips from London. But because you may be traveling within London to get to a train or bus station for the start of your day trips, we've provided the basic information you need in order to get around London by subway (Underground), bus, and taxi.

For general London travel information, call **Transport for London** at © **020/7222-1234** (www.tfl.gov.uk). You can get free bus and Underground maps and buy Travelcards and bus passes (explained below) at any major Underground station or at the London Travel Information Centres in the stations at King's Cross, Liverpool Street, Oxford Circus, Piccadilly Circus, St. James's Park, Victoria, and Heathrow Terminals 1, 2, and 3.

THE LONDON UNDERGROUND

London has the oldest and most comprehensive subway system in the world, and all of the city's train stations can be reached by subway. So can three of our day trips: to Kew Gardens, Hampstead, and Greenwich.

The subway is called the Underground or the "Tube." Thirteen Underground lines crisscross the city and intersect at various stations where you can change from one train to the next. On Underground maps, every line is color-coded, which makes planning your route easy. (See the map printed on the inside back cover of this guide.) All you need to know are the name of your stop, the Underground lines that go there, and the direction you're heading. After you figure out which line(s) to take, look on the Underground map for the name of the last stop in the direction you need to go. The name of that last stop on the line is marked on the front of the train and often on electronic signboards that display the name of the arriving train. The signage within the Underground system is clear and helpful.

Most of the Underground system operates with automated entry and exit gates. You feed your ticket into the slot, the ticket disappears and pops up again, the gate bangs open, and you remove your ticket and pass through. At the other end you do the same to get out, but the machine keeps the ticket (unless your ticket is a Travelcard or other ticket good for more than one trip, in which case it is returned to you).

Traveling to your destination by Underground may require transferring from one Underground line to another. All Underground maps clearly show where various lines converge. Signs in the stations direct you from one line to another. To get from one line to another, you go through tunnels (which the Brits call "subways"), and you may have to go up or down a level or two. If, for instance, you are trying to get to Victoria Station from Russell Square, you'll need to take the

Piccadilly Line toward Heathrow, then transfer at Green Park to the Victoria Line and travel in the direction of Brixton.

Underground service stops around midnight (a little earlier on less-used lines).

BUYING UNDERGROUND TICKETS

You can purchase Underground tickets at the ticket window in the station or from one of the automated machines found in most stations. (Machines can change £5, £10, and £20 notes.) Fares to every station are posted.

For fare purposes, the city is divided into six zones. **Zone 1** covers all of central London. **Zone 6** extends as far as Heathrow to the west and Upminster to the east. Make sure your ticket covers all the zones you're traveling through, or you may have to pay a £10 ($16) penalty fare.

At press time, a **single-fare one-way ticket** within one zone cost £1.60 ($2.65), but was set to rise to £2 ($3.30) in 2004. Tickets are valid for use on the day of issue only.

SAVING WITH TRAVELCARDS

Paying a full-price one-way fare every time you use the Underground is costly. To save money, consider buying a **Travelcard,** which allows unlimited travel by Underground *and* bus. You can purchase these cards at any Underground station ticket window, or from vending machines that take credit cards. At press time, the following Travelcards were available; expect prices to rise in 2004:

- A **1-day Travelcard for Zones 1 and 2** (everything in central London) costs £4.10 ($7); the card is valid after 9:30am weekdays and all day Saturday and Sunday.
- The **Weekend Travelcard for Zones 1 and 2,** good for a consecutive Saturday and Sunday, costs £6.10 ($10).
- A **7-day Travelcard for Zone 1** (all of central London) costs £17 ($26).
- If you're traveling by Tube or bus *before* 9:30am and still want a bargain day pass, buy a **1-day all-zone LT Card** for £8 ($12).

VISITOR TRAVELCARDS

Another way to save money on London transportation is the **Visitor Travelcard,** which you can only buy in the United States and Canada. (They are not available in London.) There are two kinds of Visitor Travelcard, the **All Zone** and the **Central Zone** (good for Zone 1 only). Both allow unlimited travel on the Tube and bus and are available in 3-, 4-, or 7-day increments. Prices for the Central Zone Travelcard are

$22 for 3 days; $27 for 4 days; and $33 for 7 days. The All-Zone Travelcard, which you can use for many of our recommended day trips (see below), costs $32 for 3 days, $43 for 4 days, and $64 for 7 days. You can buy Visitor Travelcards by contacting a travel agent; by calling **RailEurope** at © **877/257-2887** in the U.S. or 800/361-RAIL in Canada; or by going online to www.raileurope.com.

USING YOUR ALL-ZONE VISITOR TRAVELCARD FOR DAY TRIPS

We've discovered that it's often cheaper to buy an All-Zone Travelcard and pay supplemental rail fares to day-trip destinations than it is to buy a BritRail pass. The All-Zone card covers a very large area in and around London. You can use it to get to Greenwich, Hampstead, and Kew Gardens at no additional cost. For longer day trips, simply show your All-Zone Travelcard at the ticket window of a London train station and tell the clerk you want to pay the supplemental fare to your destination. This way, your fare does not begin until you reach the end of Zone 6. You can get to places like Windsor, St. Albans, Dover, Lewes, and Brighton for less than £5 ($8) return, and the costs of longer-distance day trips will also be reduced.

BY BUS

Distinctive red double-decker buses are very much a part of London's snarled traffic scene, but not all London buses are double-deckers, and some aren't red. The drawbacks to bus travel, especially for first-timers, are that you need to become acquainted with a fairly complex bus route system, and you need to know the streets of London so you can get off at the correct stop. On the plus side, riding the bus is cheaper than taking the Tube; you don't have to contend with escalators, elevators, or tunnels; and you get to see the sights as you travel.

A concrete post topped with a red or white sign reading LONDON TRANSPORT BUS SERVICE clearly marks each bus stop. Another sign shows the routes of the buses that stop there. If the sign on top is red, the stop is a request stop, meaning you must hail the approaching bus as you would a taxi. (Don't whistle; just put up your hand.) If the sign is white, the bus stops automatically. Be sure to check the destination sign in front of the bus to make certain that the bus travels the entire route. Many bus stops are handily equipped with electronic signs that announce when to expect the next buses on the routes you are traveling. On some buses you pay the driver; in others you pay the fare collector on board. Have some pound coins with you because the driver won't change banknotes. If you have a Travelcard, simply show it to the driver or the fare collector.

The bus network is divided into two fare zones. **Zone 1** covers all of central London, including the main tourist sights and train stations. **Zone 2** is everything beyond Zone 1. If you travel by bus into, from, within, or across central London (Zone 1), the bus fare for adults is £1 ($1.65). For any bus journey you take in outer London (Zone 2), the fare is 70p ($1.15).

At midnight, buses become **night buses** (with an "N" prefix), change their routes, and increase their Zone 1 fares to £1.50 ($2.50). Your 1-day bus pass and Weekend Travelcard (described above) aren't valid on night buses.

BUS PASSES

A **1-day bus pass** is a good thing to have if you plan to do much traveling by bus. The pass can be used all day but isn't valid on N-prefixed night buses. You can purchase this and bus passes for longer periods at most Underground stations, selected news agents, and the Travel Information Centres. A 1-day bus pass for central London costs £2 ($3.30). A 7-day bus pass for central London costs £8.50 ($14).

BY TAXI

Taking a taxi in London is a safe and comfortable way to get around the city. Riding in the old-fashioned and roomy black taxis is a pleasure. Today, there are also many smaller and newer-model taxis on the streets. London cabs of any size or color aren't cheap, though. The fare starts at £1.40 ($2.30) for one person, with 40p (65¢) for each additional passenger. The meter leaps 20p (32¢) every 333 feet (100m) or 90 seconds. Then there are the surcharges: 10p (16¢) per item of luggage; 60p (95¢) weeknights 8pm to midnight and 90p ($1.50) midnight until 7am; 60p (95¢) Saturday and Sunday until 8pm and 90p ($1.50) after that. Tip your cabbie 10% of the total fare.

Tips The New Oyster for Bus & Underground

Beginning in January 2004, a new plastic "smartcard" called Oyster will allow Tube and bus riders to pre-pay and save money on fares. Pre-paying by credit or debit card from machines in the Underground stations (or via telephone or online) will reduce the long queues at ticket windows, or so it's hoped. Tube and bus fares will be frozen at 2003 levels for anyone using the Oyster card. Paper tickets will remain available, but non-Oyster Underground fares in Zone 1 will jump to £2 ($3.30), and the non-Oyster cash-only bus fare outside central London will climb to £1 ($1.60). For more information on the new Oyster card, visit the website, www.oystercard.com.

You can hail a cab on the street. If a cab is available, its yellow or white FOR HIRE sign on the roof will be lighted. Stick to official London cabs. Steer clear of minicabs and unofficial car services without meters. You can order a **radio cab** by calling © **020/7272-0272** or 020/7253-5000. Be aware that if you call for a cab, the meter starts ticking when the taxi receives notification from the dispatcher.

London is one city where you don't have to worry whether the cab driver knows where he's going. When it comes to finding a street address, London cabbies are among the most knowledgeable in the world. Their rigorous training includes an exhaustive street test called "The Knowledge."

2 Day-Tripping by Train

In England, people still take trains to travel around the country. We do, too, and we recommend train over all other forms of transportation, especially if you're a first-time visitor to England. When all goes well, traveling by train is fun and convenient. In cities outside of London, the train stations are never more than a few minutes' walk or a simple bus ride from the town center.

That said, we also feel obligated to tell our readers that the train system in the U.K. has seriously deteriorated since it was privatized in the 1980s. In fact, the British rail system is currently in something of a crisis and in the midst of a multibillion-pound, 5-year restoration plan. Hopefully, things will improve by 2008. In the meantime, trains are frequently cancelled, departure tracks are changed without notice, service can be slow and sporadic (especially on Sun, a favorite day for day-trippers), and railway employees don't always have the correct information to help you on your journey. Compartments in some of the commuter lines are full of litter, and on many local trains the windows are scratched so badly you can't see out.

For all these reasons, we urge you to keep your wits about you when traveling by train in England. In the following day-trip chapters, under "Getting There," we provide information on your train options, including departure stations in London. All of our information, including fares, was correct at press time. But train information and fares in the U.K. change often, so we want to err on the side of caution and ask you to keep the following in mind:

- Always call **National Rail Enquiries** (© **08457/484-950**) the night before your train trip to verify departure times and departure stations.
- Whenever possible, choose a direct train over one that requires a change along the way. In some cases, trains going to the same

destination (such as Canterbury or Dover) depart from different London stations. From one station the train may go direct to your destination, but from the other it may not. Likewise, trains from one station may be delayed because of track work, while trains going to the same destination but from another station are running on schedule. It's always wise to ask National Rail Enquiries or information agents at the railway stations for the quickest and most direct routes to a destination.

- Arrive at the station a few minutes early—a half hour early if you need to buy a ticket or have your BritRail pass (discussed later in this chapter) validated.
- At the station, the departures board will tell you when your train is leaving (expect delays) and from what track. But tracks can get switched without an announcement being made, so always verify with a railway employee, before you board, that the train is going to your destination. Ask the employee at the gate or one of the conductors outside the train.
- When you reach your destination, verify return times to London. If there isn't a person at the ticket window, the departure times will be posted on a signboard outside or within the station.
- On some lines, Sunday is now one of the worst days to travel because there are fewer trains and they tend to be slow. Track work is often undertaken on Sunday, sometimes causing long delays or requiring that you complete part of the journey by bus. Be aware of these considerations and try to leave London earlier in the morning so you will have more time at your destination if you are delayed. We've been on trains where trips that should have taken 90 minutes turned into 3½-hour marathons.

TRAIN TYPES

The sleek, high-speed **intercity trains** that run between London and heavily traveled, main-line routes are the most dependable and the most comfortable trains you can take. You can ride these fast trains to York, Stratford-upon-Avon, and Bath. For shorter trips, such as to Brighton and Cambridge, you often take **commuter trains.** In some cases you may need to transfer to an even smaller **local train** to reach your destination. The local trains connect larger towns to smaller ones and are very basic, without toilets or food service. Smoking is not permitted on local trains, and is confined to strictly designated areas on commuter and intercity trains. To day-trip destinations such as Kew Gardens, Greenwich, or Hampstead, you can take the **London Underground.**

Train Routes in England

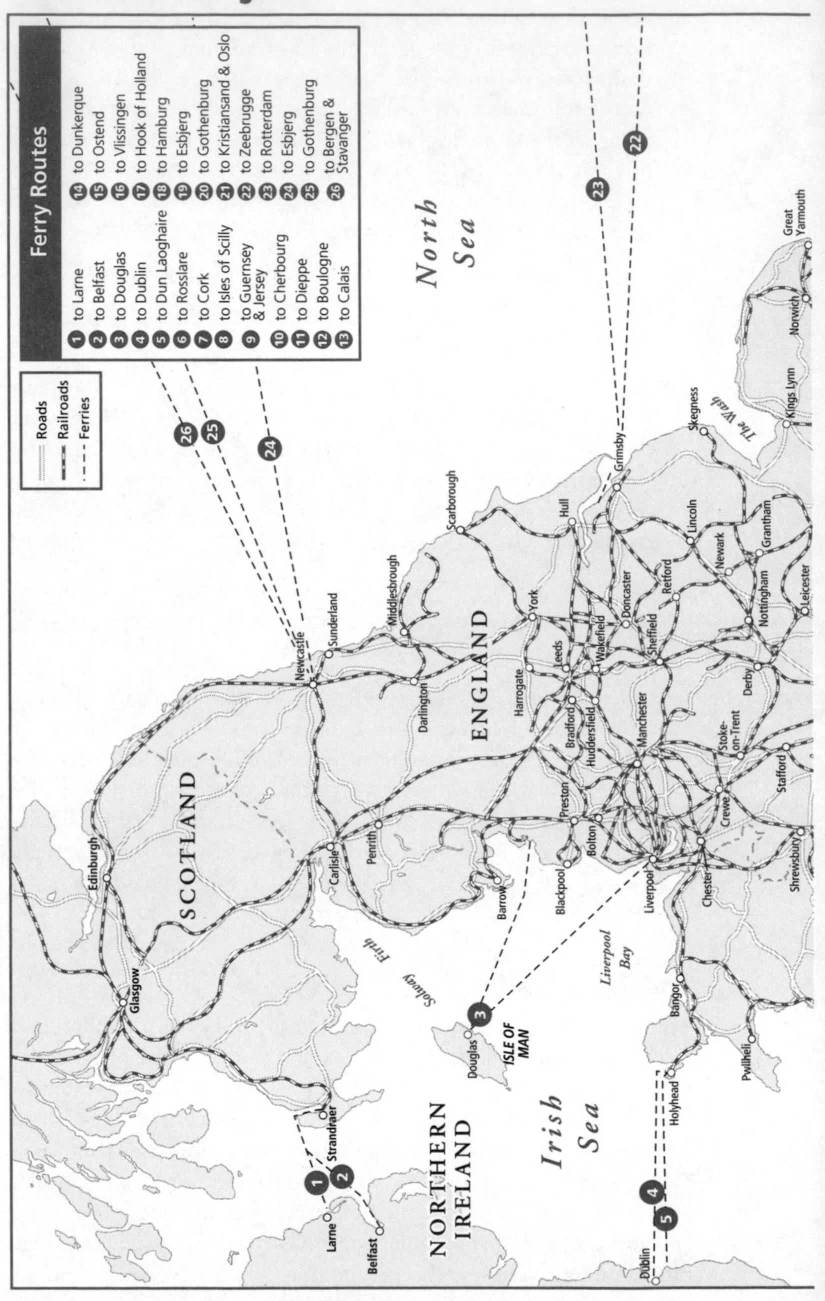

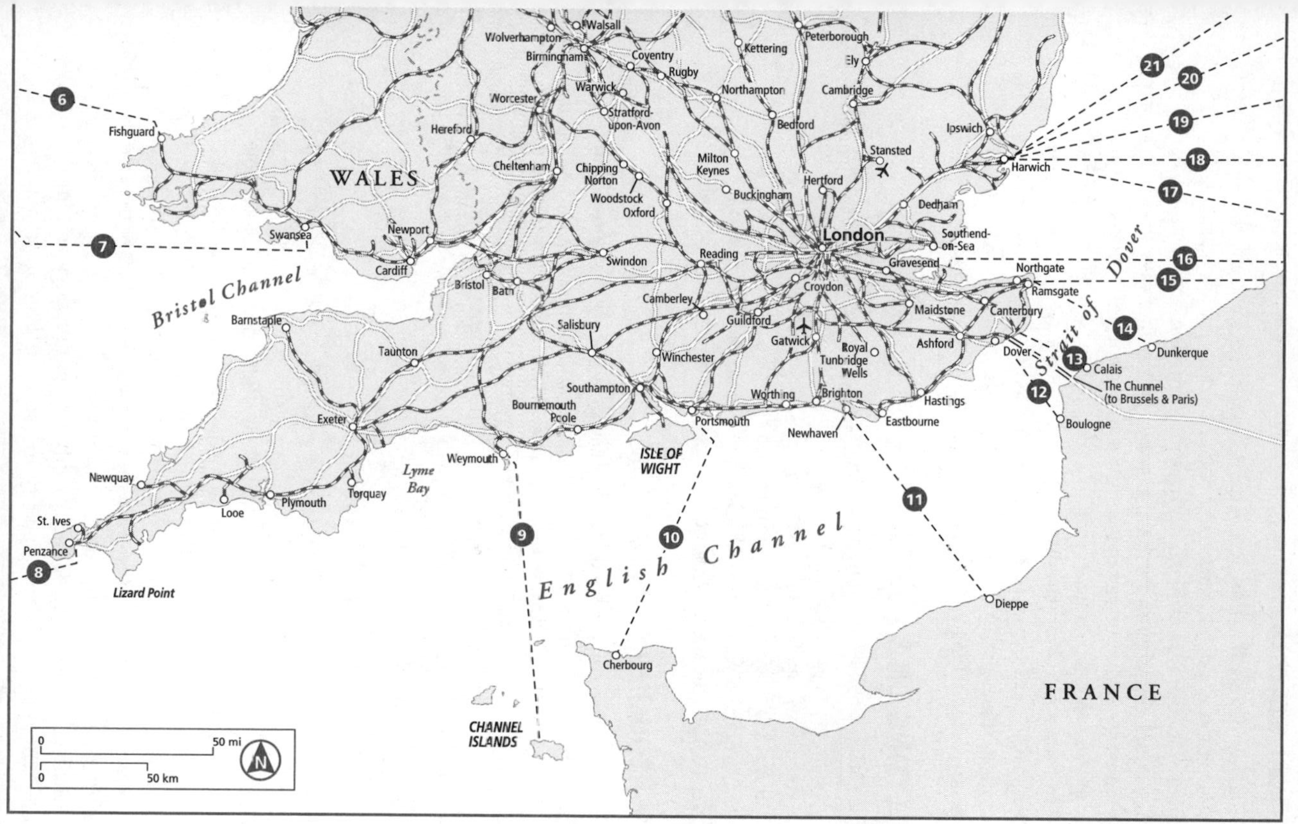
WALES
Bristol Channel
Strait of Dover
English Channel
Lyme Bay
ISLE OF WIGHT
CHANNEL ISLANDS
Lizard Point
FRANCE
London
Walsall
Wolverhampton
Birmingham
Coventry
Rugby
Kettering
Peterborough
Ely
Cambridge
Northampton
Bedford
Warwick
Stratford-upon-Avon
Worcester
Hereford
Cheltenham
Chipping Norton
Woodstock
Oxford
Milton Keynes
Buckingham
Hertford
Stansted
Ipswich
Harwich
Dedham
Southend-on-Sea
Gravesend
Northgate
Ramsgate
Canterbury
Maidstone
Ashford
Dover
Fishguard
Swansea
Newport
Cardiff
Swindon
Reading
Bristol
Bath
Croydon
Camberley
Guildford
Gatwick
Royal Tunbridge Wells
Barnstaple
Salisbury
Taunton
Winchester
Southampton
Worthing
Brighton
Hastings
Eastbourne
Newhaven
Bournemouth
Poole
Portsmouth
Exeter
Weymouth
Newquay
Looe
Plymouth
Torquay
St. Ives
Penzance
Dunkerque
Calais
The Chunnel (to Brussels & Paris)
Boulogne
Dieppe
Cherbourg
6
7
8
9
10
11
12
13
14
15
16
17
18
19
20
21
0
50 mi
0
50 km
N

LOCAL STATIONS

At many of our day-trip destinations outside of London, the local train station is a small, one-person operation. Sometimes (particularly on Sun) no one is available to help with information or ticket sales, or the station closes down in the afternoon. You will always find train schedules posted in or just outside the station, but don't expect much in the way of basic services.

In these small local stations there are often only two tracks with an overpass to get from one side to the other. When you're returning to London, make sure you're on the correct side of the track. There is usually a sign telling you which side is for the London-bound train.

GETTING ON & OFF

Except on small local trains, an announcement is usually made before the train arrives at each station. Station stops are short, so be ready to disembark when the train comes to a halt. In newer trains, you push a well-marked button to open the door automatically. In older trains, you need to open the door yourself. It may open from the inside, or you may have to open the window and reach outside to turn the door handle.

SCHEDULING YOUR DAY TRIP

For the most current train schedules and fares, call **National Rail Enquiries** at ✆ **08457/484-950** in the United Kingdom. You can also find timetable information online at www.nationalrail.com, but you should always call National Rail Enquiries the night before your journey to verify times and departure station. Throughout this book we provide basic schedule information with our coverage of each day-trip destination.

BUYING YOUR TRAIN TICKET

Before you board the train, purchase your ticket with cash or credit card at a ticket window. If you have a BritRail pass (see "Using BritRail Passes," below), you must have it validated at a ticket window before your first journey. After that, you don't have to bother with buying tickets; just board the train. At the platform barrier you will have to feed your ticket through a turnstile or show your BritRail pass in order to enter. The same procedure applies at the end of the line, though very small stations have no turnstiles.

Different train lines use slightly different terminology and impose different restrictions, but generally speaking, in England a one-way train ticket is a **single.** A round-trip ticket is a **return.** If you go on a day trip, ask for a **day return.** After 9:30am you can get a **cheap day return.** In the chapters that follow, we list the cheapest fares available for same-day travel. When purchasing your tickets, be sure to ask if any time restrictions might affect your plans.

When you buy your ticket, you must choose between first and standard (second) class. First-class tickets cost about one-third more than standard class. The first-class cars have roomier seats, but you can travel quite comfortably in standard class, and some commuter trains have no first-class cars. If you want a first-class ticket, you must request one—otherwise the agent will sell you a standard-class ticket.

First-class service on some intercity train routes includes free coffee, tea, beverages, and snacks served at your seat, plus a free newspaper and a higher standard of personal service. Standard-class passengers can buy sandwiches and drinks in a cafe car. On some lines an employee comes through with a food and beverage trolley.

Local trains do not offer first-class service or food service.

USING ALL-ZONE TRAVELCARDS

Financially speaking, purchasing an **All-Zone Travelcard** for the London Underground and using it for your longer day trips may be better than buying a BritRail pass. An All-Zone Travelcard (described above) will get you to Greenwich, Hampstead, and Kew Gardens at no additional charge. To destinations that are further afield but still within commuting distance of London (such as Brighton, Hampton Court, St. Albans, Knole, Sissinghurst, Canterbury, Rye, Windsor), you can show your All-Zone Travelcard at the ticket window in London and pay a supplemental fare, usually under £5 ($8) for a day-return ticket.

USING BRITRAIL PASSES

If you plan to travel around England by train, consider purchasing a **BritRail pass.** These must be purchased before you arrive in England. BritRail passes are convenient because you don't have to stand in line to buy train tickets; if a train is in the station, you can just hop on. But if you're going to be mostly in London and making just one or two short day trips, it makes more sense to buy an All-Zone Travelcard (see above) instead; this will provide unlimited transport within London and allow you to travel outside the capital for a relatively small supplemental fee. BritRail passes can be ordered through a travel agent or by contacting **RailEurope** (**© 877/257-2887** in the U.S., or 800/361-RAIL in Canada; www.raileurope.com). The BritRail passes most pertinent to day-trippers are:

BritRail Days Out from London Pass This pass covers a large area around London and makes the most sense for day-trippers. The pass gets you to Cambridge, Oxford, Canterbury, Dover, Winchester, Salisbury, and everywhere in between. But if you are taking day trips to Hampton Court or Windsor, places closer to London, you'll be better off paying the regular train fares from London or getting an All-Zone Travelcard. A Days Out from London Pass costs $89 for first-class travel for any 2 days in an 8-day period; standard class is $59. Four-day and 7-day Days Out from London passes are also available.

BritRail Flexipass This pass allows you travel any 4, 8, or 15 days within a 2-month time period. Dollarwise, it makes sense only if every one of your day-trip destinations is to a place some distance from London, such as Stratford-upon-Avon, Bath, York, or Moreton-in-Marsh. A 4-day, first-class Flexipass is $355 for adults, $305 for seniors over 60. The Flexipass allows you to visit Wales and Scotland in addition to every place we list in this guide.

BritRail Family Pass This pass makes traveling with kids cheaper and easier. Buy any adult or senior pass, and you get a free youth pass (ages 5–15) of the same type and duration. Children under 5 travel free at all times.

LONDON'S TRAIN STATIONS

London has 11 major train stations, so getting to the right station to catch your train is important. (Throughout this book, we always tell you which London station serves the particular destination we're describing.) The Underground (subway) serves all of London's train stations. In every station, a large overhead display, usually near the platforms, lists the departing trains and platforms.

Below we list our day-trip destinations after the stations from which you'll most likely be departing, but please note: It's sometimes possible to use more than one station, and service may change depending on day of the week, track work, and other considerations. It's always a good idea to check with **National Rail Enquiries** at © **08457/484-950** before setting off.

If you're day-tripping from London, you'll depart from one of the following stations:

Charing Cross Station Trains from here travel southeast to Battle, Canterbury, Dover, Rye, Staplehurst (for Sissinghurst), and English Channel ports that connect with ferry service to the Continent.

Euston Station Trains from this station head to St. Albans and north to the Lake District and up to Scotland.

King's Cross Station Trains from here travel to St. Albans and destinations in the east of England, including Cambridge and York.

Paddington Station Trains from Paddington travel southwest to Windsor and Bath and northwest to Moreton-in-Marsh, Oxford, and Stratford-upon-Avon.

Victoria Station Head here for trains traveling to the south and southeast of England, including Bearsted (for Leeds Castle), Brighton, Canterbury, Hever, Lewes, Rochester, and Sevenoaks (for Knole).

Waterloo Station This station is primarily for trains going to the south of England, including Hampton Court, Salisbury, Winchester, and Windsor. Waterloo Station is connected to Waterloo International, the terminal at which Eurostar trains arrive from and depart for Paris and Brussels.

3 Day-Tripping by Coach (Bus)

A long-distance touring bus in England is a **coach.** Buses are what you take for local transportation. The main, long-distance coach company is **National Express** (✆ **0990/808080;** www.nationalexpress.com). Their bus routes cover the entire country, and their comfortable coaches are equipped with reclining seats, a toilet, and often a food and beverage service. Tickets usually cost half of what the train fare costs, and are even cheaper if you buy a return ticket. The one drawback, at least for the busy day-tripper without much time, is that coaches may take twice as long as the train—if the train is running on time, that is.

If you travel by coach from London, you'll depart from **Victoria Coach Station,** Buckingham Palace Road (✆ **020/7730-3466;** Tube: Victoria), located just 2 blocks from Victoria Station. Coach stations in cities outside of London are always close to the city center, often next to the train station.

National Express offers a **Tourist Trail Pass** for unlimited travel on their extensive network, which covers all of England. A 2-day pass costs £49 ($81); a 5-day pass for use within any 30 consecutive days costs £85 ($140). An 8-day pass is also available. The passes are a money-saving option if you plan to travel fairly far afield from London on your day trips (for example, to Moreton-in-Marsh, York, Bath, Salisbury, Stratford-upon-Avon, or Winchester).

4 Day-Tripping by Car

We strongly recommend that people making day trips from London, especially first-time travelers, travel by train or coach (bus) instead of by car. Much of a car trip can be spent on motorways without much scenery, so what's the point? Most of our day trips are localized adventures in one place or town and don't require any driving. Our subsidiary sights—Stonehenge, say, which is 9 miles (14km) from Salisbury—can easily be reached by bus or taxi from the primary day-trip destination.

But having a car does open up regions of the English countryside for deeper exploration. In areas such as the Cotswolds, where trains do not serve villages and where local bus service is sporadic or infrequent, having a car can be handy. And if you're exploring several of the houses, gardens, and castles of Kent and Sussex, you can reach them more easily by car than by train or coach.

In fact, a car is a cost-effective and reasonable alternative to public transportation only if you plan to group several of our day trips into a road trip on which you visit multiple destinations and spend a night or two outside the capital. This way, you can cover a lot of ground. For instance, you might want to rent a car at Gatwick Airport, drive from there to Knole and Hever, then spend the night in Rye, with a visit the next day to Sissinghurst and Battle. Or, you may want to drive from Heathrow Airport to Salisbury (with a stop at Stonehenge en route), and use that city as an overnight base from which to visit Wilton House, as well as nearby Winchester and Chawton, before you return to London. Or, you might want to rent a car at Heathrow and drive west to Oxford for the night, make a stop at Blenheim, then continue on to Bath the next day before settling for the night in the Cotswolds. While our focus in this book is on day trips, we do mention places that might warrant an overnight stay, and we recommend our favorite hotels in each.

Overall, though, for your single day-trip excursions outside of London, trains and buses are far better options than cars. Even if you plan on visiting two or more of our day-trip destinations in a single day—combining Sissinghurst and Rye, for instance—you'll still find it less expensive and just as quick to travel by train. Remember that you can always hire a taxi to meet you at a train station and take you to a great house or garden or castle in the country. In every day-trip chapter, we give you the local numbers of taxi companies.

BEFORE YOU RENT A CAR

Driving in England requires real skill and dexterity, and it's not for the faint of heart. If you are a nervous driver at home, in your own car, do not put yourself through the ordeal of driving in England. Before you even consider renting a car, ask yourself if you'd be comfortable driving with a steering wheel on the right-hand side of the vehicle while shifting with your left hand. (You can get an automatic, but it costs considerably more.) Remember, you must drive on the left and pass on the right. Two essential rules for drivers are: Always look to the right, the direction from which oncoming traffic will approach; and, to ensure you're on the left side of the road, make certain that the center of the road is to your right.

RENTING A CAR

Do yourself a favor: Forget about renting a car in London. Driving in the city is an endurance test, and given the fact that drivers are now assessed £5 ($8) a day "congestion charge" to use a car in central London, it can be incredibly expensive as well. If you want to travel with Londoners on their own turf (or in their own tunnels), the Tube (Underground) is a great way to go. If you want a car to explore the countryside, you can rent one for the day, either at Heathrow or Gatwick airports, or in a hub city or town after you arrive. It's a good idea to reserve the car before you arrive.

Americans renting a car in England need a valid U.S. driver's license that you've had for at least 1 year. The same holds true for Canadians, Australians, and New Zealanders. In most cases, depending on the agency, you must be at least 23 years old (21 in some instances, 25 in others) and no older than 70. (Some companies have raised the maximum age to 75.)

RENTAL CAR COSTS

The price of renting a car depends on a host of factors, including the size of the car, the length of time you keep it, where and when you pick it up and drop it off, and how far you drive it. Asking a few key questions can save you money. Here are some factors to keep in mind when renting a car in England:

- You can often get a lower car rental rate if you reserve 7 days in advance using a toll-free reservations number.
- Find out if the quoted price includes the 17.5% VAT (Value-Added Tax).
- A rental package with unlimited mileage is usually your best option.
- Weekend rates may be lower than weekday rates.
- Don't forget to mention membership in AAA, AARP, frequent-flier programs, and trade unions. These usually entitle you to discounts ranging from 5% to 30%. Ask your travel agent to check any and all of these rates.
- Most car rentals are worth at least 500 miles (800km) on your frequent-flier account.
- Some airlines offer package deals that include car rental.

INSURANCE FOR CAR RENTALS

On top of the standard rental prices, other optional charges apply to most car rentals. The **Collision Damage Waiver (CDW),** which limits your liability for damages caused by a collision, is covered by many credit card companies if you pay with their credit card. Check with your credit card company before you go so you can avoid paying this fee (as much as $15 per day).

The car rental companies also offer **additional liability insurance** (if you harm others in an accident), **personal accident insurance** (if you harm yourself or your passengers), and **personal effects insurance** (if your property is stolen from your car). If you have insurance on your car at home, you're probably covered for most of these unlikelihoods. If your own insurance doesn't cover you for rentals, or if you don't have auto insurance, you should consider these additional types of coverage.

Although not as common a practice as in the United States, some international companies also offer **refueling packages,** in which you pay for an entire tank of gas up front. The price is usually fairly competitive with local gas prices, but you don't get credit for any gas remaining in the tank. If you reject this option, you pay only for the gas you use, but you have to return the car with a full tank or face costly per-gallon charges for any shortfall. If you think that a stop at a gas station on the way back to the airport will make you miss your plane, then by all means take advantage of the fuel purchase option. Otherwise, skip it.

CAR RENTALS ON THE WEB

As with other aspects of planning your trip, using the Internet can make comparison-shopping for a car rental much easier. All the major booking websites—**Expedia** (www.expedia.com), **Frommers** (www.frommers.com), **Travelocity** (www.travelocity.com), and **Yahoo! Travel** (http://travel.yahoo.com), for example—have search engines that can dig up discounted car rental rates. Just enter the size of the car you want, the pickup and return dates, and the city where you want to rent, and the site returns a price. You can even make the reservation through these sites.

WHERE TO RENT A CAR

You'll save yourself time, bother, and expense if you rent a car at one of London's two major airports, Heathrow or Gatwick. Both are connected to the city by excellent public transportation: You can reach Heathrow on the Underground for a basic fare of £3.70 ($6); or you can reach it on the **Heathrow Express,** which makes the trip from Paddington Station in just 15 minutes for £12 ($19) standard class. The **Gatwick Express** connects Victoria Station with Gatwick Airport in a half hour; the fare is £11 ($18) standard class.

From both airports you can easily get onto the M25, the ring road that encircles London, and from the M25 you can easily access the

Major Car Rental Agencies

Alamo
© 800/327-9633 (U.S.)
© 0800/272-200 (U.K)
www.alamo.com

Avis
© 800/331-1212 (Continental U.S.)
© 0990/900-500 (U.K.)
www.avis.com

Budget
© 800/527-0700 (U.S.)
© 0541/565-656 (U.K.)
www.budgetrentacar.com

Hertz
© 800/654-3131 (U.S.)
© 08708/448-844 (U.K.)
www.hertz.com

National
© 800/CAR-RENT (U.S.)
© 0990/565-656 (U.K.)
www.nationalcar.com

major roads leading to all parts of the country. When renting a car for airport pickup, be sure to ask where the facility is located and how you can reach it—some agencies are located far from the terminals and do not provide shuttle service, making them difficult and costly to reach.

Alternatively, you may want to take a train to a major city outside London and rent a car there. However, options can be limited in all but major cities.

MOTORWAYS, DUAL CARRIAGEWAYS & ROUNDABOUTS

What is commonly known as a freeway in some countries, the Brits call a **motorway** (indicated as "M" plus a number on maps). A two-way road is a **single carriageway,** and a four-lane divided highway (two lanes in each direction) is a **dual carriageway.** Country roads, some of them paved-over tracks dating back centuries, are full of twists and turns and are often barely wide enough for two cars to pass.

One element of British roads that invariably throws non-native drivers is the **roundabout**—a traffic junction where several roads meet at one traffic circle. On a roundabout, the cars to your right (that is, those already on the roundabout) always have the right of way.

On certain sections of the motorway, where speeding is especially dangerous, speed cameras have recently been installed. The cameras take a photograph of any car exceeding the speed limit so the police can trace the culprit. You will see a camera symbol upon entering these areas. Surveillance cameras have also been installed at some traffic lights to catch anyone who runs a red.

Before you arrive in England, or before you leave on your car journey, find and purchase a good-quality, large-scale road map with a scale of 3 miles to 1 inch or 2km to 1 centimeter.

RULES OF THE ROAD

You need to know some general facts if you're going to drive in England.

- In England, all distances and speed limits are shown in miles and miles per hour (mph). If you need to translate from the metric system, a kilometer is 0.62 of a mile, and a mile is 1.61km.
- Speed limits are usually:

  30mph (48kmph) in towns

  40mph (65kmph) on some town roads where posted

  60mph (97kmph) on most single carriageway (2-way) roads

  70mph (113kmph) on dual carriageways and motorways
- Road signs are usually the standard international signs. Buy a booklet (available at many shops and in airports) called *Highway Code* for about £1 ($1.60) before you set out, or visit www.highwaycode.gov.uk. The information in the booklet and on the website is essential for driving in England.
- The law requires you to wear a seat belt. If you have children, make sure that you ask the car rental agency about seat belts or car seats before you rent.
- At roundabouts, traffic coming from the right has the right of way.
- You can pass other vehicles only on the right.
- Parking in the center of most towns is difficult and expensive. Make sure you read all posted restrictions, or park in a lot.
- You must stop for pedestrians in cross walks marked by striped lines (called **zebra crossings**) on the road. Pedestrians have the right of way.

EMERGENCIES ON THE ROAD

All motorways have emergency telephones stationed about .6 miles (1km) apart. The phone operator will obtain emergency or automotive services if you require them. If you must pull over to the side of the motorway, park as close to the far edge of the shoulder as possible. Motorway service stations are usually about 25 miles (40km) apart and occasionally as far as 50 miles (81km) apart.

FILLING THE TANK

Petrol (gasoline) stations are self-service. The green filler pipe is for unleaded petrol, the red filler pipe is for leaded petrol, and the black filler pipe is for diesel fuel. Petrol is often cheapest at supermarkets, but going to a motorway service station is more convenient. Petrol is purchased by the liter (3.78 liters equals 1 gal.). Expect to pay about 84p ($1.40) per liter (approximately $5.30 per gal.) for unleaded petrol.

5 Traveling Locally from Your Destination

USING LOCAL BUSES

In some of our day trips we list major attractions that are several miles from the principal day-trip destination. To reach these places—Jane Austen's House in Chawton, for instance, which is 17 miles (28km) from Winchester—your best bet is a taxi or a local bus. We provide current local bus information whenever possible, but it's important for you to double-check times and services at the local tourist information center (in Winchester, for example, if you're going to Chawton). Local bus service is reliable, but local timetables may not suit your schedule.

If your train station is a little ways from the town center and you don't want to walk, there will almost always be a local bus that travels between the station and the center of town. Have some pound and smaller coins with you because drivers usually won't take banknotes.

TAKING A TAXI

To reach subsidiary sites from some of our primary day-trip destinations, you can save yourself a lot of time and bother by taking a taxi instead of waiting for a local bus or renting a car. But in only one of our day trips, to Monk's House (Virginia Woolf's country home in Rodmell, Sussex) and nearby Charleston (Vanessa Bell and Duncan Grant's house), is it necessary to take a taxi if you want to see both places in 1 day.

In the "Getting Around" section in every day trip we provide the numbers for local taxi companies. Reserve a taxi in advance, or you may have to wait for an hour or more once you arrive at the train station.

Our general experience with local taxis is that the fare is between £8 ($13) and £15 ($25) per ride.

RENTING A BICYCLE

England is a wonderful country for cycling. Though it may be difficult to fit a bicycle journey into your day-trip itinerary, it's not impossible and it can add a lot to your enjoyment of a region. If there is a particularly charming, scenic, or interesting bike route in or around a day-trip destination, we tell you about it under "Outdoor Activities." These are not marathon 20-mile (32km) rides, but easygoing jaunts. We'll also tell you where you can rent a bike locally.

ESCORTED TOURS

Maybe you only have time for a trip or two outside of London and don't want to bother with train schedules, admission hours, and other details. If so, an escorted tour can be an easy and cost-effective alternative to making day trips on your own. Keep in mind, though, that the ease of an escorted tour comes at a price—a loss of flexibility. On an escorted tour you won't be able to linger on the lawns at Leeds Castle or dawdle in front of a painting at Hampton Court if the coach is ready to pull out of the car park.

Below is a sampling of tour companies that offer half- and full-day tours from London. For a list of others, visit the Britain & London Visitor Centre, 1 Regent St., Piccadilly Circus, London W1, and Tourist Information Centres elsewhere around the country. Prices usually include admission fees as well as pickup in central London and at some central London hotels.

- **Astral Travels,** 72 New Bond St. (✆ **0870/902-0908;** www.astraltravels.co.uk), offers a sights-filled full-day tour of Stratford-upon-Avon, the Cotswolds, and Oxford for £49 ($78), and a trip to Canterbury, the Kent countryside, and Leeds Castle for £51 ($82).
- **London Tourism** (✆ **01844/343-132;** www.london-tourism.com), a private firm and not an official government tourism agency, offers full-day outings to Sissinghurst Castle Garden and other scenic spots in Kent for £60 ($96) adults and £58 ($93) children; to Windsor and Hampton Court Palace, with a cruise on the Thames, for £55 ($88) adults and £47 ($75) children; and to Oxford, Stratford-upon-Avon, and Warwick Castle for £53 ($85) adults and £45 ($72) children.
- **Sightseeingtours.co.uk** (✆ **0870/745-1046;** www.21stcenturytravel.co.uk) offers tours that include a full day in Bath and the

Cotswolds, with a cream tea, for £50 ($80) adults and £48 ($76) children, and a half-day at Leeds Castle for £30 ($48) adults and £27 ($42) children.

6 Saving Money on Admissions

If you plan to make several day trips and visit a number of historic properties, consider arming yourself with the **Great British Heritage Pass.** The pass gives you free entry to hundreds of properties throughout the U.K. that are associated with the National Trust and English Heritage, including many in London and many of those we visit on our day trips. A shortlist of these properties you might visit is Blenheim Palace, Dover Castle, Fenton House in Hampstead, Hampton Court, Hever Castle, Mompesson House in Salisbury, Rochester Castle, the Roman Baths and Pump Room in Bath, Shakespeare's Birthplace in Avon, Sissinghurst Castle Garden, Stonehenge, Warwick Castle, Winchester City Mill, and Windsor Castle.

Prices: 4 days, £22 ($35); 7 days, £35 ($56); 15 days, £46 ($74); and 1 month, £60 ($96).

Before you jump in and purchase the pass, check admission fees for the properties you might want to visit and do a little math. Fees vary but usually run between £8 ($13)and £12 ($19) per property. If you plan to visit only one or two properties, the pass is not cost effective. If, however, you plan to make several trips out of London and visit four or more properties, the pass may provide a substantial savings. Remember, too, that many National Trust properties are closed November through March, so if you are visiting during those months, the pass may be of little use to you.

The pass is only available to non-residents of the U.K., but it can be purchased before or after your arrival in Britain. In the U.S. and Canada, you can purchase the pass from travel agents; or by calling **RailEurope** (© **877/257-2887** in the U.S.; 800/361-RAIL in Canada); or by going online at www.raileurope.com. In Britain, you can purchase the pass from the **Britain & London Visitor Centre,** 1 Regent St., Piccadilly Circus, London W1 (Tube: Piccadilly); or from Tourist Information Centres at airports, ports, and major cities throughout England. For more information about the Great British Heritage Pass, including a full list of properties, visit www.visitbritain.com/world/heritagepass.

Trip 1

Bath

The Romans channeled Bath's hot, sulfurous waters into elaborate thermal pools some 2,000 years ago. But it was 18th-century ladies and dandies who created one of England's most elegant and beautiful cities when they began coming to Bath to take the waters and enjoy the season amid terraced houses on elegant squares and curving crescents. These days, millions of visitors come to this city of soft, mellow stone—designated by UNESCO

Bath

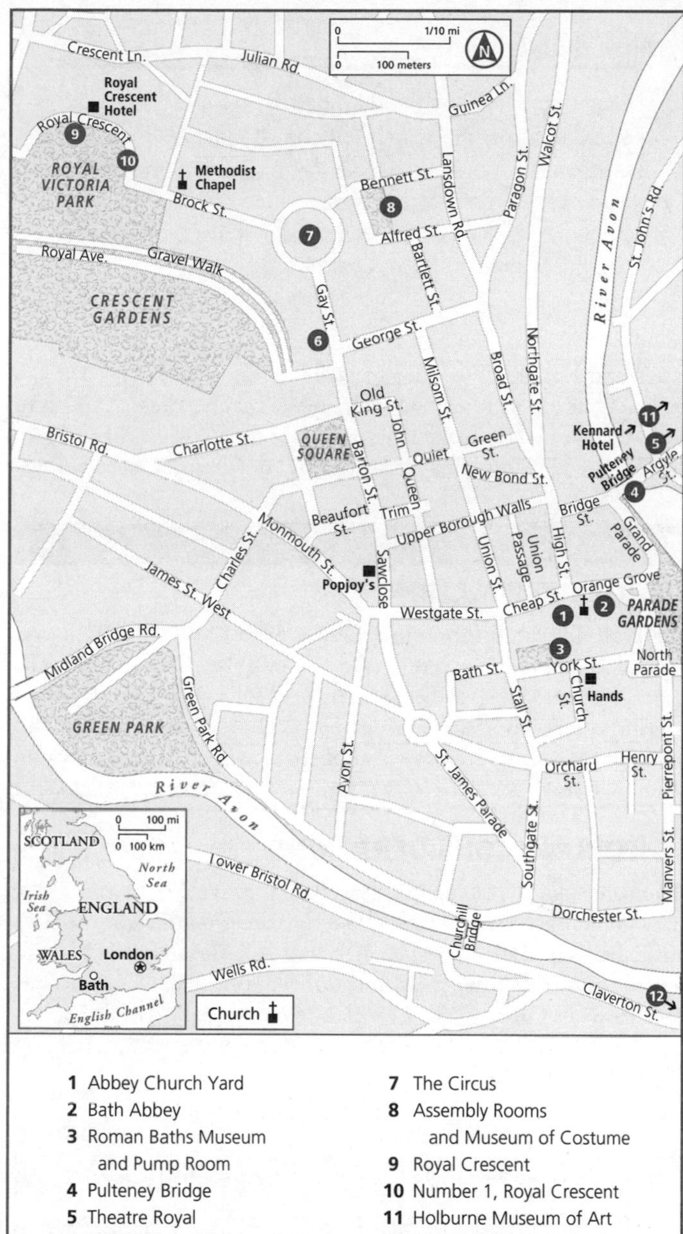

1 Abbey Church Yard
2 Bath Abbey
3 Roman Baths Museum and Pump Room
4 Pulteney Bridge
5 Theatre Royal
6 Jane Austen Centre
7 The Circus
8 Assembly Rooms and Museum of Costume
9 Royal Crescent
10 Number 1, Royal Crescent
11 Holburne Museum of Art
12 American Museum

Bath Highlights

- Exploring the ancient Roman baths.
- Strolling across shop-lined Pulteney Bridge.
- Visiting the Museum of Costume—one of the world's leading collections of fashion.
- Admiring the elegant town houses of Royal Crescent, and touring Number 1, Royal Crescent.

as a World Heritage Site—not to take the waters (although that can be done) but simply to enjoy Bath's unique beauty. There's enough to do and see in Bath to make it a good place for an overnight stop; see the last section in this chapter for hotel recommendations.

1 Essentials

VISITOR INFORMATION

The **Bath Tourist Information Centre** (✆ **01225/477-101;** www.visitbath.co.uk) is in the center of town, in Abbey Church Yard. The center is open May 1 to September 30, Monday to Saturday from 9:30am to 6pm and Sunday from 10am to 4pm; and October 1 to April 30, Monday to Saturday from 9:30am to 5pm and Sunday from 10am to 4pm.

SCHEDULING CONSIDERATIONS

You might want to plan your visit to Bath to coincide with one of the many events the city hosts throughout the year. These include the **Bath Music Festival** in late May and early June, and **Mozartfest** in November. For information on these and other events in Bath, contact the **Bath Festivals Office** (✆ **01225/463-362;** www.bathfestivals.org.uk).

GETTING THERE

BY TRAIN

Trains run about every half hour from London's Paddington Station to Bath. The trip takes 90 minutes, with the first train departing at 5:05am and the last train returning to London at 10:57pm. The "Saver Return" fare is £40 ($64). For information, call ✆ **08457/484-950** or go to www.railtrack.co.uk. The Bath train station is at the south edge of the city center, off Dorchester Street, about a 5-minute walk down Manvers Street from Bath Abbey and Grand Parade.

BY CAR

Bath is 115 miles (185km) west of London. The M4 links London with Bath, and the trip usually takes about 2 hours. Most of the city center is closed to traffic, and much of the street parking is reserved for residents. It's easiest to use the city's Park and Ride facilities, well marked from entrance routes into the city; the most convenient when entering the city from the M4 from London is Lansdown, on the north side of the city. The facilities operate Monday to Saturday 7:15am to 7:30pm; parking is free. Buses to the city center leave about every 10 to 15 minutes and cost £1.40 ($2.30) return.

BY BUS

National Express buses leave London's Victoria Coach Station for Bath every hour, with some half-hourly departures. Travel times vary from 3 hours and 15 minutes for the direct trip to 4 or even close to 5 hours for trips that require a change. The fare is £21 ($34) return. The bus station is on Manvers Street, near the train station. For more information, call ✆ **08705/808-080** or go to www.nationalexpress.com.

GETTING AROUND

City buses run from the train station to locations around town, but most places are within walking distance. There is a taxi rank outside the station, or you can call **AA Taxis** (✆ **01225/460-888**). The center is compact, and many streets are open only to pedestrian traffic, making it easy to get around Bath on foot. The easiest way to get from the south side of the city center (where Bath Abbey and the Roman Baths are located) to the north side (for the Assembly Rooms, Circus, and Royal Crescent) is to follow High Street north as it becomes Broad Street and Lansdown Road, then turn left (west) onto Bennett Street.

2 A Day in Bath

The lively center of the city is pedestrian-only. Start your tour at ❶ **Abbey Church Yard,** adjacent to ❷ **Bath Abbey** (✆ **01225/422-462;** www.bathabbey.org). This airy cathedral was established in the 8th century and rebuilt in the 16th century with a graceful fan-vaulted ceiling and large expanses of glass that fill the church with light; little wonder the cathedral is known as the "Lantern of the West." Bath Abbey is open Monday to Saturday from 9am to 6pm in summer and from 9am to 4:30pm in winter; on Sunday it's open from 1:15 to 2:45pm and 4:45 to 5:30pm in summer and from 1:15 to 2:45pm in winter.

Just across Abbey Church Yard is the ❸ **Roman Baths Museum and Pump Room** (✆ **01225/477-785;** www.romanbaths.co.uk), the bath complex built by the Romans that remains, in part, just as they left it. A terrace overlooks the large pool where legionnaires once soaked in waters that continue to bubble forth at 116°F (47°C) at the rate of about 240,000 gallons a day. In a maze of subterranean chambers, which you navigate with the aid of an excellent self-guided audio commentary, are the remains of steaming pools and saunas, surrounded by elaborate paving. You can sample Bath water in the adjacent Pump Room, though you may opt to sip coffee or tea instead, to the musical accompaniment of a string trio. The complex is open November to February, daily from 9:30am to 5:30pm (last entry at 4:30pm); March to June and September to October, daily from 9am to 6pm. (last entry at 5pm); and July to August, daily from 9am to 10pm (last entry at 9pm). Admission is £8.50 ($14) for adults, £7.50 ($12) for seniors and students, £4.80 ($7.70) for children 6 to 16, and £22 ($35) for families of up to two adults and two children. A combined ticket to the Roman Baths and the Museum of Costume (see below) costs £11 ($18) for adults, £9.50 ($15) for seniors and students, £6.20 ($10) for children 6 to 16, and £30 ($48) for families of up to two adults and four children.

The Grand Parade leads a few blocks north to ❹ **Pulteney Bridge,** an 18th-century span over the Avon River modeled on the Ponte Vecchio in Florence—and like its Italian counterpart, it is lined with shops. Return to the west bank of the bridge and follow Upper Borough Walls Street through the city center to the ❺ **Theatre Royal** (**✆ 01225/448-844;** www.theatreroyal.org.uk), one of Britain's oldest working stages. If you're unable to attend a performance, you might be around to join one of the tours on the first Wednesday of every month at 11am and every Saturday at noon; the fee is £3 ($4.80) for adults and £2 ($3.20) for children. The house next to the theater was once the home of Beau Nash, an 18th-century arbiter of taste and a high-living gambler who is credited with putting Bath on the map as a fashionable watering hole.

Gay Street leads north past Queen Square to the ❻ **Jane Austen Centre** (**✆ 01225/443-000;** www.janeausten.co.uk), a rather dull but informative collection of text-heavy displays that honor the ever-popular novelist of late-18th- and early-19th-century manners. Jane visited Bath twice in the late 18th century and lived here from 1801 to 1806; she drew lavishly from her experiences here for her novels. The most satisfying part of a visit is the gossipy introductory lecture; among the juicy tidbits you'll glean is how Jane came to loathe Bath, where she and her mother and sister fell upon hard times. The center is open Monday to Saturday from 10am to 5:30pm; Sunday from 10:30am to 5:30pm. Admission is £4.45 ($7.10) for adults, £3.65 ($6) for seniors and students, £2.45 ($3.90) for children 6 to 15, and £12 ($19) for families of up to two adults and four children.

From the Jane Austen Centre, Gay Street continues north to ❼ **The Circus,** where three semicircular terraces of Regency town houses surround a circular park. The ❽ **Assembly Rooms and Museum of Costume** (✆ **01225/477-789;** www.museumofcostume.co.uk), just east of the Circus on Bennett Street, evoke a lifestyle in which balls and gossip ranked high among priorities. You can walk through the four elegant rooms that were the center of 18th-century Bath social life, then go downstairs to view the finery in which a lady or dandy of the time would have danced away an evening; this is one of the world's leading collections of fashion. Just as intriguing as historic fashions are creations by Versace and other contemporary designers. Hours are daily from 10am to 5pm (last admission 4:30pm). Admission to the Assembly Rooms is free and to the museum is £5.50 ($9) for adults, £4.50 ($7) for seniors and students, £3.75 ($6) for children 6 to 18, and £15 ($24) for families of up to two adults and four children. A combined ticket to the Museum of Costume and the Roman Baths costs £11 ($18) for adults, £9.50 ($15) for children, £6.20 ($10) for children 5 to 16, and £30 ($48) for families of up to two adults and four children.

Brock Street leads west from The Circus to Royal Victoria Park and the amazing ❾ **Royal Crescent,** a majestic semicircle of elegant town houses and one of the most distinctive examples of residential architecture in the world. At ❿ **Number 1, Royal Crescent** (✆ **01225/428-126;** www.bath-preservation-trust.org.uk/museums/no1) you can step into one of the town houses, a spacious "corner" house whose

The Beau of Bath

Bath was a sleepy, inelegant little place when Beau Nash arrived in 1705 to try his hand at some games of chance. Nash, then 31, had more or less given up law and made his living by gambling. He was well known in London social circles for his looks, charm, aplomb, and stylish attire. He was lucky in Bath, decided to stay on as assistant to the town's master of ceremonies, and soon made his mark by enforcing dress codes and rules of behavior at dances, installing streetlights, and improving lodgings. He put Bath on the map as one of Europe's fashionable spas, with a sparkling new Pump Room for taking the waters, Assembly Rooms for dances, terraces on handsome houses, and other improvements we still enjoy today. Bath staged a grand funeral ceremony when Nash died in 1761 at age 87—and the elegant town continues to pay tribute to Beau Nash with its perfectly preserved beauty.

tenants included, in 1776, the duke of York, second son of George III. The Bath Preservation Trust has restored the house using only paint, wallpapers, fabrics, and other materials available in the 18th century, and furnished the three floors with a superlative collection of period antiques; one of the more amusing pieces is a card table in the study—a handy piece of equipment given the popularity of gambling in Georgian Bath. The house is open mid-February to October, Tuesday to Sunday from 10:30am to 5pm; and in November, Tuesday to Sunday from 10:30am to 4pm. Admission is £4 ($6) for adults; £3.50 ($6) for seniors, students, and children 6 to 18; and £10 ($16) for families of up to two adults and two children.

MORE THINGS TO SEE & DO

⓫ **Holburne Museum of Art** When this mansion was Bath's finest hotel, Jane Austen kept an eye on the fashionable clientele from her house nearby. Now the elegant rooms house silver, glass, and other decorative objects, as well as paintings by Joseph Turner and other masters, collected by 19th-century Bath resident Sir William Holburne.

Great Pulteney St. ✆ **01225/466-669.** www.bath.ac.uk/Holburne. Admission £4 ($6) adults, £3.50 ($6) seniors, £1.50 ($2.40) children, £7 ($11) families of up to 2 adults and 2 children. Mid-Feb to mid-Dec, Tues–Sat 10am–5pm, Sun 2:30–5pm.

⓬ **American Museum** On display at 19th-century Claverton Manor are quilts, folk art, Shaker pieces, and the other holdings of Britain's only museum devoted to Americana; the 125 acres (51 hectares) of gardens, including a replica of the one at Mount Vernon, spill down the hillside. The museum is closed most of the winter, except from mid-November to mid-December, when the rooms are decorated for Christmas.

Off the Ave., Bathwick Hill. ✆ **01225/460-503.** www.americanmuseum.org. Admission £6 ($10) adults, £5.50 ($9) seniors and students, £3.50 ($6) children. Mar 22–Nov 2, Tues–Sun 2–5pm; Nov 22–Dec 13, Tues and Thurs–Sun 1–4pm, Wed 1–4pm and 5:30–7:30pm. Bus: 18 to the museum from the train station and other stops in the city center.

ORGANIZED TOURS

Among the many walking tours of Bath (the Tourist Information Centre has a complete list), you get the best overview on the free, 2-hour **Mayor of Bath's Honorary Civic Walking Tour,** with stops at the Pump Room, Pulteney Bridge, Royal Crescent, and other architectural gems. The tour departs from outside the Abbey Church Yard entrance to the Pump Room from May to October, daily at 10:30am; Monday to Friday and Sunday at 2:30pm; and Tuesday, Friday, and Saturday at 7pm. From November to April, tours depart daily at 10:30am, Monday to Friday at 2pm, and Sunday at 2:30pm. The 90-minute tours of **Bizarre Bath** (✆ **01225/335-124;** www.bizarrebath.co.uk) use street theater for a humorous look at the city. Tours leave from in front of the

Huntsman Inn in North Parade Passage every evening at 8pm from April 1 to September 28, and cost £5 ($8) for adults, £4.50 ($7) for students; purchase tickets, in cash, at the time of the walk. The **Jane Austen Centre** (✆ **01225/443-000;** www.janeausten.co.uk) sponsors walking tours that focus on the novelist's residences and settings for her novels and are conducted daily at 1:30pm from June to September, and Saturday and Sunday at 1:30pm from October to May. Walks begin in Abbey Church Yard and cost £3.50 ($6) for adults; £2.50 ($4) for seniors, students, and children.

OUTDOOR ACTIVITIES

Skiffs, punts, and canoes are available for rental from the **Victorian Bath Boating Station,** on the River Avon beneath the Pulteney Bridge (May–Sept daily 10am–6pm; ✆ **01225/466-407**). The nearby Kennet and Avon Canal towpath is one of many local places ideal for hiking, cycling, and boating; the **Bath and Dundas Canal Company** (✆ **01225/722-292**) at the canal information office rents bikes as well as well as canoes and other boats. It's 5 miles (8km) south of Bath on the A36 at Monkton Combe. (Take bus no. 4, 5, or 6 from the train station.) Soaks and other water-related treatments are once again available in Bath at the luxurious new **Bath Spa,** next to the Roman Baths (✆ **1225/780-308;** www.bathspa.co.uk), scheduled to open in 2004.

3 Shopping

One of Bath's liveliest shopping venues is the **Green Park Arts and Craft Market,** in the historic Green Park train station, north of the center off Charles Street; the market is open from 9am to 5pm Tuesday through Sunday and hosts vendors selling everything from antiques to crafts to farm produce. Vendors at the **Bartlett Street Antique Centre,** near the Assembly Rooms on Bartlett Street, open Monday to Saturday from 9am to 5pm, sell jewelry, silver, prints, and other easily portable items. Vendors in the **Bath Saturday Antiques Market,** in the Old Cattle Market on Bath Walcot Street, sell collectibles of an unusually high quality Saturday from 6:30am to 2:30pm. Quill pens, needlepoint kits, and other items associated with Jane Austen are for sale in the gift shop of the **Jane Austen Centre** (✆ **01225/443-000**).

4 Where to Dine

Hands LIGHT FARE/TEA These bright, airy rooms next to Bath Abbey are especially popular for morning coffee and at teatime. Breakfast and lunchtime sandwiches and salads are available, too.

Moments **Soaking up Bath**

Bath was designed to be admired, so find a vantage point and just soak in the architectural grandeur of the place—two of the best are Royal Victoria Park, looking toward the Royal Crescent, and the Grand Parade, looking toward Pulteney Bridge.

Abbey St. ✆ **01225/463-928.** Most items £3.50–£7 ($6–$11). MC, V. Tues–Sat 9:30am–5:30pm; Sun 11am–4:30pm.

No. 5 Bistro FRENCH A welcoming, casual air pervades this handsome restaurant at the east end of Pulteney Bridge, where chef Michel Lemoine serves fresh fish, hearty soups, and other memorable dishes.

5 Argyle St. ✆ **01225/444-499.** £13–£14 ($20–$22). AE, MC, V. Tues–Sat noon–2:30pm; Mon–Thurs 6:30–10pm; Fri–Sun 6:30–10:30pm.

Popjoy's MODERN BRITISH/CONTINENTAL This 1720 home built for Julia Popjoy, mistress of the dandy Beau Nash, provides an elegant setting in which to enjoy seafood and innovative modern British cuisine.

Beau Nash House, Saw Close. ✆ **01225/460-494.** Main courses £15–£23 ($24–$37). AE, DC, MC, V. Mon–Sat noon–2:30pm and 6–11pm.

5 Extending Your Trip

Bath is so engaging that you may well want to spend the evening taking in a play at the Royal Theatre or enjoying a leisurely dinner, and continue your sightseeing the next day. Plus, Bath is a handy base from which to explore the nearby Cotswolds.

Kennard Hotel Just across the Pulteney Bridge from the city center, this handsome town house was built as lodgings in 1794 and still treats guests to tidy and comfortable accommodations, an attractive breakfast room, and a gracious welcome.

11 Henrietta St. ✆ **01225/310-472.** www.kennard.co.uk. £48–£118 ($77–$189) double. MC, V.

Royal Crescent Hotel These elegant, interconnected town houses not only boast the best address in town but provide elegant accommodations as well as a delightful garden and beautiful pool and spa.

16 Royal Crescent, Bath, Somerset BA1 2LS. ✆ **01225/823-333.** www.royalcrescent.co.uk. From £170 ($272) double. Check the website for special offers. AE, MC, V.

Trip 2

Battle

If you ever studied English history, the year 1066 probably rings a bell. In that year, in a battle that changed the course of English history, Duke William of Normandy defeated Harold, king of England, at the Battle of Hastings. After the battle, William became known as William the Conqueror. He had himself crowned king at Westminster Abbey and Winchester and began construction of the Tower of London and other fortifications. For taxation

Battle Highlights

- Walking the battleground where King Harold of England fought Duke William of Normandy.
- Exploring the ruins of Battle Abbey.

purposes, the new monarch compiled a list of every property and building in his newly conquered land. The list became the famous Domesday Book, which is today a unique record of England in the 11th century. But all this history started with a battle, and that's where Battle comes into the viewfinder. In the town, preserved behind high brick walls, is the battlefield where Saxon and Norman soldiers clashed on that fateful day in 1066. For anyone with an interest in history, Battle is a memorable spot to visit. Located 57 miles (92km) south of London, Battle makes a memorable day trip.

1 Essentials

VISITOR INFORMATION

The **Battle Tourist Information Centre,** 88 High St. (✆ **01424/773-721;** www.battletown.co.uk), across from Battle Abbey, has a free pamphlet that includes a town map. The center is open daily, from 10am to 6pm in summer and from 10am to 4pm in winter.

SCHEDULING CONSIDERATIONS

The battlefield site is open daily until 6pm in summer, until 5pm in October, and until 4pm November through March. The last audio tours are issued 1 hour before closing.

GETTING THERE

BY TRAIN

Battle is a stop on the London–Hastings line, and direct train service is available from London's Charing Cross Station. The trip takes about 90 minutes. A standard day return costs about £16 ($26). The first direct train from London departs at 7:43am; the last direct train to London departs Battle at 8:57pm. For train schedules and information, call **National Rail Enquiries** at ✆ **08457/484-950.**

BY BUS

There is currently no daytime coach service from London to Battle.

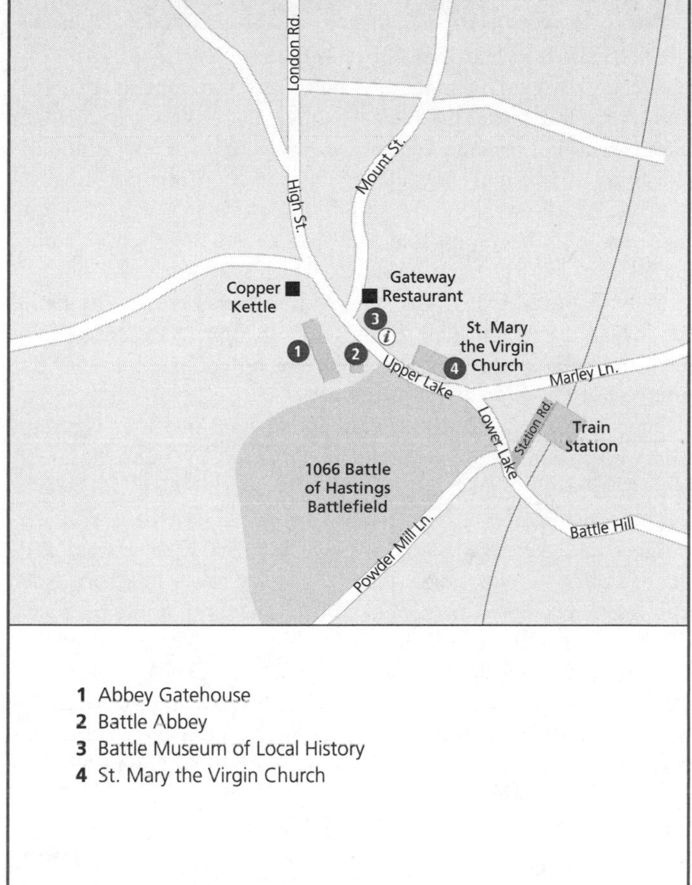

BY CAR

Battle is about 6 miles (9.5km) north of Hastings on A2100. From London, head southeast towards the coast and Hastings on A21, cutting south at Sevenoaks and continuing along A21 to Battle via A2100. Free parking lots are located near the entrance to the battlefield.

GETTING AROUND

To reach the battlefield from the train station, take Station Road to Lower Lake, and follow Lower Lake north as it becomes Upper Lake; the easy walk takes about 10 minutes. Taxis are usually available outside the station, or you can reserve one by calling **Town Country** (✆ **01424/772-222**) or **4167 Cars** (✆ **01424/774-167**). Walking is the only way to see the battlefield.

2 A Day in Battle

The **1066 Battle of Hastings Abbey and Battlefield** (✆ **01424/773-792**), hidden behind high walls on High Street, is the one site that you want to see in Battle. This ancient battleground offers a fascinating journey back in time, and you should give yourself at least 2 unhurried hours to take it all in. The preservationist organization English Heritage, which owns the site, has done a clever job of making the experience both interesting and informative. You are given an audio guide when you pay for your ticket, which will guide you along a pathway that runs through the field, with markers keyed to the audio text. The site is open daily from 10am to 6pm (Oct until 5pm, Nov–Mar until 4pm). Admission is £5 ($8) for adults, £3.80 ($6) for seniors, and £2.50 ($4.10) for children.

Enter through the ❶ **Abbey Gatehouse,** built in 1338. The tour starts with an outdoor video presentation that fills you in on the major events leading up to the battle. Next comes an exhibition, "Prelude to Battle," which uses text panels to draw you deeper into the story of the intrigues and the royal power struggle between King Harold and Duke William of Normandy. Finally, you walk onto the battlefield itself, where descriptive panels linked to the audio tour line the pathway. The battle's events unfold as seen through the eyes of three different narrators: Aelfric, a Saxon thane; Henri, a French knight; and Edith, the wife of King Harold. As you tour the battlefield, you can follow the story and tactics used by both sides from these three perspectives. The complete tour takes about an hour; a shorter version takes about 45 minutes.

❷ **Battle Abbey,** the great church that William constructed to mark the spot where King Harold was slain, was destroyed by Henry VIII in 1539. Today it's an atmospheric ruin.

Leaving the Battle Abbey site, turn left and cross High Street to reach the small ❸ **Battle Museum of Local History** (✆ **01424/775-955**). Among the artifacts on display are the only battle-axe discovered from the Battle of Hastings site, and early-19th-century engravings of the Bayeux Tapestry (which chronicled the battle). The museum is

---

Moments Incendiary Traditions

Sitting in the front hallway of the Almonery, the building on High Street that houses the Copper Kettle restaurant, is one of the oldest Guy Fawkes effigies in the country. Bearded and dressed in black and red with a pointed hat, the figure is paraded around town before a bonfire is lit on Guy Fawkes Night, November 5.

---

open April through October, Monday to Saturday from 10:30am to 4:30pm, and Sunday 2 to 5pm. Admission is £1 ($1.60).

Heading back down High Street, you reach Upper Lake and ❹ **St. Mary the Virgin Church** (✆ **01424/773-649**), originally built on the battlefield but now standing outside the walls. The church has a magnificent Romanesque nave, a Norman font with medieval cover, rare 14th-century wall paintings, and the gilded alabaster tomb of Sir Anthony Browne, to whom Henry VIII granted the Battle Abbey. The church is open Easter through September, Monday to Friday from 10:30am to 4:30pm; October through Easter, Wednesday to Friday from 10am to noon.

3 Shopping

Friar House, High Street (✆ **01424/777100**), dates back to 1642 and sells pottery made in 17th-century style.

4 Where to Dine

Copper Kettle LIGHT FARE/TEAS Located in the Almonery, a lovely, beamed medieval hall (where the Town Council meets) with a pretty walled garden, this is an atmospheric spot for a simple lunch or afternoon tea.

High St. ✆ **01424/772-727.** Lunch £4–£5 ($7–$8). No credit cards. Mon–Sat 9:30am–4:30pm.

Gateway Restaurant TRADITIONAL BRITISH For hearty and traditional home-cooked English food, try this spot. Lunch specials usually include several old-fashioned pies: steak, ale, and mushroom; steak and kidney; and chicken, leek, and bacon. You can also get toasted sandwiches, an all-day brunch, or an afternoon cream tea.

78 High St. ✆ **01424/772-056.** Lunch £4.50–£5.50 ($7–$9); cream tea £4 ($6). No credit cards. Daily 9am–5:30pm.

Brighton

On the Sussex coast, a mere 50 miles (80km) south of London on the English Channel, Brighton is England's most famous and popular seaside town. It was a small fishing village until the prince regent, a fun-loving dandy who reigned as George IV from 1820 to 1830, became enamored of the place and had the Royal Pavilion built. Where royalty moves, fashion follows, and Brighton eventually became one of Europe's most fashionable towns. The long terraces of Georgian

Brighton Highlights

- Touring the extravagant Royal Pavilion.
- Promenading along the seafront.
- Visiting the Brighton Art Gallery's top-notch furniture collection.

town homes that you see everywhere in Brighton date from that period. Later in the 19th century, when doctors prescribed breathing sea air as a cure-all, the Victorians descended en masse. Today, Brighton is a popular place for weekend getaways. People come to hang out on the long stretch of beach, shop, stroll, and party the night away at clubs and discos. You may find you want to spend more than 1 day in Brighton, so we've recommended some hotels at the end of this chapter. If you do decide to spend more than a day in Brighton, consider combining this trip with a visit to nearby Monk's House and Charleston (see trip 14).

1 Essentials

VISITOR INFORMATION

Brighton's **Tourist Information Centre,** 10 Bartholomew Sq. (© **0906/711-2255;** www.tourism.brighton.co.uk), is opposite the town hall, about a 10-minute walk south from the train station. The center is open Monday through Friday from 9am to 5:30pm, on Saturday from 10am to 5pm, and on Sunday from 10am to 4pm.

SCHEDULING CONSIDERATIONS

You might want to time your visit to coincide with the **Brighton International Festival** (© **01273/292-950;** www.brighton-festival.org.uk) in May. One of England's best-known arts festivals, it features a wide array of drama, literature, visual art, dance, and concert programs ranging from classical to hard rock.

GETTING THERE

BY TRAIN

Connex South Central runs over 40 direct trains a day from London's Victoria Station, with the first trains departing at 8:02am (later on weekends), and returning to London hourly until almost 10pm. The trip takes about an hour; an off-peak (after 9:30am) return ticket costs £15 ($24). For train schedules and more information, call **National Rail Enquiries** (© **08457/484-950**).

Brighton

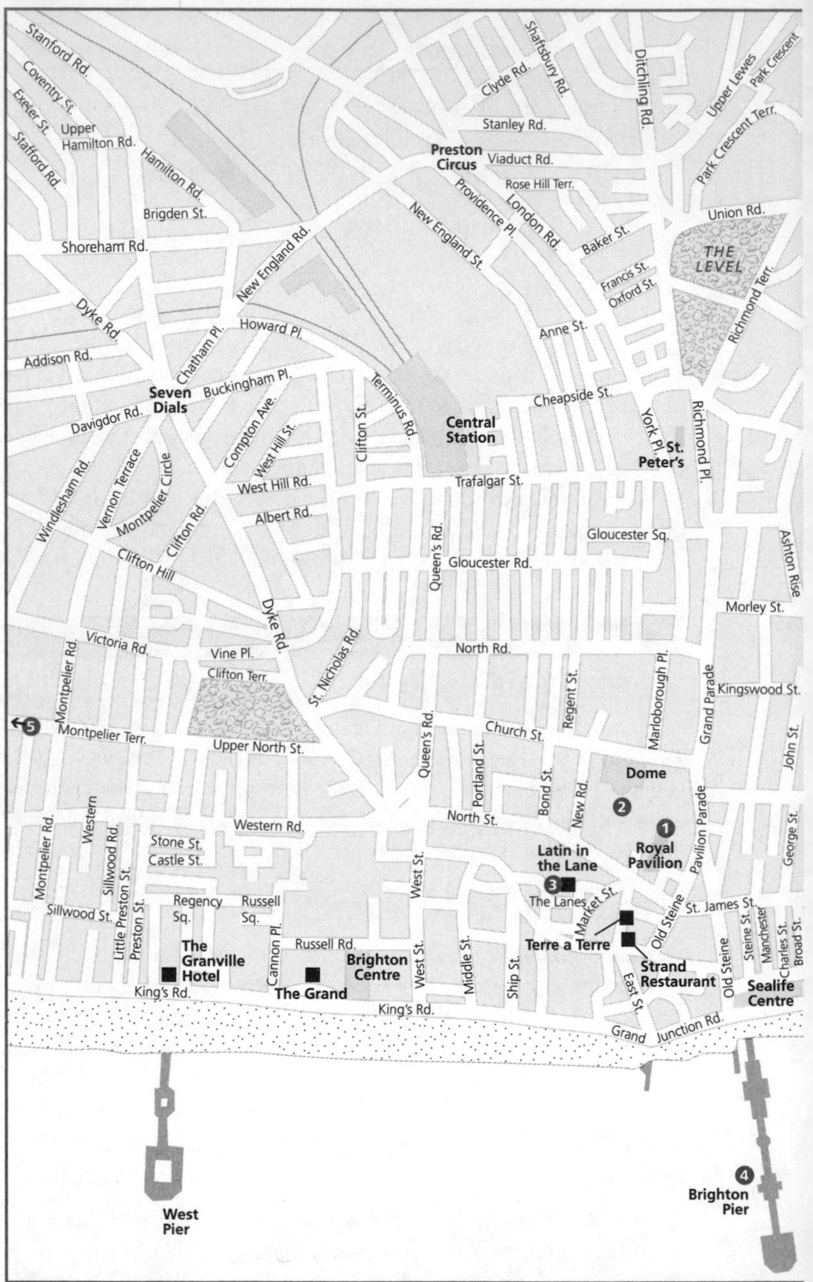

Stanford Rd.
Coventry St.
Exeter St.
Stafford Rd.
Upper Hamilton Rd.
Hamilton Rd.
Brigden St.
Shoreham Rd.
Dyke Rd.
Addison Rd.
Davigdor Rd.
Seven Dials
Chatham Pl.
Howard Pl.
New England Rd.
Buckingham Pl.
Compton Ave.
West Hill St.
West Hill Rd.
Albert Rd.
Windlesham Rd.
Vernon Terrace
Montpelier Circle
Clifton Rd.
Clifton Hill
Victoria Rd.
Vine Pl.
Clifton Terr.
Montpelier Rd.
Montpelier Terr.
Upper North St.
Dyke Rd.
St. Nicholas Rd.
Clifton St.
Terminus Rd.
Central Station
Preston Circus
Viaduct Rd.
Stanley Rd.
Clyde Rd.
Shaftsbury Rd.
Ditchling Rd.
Upper Lewes
Park Crescent
Park Crescent Terr.
Rose Hill Terr.
Providence Pl.
London Rd.
New England St.
Baker St.
Union Rd.
THE LEVEL
Francis St.
Oxford St.
Richmond Terr.
Anne St.
Cheapside St.
York Pl.
St. Peter's
Richmond Pl.
Trafalgar St.
Gloucester Sq.
Queen's Rd.
Gloucester Rd.
Ashton Rise
Morley St.
North Rd.
Regent St.
Marlborough Pl.
Grand Parade
Kingswood St.
Church St.
Queen's Rd.
Portland St.
Bond St.
New Rd.
Dome
John St.
Pavilion Parade
George St.
North St.
Western Rd.
Western
Sillwood Rd.
Stone St.
Castle St.
Latin in the Lane
Royal Pavilion
The Lanes
Market St.
West St.
St. James St.
Sillwood St.
Little Preston St.
Preston St.
Regency Sq.
Russell Sq.
Cannon Pl.
Russell Rd.
Terre a Terre
Old Steine
Steine St.
Manchester
Charles St.
Broad St.
The Granville Hotel
Brighton Centre
Middle St.
Ship St.
Strand Restaurant
East St.
Old Steine
Sealife Centre
King's Rd.
The Grand
King's Rd.
Grand Junction Rd.
West Pier
Brighton Pier

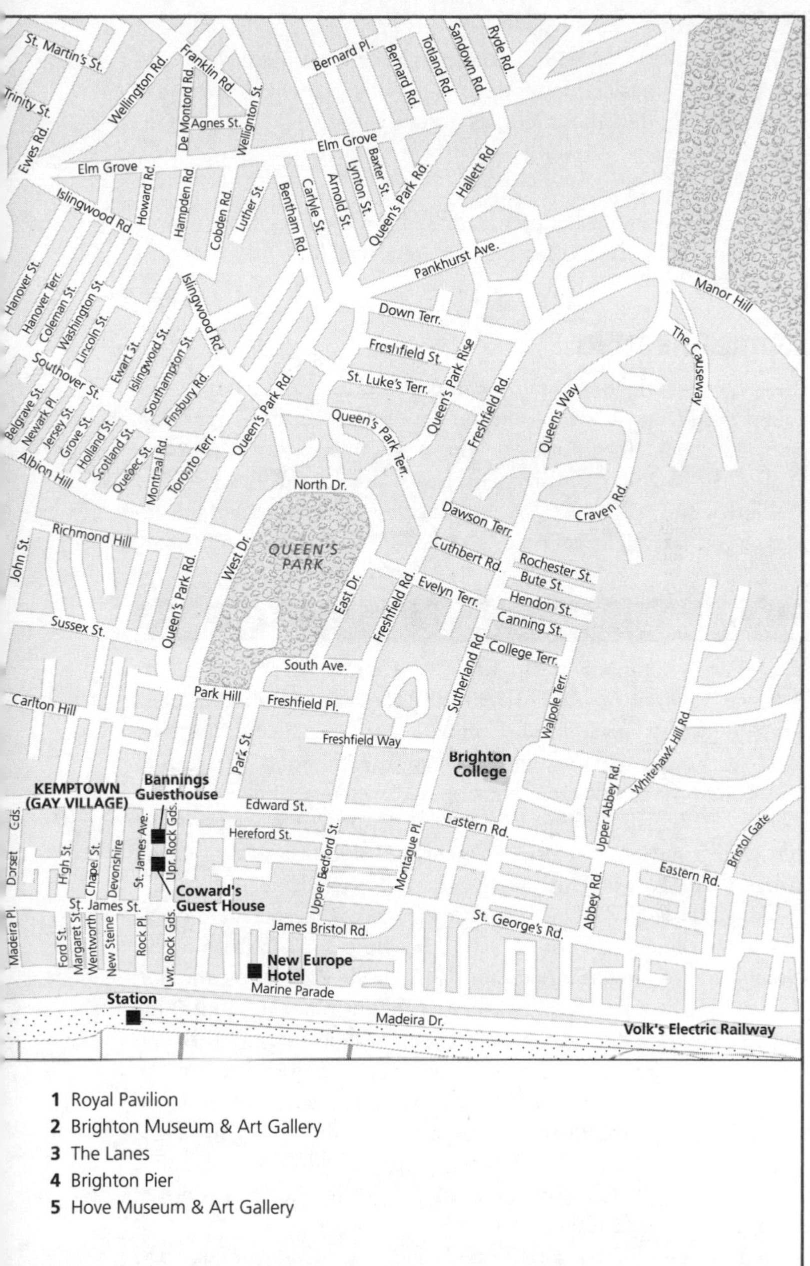
St. Martin's St.
Trinity St.
Ewes Rd.
Wellington Rd.
Franklin Rd.
De Montford Rd.
Agnes St.
Wellington St.
Bernard Pl.
Bernard Rd.
Totland Rd.
Sandown Rd.
Ryde Rd.
Elm Grove
Elm Grove
Howard Rd.
Hampden Rd.
Cobden Rd.
Luther St.
Bentham Rd.
Carlyle St.
Arnold St.
Lynton St.
Baxter St.
Queen's Park Rd.
Hallett Rd.
Islingwood Rd.
Pankhurst Ave.
Manor Hill
Hanover St.
Hanover Terr.
Coleman St.
Washington St.
Lincoln St.
Islingwood Rd.
Down Terr.
Freshfield St.
Queen's Park Rise
St. Luke's Terr.
Freshfield Rd.
The Causeway
Southover St.
Ewart St.
Islingword St.
Southampton St.
Finsbury Rd.
Queen's Park Rd.
Queen's Park Terr.
Queens Way
Belgrave St.
Newark Pl.
Jersey St.
Grove St.
Holland St.
Scotland St.
Quebec St.
Montreal Rd.
Toronto Terr.
Albion Hill
North Dr.
Dawson Terr.
Craven Rd.
Richmond Hill
John St.
West Dr.
QUEEN'S PARK
Cuthbert Rd.
Rochester St.
Bute St.
Queen's Park Rd.
East Dr.
Freshfield Rd.
Evelyn Terr.
Hendon St.
Canning St.
Sussex St.
Sutherland Rd.
College Terr.
South Ave.
Walpole Terr.
Park Hill
Freshfield Pl.
Carlton Hill
Whitehawk Hill Rd
Freshfield Way
Park St.
Brighton College
KEMPTOWN (GAY VILLAGE)
Bannings Guesthouse
Edward St.
Upper Abbey Rd.
Eastern Rd.
Hereford St.
Bristol Gate
Dorset Gds.
High St.
Chapel St.
Devonshire
St. James Ave.
Upr. Rock Gds.
Upper Bedford St.
Montague Pl.
Eastern Rd.
Coward's Guest House
Abbey Rd.
St. James St.
St. George's Rd.
Madeira Pl.
Ford St.
Margaret St.
Wentworth
New Steine
Rock Pl.
Lwr. Rock Gds.
James Bristol Rd.
New Europe Hotel
Marine Parade
Station
Madeira Dr.
Volk's Electric Railway
1 Royal Pavilion
2 Brighton Museum & Art Gallery
3 The Lanes
4 Brighton Pier
5 Hove Museum & Art Gallery

BY BUS

National Express (✆ **0990/808-080;** www.nationalexpress.com) runs hourly buses from London's Victoria Coach Station. A same-day return ticket for the 2-hour journey costs £9 ($14).

BY CAR

The M23 from central London leads to Brighton. The drive should take about 1 to 1½ hours, but if roads are clogged, the trip may take twice as long.

GETTING AROUND

The center of Brighton is fairly compact, so the easiest way to get around is on foot; the walk from the train station to the Royal Pavilion takes about 10 minutes. **Brighton and Hove Bus Company** (✆ **01273/886-200**) offers frequent service along the main streets; the local fare is £1.20 ($1.90). Taxis are usually available at the train station, or you can call **Streamline** (✆ **01273/747-474**) to reserve one.

2 A Day in Brighton

Start your explorations at Brighton's one must-see attraction, the ❶ **Royal Pavilion** (✆ **01273/290-900**). Set in a small landscaped park bounded by North Street, Church Street, Olde Steine, and New Road, the Royal Pavilion is one of the most extraordinary palaces in Europe. John Nash redesigned the original farmhouse and villa on this site into an Indian fantasy of turrets and minarets for George IV (when the king was still prince regent). The fun- and food-loving George lived here with his mistress, Lady Conyngham, until 1827. The king's brother, William IV, and their niece, Queen Victoria, also used the pavilion. Give yourself about an hour for a leisurely walk-through tour of the sumptuous and fantastically extravagant interior. The Long Gallery has a color scheme of bright blues and pinks; the Music Room has a domed ceiling of gilded, scallop-shaped shells; and the king's private apartments on the upper floors epitomize the Regency lifestyle of the rich and royal. The Queen Adelaide Tea Room is a nice spot to have lunch or afternoon tea. The Royal Pavilion is open daily from 10am to 5:15pm (Apr–Sept 9:30am–5:45pm). Admission is £5.80 ($9) for adults, £4 ($4.50) for students and seniors, £3.40 ($4) for children under 16.

On the west side of the Royal Pavilion's gardens, you find the ❷ **Brighton Museum & Art Gallery** (✆ **01273/290-900**). Admission is free to this small, attractive museum with interesting collections of Art Nouveau and Art Deco furniture, glass, and ceramics, plus

Moments Catcreep-ing through Brighton

Exploring Brighton's catcreeps and twittens takes you into a secretive, hidden side of this otherwise flamboyant seaside town. Catcreeps are flights of steps connecting two roads at different levels on a hillside, and a twitten is a Sussex word used to describe a narrow path between two walls or hedges, or wall and hedge, usually leading from one street to another. You'll find catcreeps and twittens around The Lanes.

a fashion gallery. The museum is open Monday, Tuesday, and Thursday through Saturday from 10am to 5pm; Sunday from 2 to 5pm.

From the museum, head south on New Road, turning south on North Street, and south again on Market Street. This brings you to ❸ **The Lanes,** the warren of narrow streets that was Brighton's original fishing village. Today the area is filled with small shops. After you've browsed The Lanes, continue south on Market Street and then follow East Street down to the seafront. Brighton and neighboring Hove stretch along the English Channel, and the entire seafront is a pebbly public beach used for swimming and sunning. Stroll along the wide promenade and out to sea on the town's famous and tackily entertaining amusement area, ❹ **Brighton Pier.** The pier was built in the late 19th century when Brighton became a major holiday resort. At night, all lit up with twinkling lights, it's cheerily irresistible, even though you won't find much more than junk food and arcade games. Admission is free and it's open round the clock.

MORE THINGS TO SEE & DO

❺ **Hove Museum & Art Gallery** In the town that adjoins Brighton to the west, the Hove Museum is housed in an impressive Victorian villa and contains a good collection of 20th-century paintings and drawings, 18th-century furniture and decorative art, and the "Hove to Hollywood" film collection featuring film of the town in 1900 by local moviemakers. (The British film industry started in Hove.) The museum is about a 15-minute walk from the Royal Pavilion.

19 New Church Rd. ✆ **01273/290-200.** Free admission. Tues–Fri 10am–5pm; Sat–Sun 10am–4:30pm.

ORGANIZED TOURS

At 8pm on the first Saturday of every month, a 90-minute **Ghost Walk** departs from Brighton Town Hall, The Lanes, visiting ancient graveyards and finishing at a haunted inn. The **Quadrophenia Walking Tour,** reliving The Who's cult classic film about mods and rockers in 1964 Brighton, leaves at 2pm from Brighton Town Hall on the first Saturday of most months and visits all the Brighton locations featured in the film, with behind-the-scenes stories and commentary about the real-life events that inspired it. Each walk costs £5 ($8). For more information on these and other special guided walks, visit the website www.brightonwalks.com or call ✆ **01273/888-596.** You can buy your tickets on the spot without advance reservations, but it's a good idea to call first to verify times.

OUTDOOR ACTIVITIES

The entire seafront is an uninterrupted beach available for sunning and swimming, though the water in the English Channel is more than brisk and the pebbly shoreline not exactly conducive to lolling. If you're into sunbathing *au naturel,* you're in luck: Brighton has the only nude beach in England, about a mile (1.5km) west of Brighton Pier. You can walk there along the promenade above the beach or take Volk's Electric Railway, England's oldest, along Madeira Drive to the marina.

3 Shopping

The Lanes, Brighton's original fishing village, is now a warren of narrow streets filled with small shops selling upscale goods and many tourist trinkets. **North Laines** has more interesting shops, including some trendy outfitters. **Duke Street** and **Upper North Street** are good for antiques. Shops in Brighton are generally open Monday through Saturday between 10am and 6pm, with a later closing on Thursday or Friday. During the summer tourist season, some shops are open on Sunday and closed on Monday.

4 Where to Dine

Latin in the Lane ITALIAN/SEAFOOD At this restaurant you can sample Italian antipasti, such as melon with Parma ham or mixed salami with fresh figs, and then go on to pastas or fish, which comes fresh from the market every day. The seafood risotto with wild mushrooms, cream, and white wine is good, and so is the casserole of fresh, seasonal seafood and the mussels in white wine, parsley, and garlic.

10/11 King's Rd. ✆ **01273/328-672.** Main courses £6–£14 ($10–$22). AE, DC, MC, V. Daily noon–2:15pm and 6:30–11pm.

Strand Restaurant MODERN BRITISH/SEAFOOD One of the hippest (and friendliest) places for dining is the bow-fronted Strand. The ever-changing (but fixed-price) menu is an extremely good value. Herby homemade vegetable soup, pâté, or mussels cooked with fresh cream, wine, and garlic may be followed by chicken breast with leeks and blue cheese sauce, artichoke-and-pesto lasagna, or lamb chops with gravy and a dessert.

6 Little East St. ✆ **01273/747-096.** Main courses £8–£15 ($13–$24). AE, DC, MC, V. Daily 12:30–10pm.

Terre à Terre VEGETARIAN Considered the finest vegetarian restaurant in England, Terre à Terre elevates meatless cuisine into the art it should be but rarely is. The food is impeccably fresh and beautifully presented. You can eat your way through the menu with the Terre à Tapas, a superb selection of all their best dishes, big enough for two.

71 East St. ✆ **01273/729-051.** Reservations essential weekends. Main courses £10–£11 ($16–$18). DC, MC, V. Mon 6–10:30pm; Tues–Sat noon–10:30pm; Sun 10am–10:30pm (brunch 10am–1pm).

5 Extending Your Trip

The Grand The grandest place to stay in Brighton is the Grand, a huge, dazzling-white resort hotel built on the seafront in 1864. The only five-star luxury hotel in Brighton, it has 200 spacious and predictably gorgeous guest rooms with big tile bathrooms.

King's Rd., Brighton, E. Sussex BN1 2FW. ✆ **01273/224-300.** Fax 01273/224-321. www.grandbrighton.co.uk. £230–£250 ($368–$400) double. Rates include English breakfast. AE, DC, MC, V.

Brighton's Gay & Lesbian Hotels & B&Bs

Several hotels and B&Bs in Brighton cater to gay and lesbian visitors. **Bannings Guesthouse,** 14 Upper Rock Gardens, Brighton, Sussex BN2 1QE (✆ **01273/681-403;** www.bannings.co.uk), is a snug Georgian town house for women only. It has six bedrooms, all with private bathrooms, that cost £45 to £50 ($72–$80) double, breakfast included. **Coward's Guest House,** 12 Upper Rock Gardens, Brighton, Sussex BN2 1QE (✆ **01273/692-677**), is a dapper, Regency-era town house that caters to men. It has six bedrooms with private bathrooms that rent for £45 to £60 ($72–$96) double, breakfast included. The **New Europe Hotel,** 31–32 Marine Parade, Brighton, Sussex BN2 1TR (✆ **01273/624-462;** fax 01273/624-575; www.legendsbar.co.uk), is the largest (30 rooms) gay-owned and -operated hotel in Brighton. A double room with private bathroom costs £60 to £65 ($96–$104), breakfast included. The hotel is also the home of Legends, one of the most popular gay clubs in town.

The Granville Hotel *Kids* Located opposite the West Pier, Granville's is a good choice if you're looking for a smaller hotel on the seafront. A former town house, this place has 24 individually designed rooms, all with private bathrooms and some with four-poster beds. The hotel is completely nonsmoking and welcomes families with children.

124 Kings Rd., Brighton, E. Sussex BNT 2FA. ✆ **01273/326-302.** Fax 01273/728-294. www.granvillehotel.co.uk. £85–£145 ($136–$232) double. Rates include breakfast. MC, V.

Trip 4

Cambridge

Cambridge, like Oxford, is forever linked with the venerable university that has flourished here on the banks of the River Cam for 7 centuries. Obviously, the chance to step into a few of the 31 colleges and view their architectural wonders is what brings many visitors to Cambridge. But you're in for a pleasant surprise—this town that rises from marshy lands known as fens is itself a gem, an appealing blend of

Cambridge Highlights

- A concert by the internationally famous King's College Choir.
- The eclectic Fitzwilliam Museum, where you can see the first draft of Keats's "Ode to a Nightingale."
- The Tower at beautiful Queens' College, where the great scholar, Erasmus, lived from 1510 to 1514.
- Punting along the River Cam.

busy markets and shops, medieval architecture, and grassy riverside meadows. There's even a nice 21st-century buzz to the place, as dot-commers settle into what has become known as "Silicon Fen." You'll want to spend a whole day in Cambridge, so get an early start. If you decide to extend your visit, see the last section in this chapter for nightlife and hotel recommendations.

1 Essentials

VISITOR INFORMATION

The **Tourist Information Centre (TIC),** Wheeler Street (✆ **01223/322-640;** www.cambridge.gov.uk/leisure/tourism.htm), is behind the Guildhall and provides information on transportation and sightseeing, as well as useful maps. The office is open all year, Monday to Friday 10am to 5:30pm, Saturday 10am to 5pm, Sunday 11am to 4pm. To find out more about Cambridge University, including opening times for the colleges, it's best to surf the extensive website, www.cam.ac.uk, which has links to websites for each college; or call ✆ **01223/337-733.**

SCHEDULING CONSIDERATIONS

What colleges you are able to see depends upon when you visit, since many close during exam periods (in May and June) and are open for limited hours during terms, which in general run from mid-January to mid-March, mid-April to mid-June, and mid-October to mid-December. You'll only be able to hear the King's College Choir during terms and the first half of July. The colleges are most crowded with visitors during the summer holidays. Keep in mind that the Fitzwilliam Museum and Kettle's Yard are closed on Monday.

Cambridge

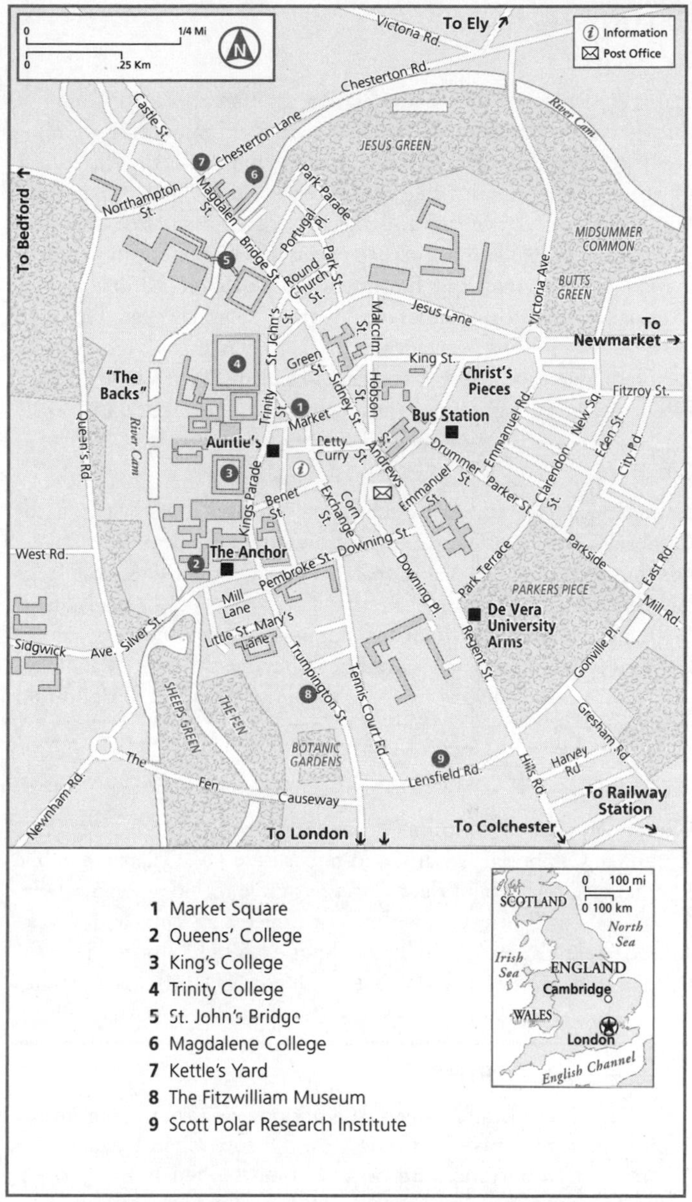
0
1/4 Mi
0
.25 Km
N
Information
Post Office
To Ely
Victoria Rd.
Chesterton Rd.
River Cam
Castle St.
Chesterton Lane
JESUS GREEN
To Bedford
Northampton St.
Magdalen St.
Park Parade
Portugal Pl.
Bridge St.
MIDSUMMER COMMON
Round Church St.
Park St.
BUTTS GREEN
Victoria Ave.
Jesus Lane
Malcolm St.
To Newmarket
St. John's St.
King St.
"The Backs"
Green St.
Hobson St.
Christ's Pieces
Fitzroy St.
Trinity St.
Sidney St.
Market
Bus Station
Emmanuel Rd.
New Sq.
Queen's Rd.
River Cam
Auntie's
Petty Curry St.
St. Andrews St.
Drummer St.
Eden St.
City Rd.
Emmanuel St.
Parker St.
Clarendon St.
Kings Parade
Benet St.
Corn Exchange St.
Downing St.
Parkside
West Rd.
The Anchor
Pembroke St.
Park Terrace
East Rd.
Mill Lane
Downing Pl.
PARKERS PIECE
Mill Rd.
De Vera University Arms
Little St. Mary's Lane
Silver St.
Sidgwick Ave.
Regent St.
Gonville Pl.
Trumpington St.
Tennis Court Rd.
SHEEPS GREEN
THE FEN
Gresham Rd.
BOTANIC GARDENS
Lensfield Rd.
Hills Rd.
Harvey Rd
The Fen Causeway
Newnham Rd.
To Railway Station
To London
To Colchester
1 Market Square
2 Queens' College
3 King's College
4 Trinity College
5 St. John's Bridge
6 Magdalene College
7 Kettle's Yard
8 The Fitzwilliam Museum
9 Scott Polar Research Institute
0 100 mi
0 100 km
SCOTLAND
North Sea
Irish Sea
ENGLAND
Cambridge
WALES
London
English Channel

GETTING THERE

BY TRAIN

Trains depart from King's Cross Station as often as every 15 minutes throughout the day, but try to take a train at 15 minutes or 45 minutes past the hour—these are the fast trains and make the trip in just 45 minutes. (Other trains take a bit over an hour.) The first train from London departs at 4:30am and the last train returns to London at 11:20pm. The standard day return fare is £18 ($29). For more information, call **National Rail Enquiries** (✆ **08457/484-950**) or go to www.nationalrail.co.uk. The Cambridge train station is located south of town on Station Road. You can walk or take a bus or taxi from the train station to Market Square and the center of town, about a mile (1.5km) away; buses run about every 15 minutes and the fare is £.80 ($1.30).

BY BUS

National Express buses leave London's Victoria Coach Station for Cambridge every half hour to hour throughout the day. Try to take a bus that makes the trip in less than 2 hours—some make more stops and take quite a bit longer. The return fare is £15 ($23). An advantage to taking the bus rather than the train is the central location of the Cambridge bus station, on Drummer Street at the edge of the city-center pedestrian zone. For more information, call ✆ **08705/808-080** or go to www.nationalexpress.com.

BY CAR

Cambridge is about 60 miles (97km) north of London on the M11. Parking in Cambridge is scarce and rather expensive. There are public lots scattered throughout the city center; these include Lion Yard Car Park, Grafton Centre Car Park, Park Street Car Park, and Queen Anne Terrace Car Park. You'll pay about £1.40 ($2.30) per hour for parking, and about £12 ($19) for 4 or 5 hours. The park-and-ride sites

---

Tips **Cycling 101**

The significant brainpower at Cambridge does not come into play when students mount bicycles, the town's most common form of transportation. Be on your guard when you step off curbs—always look both ways—and be on the lookout for cyclists roaring up behind you when you saunter down paths along the Backs and on such greenswards as Parker's Piece. If you wish to follow the old adage, "If you can't beat them, join them," rent a bicycle and pedal around town yourself. (See "Outdoor Activities," below.)

---

in outlying areas (well marked from entrances to the city) are less expensive, and regular bus service connects them with the city center.

GETTING AROUND

Cambridge (pop. 111,000) is an easily walkable city with two main streets. **Trumpington Road**—which becomes Trumpington Street, King's Parade, Trinity Street, and finally St. John's Street—runs parallel to the River Cam and provides easy access to several of the colleges. **Bridge Street,** the city's main shopping zone, starts at Magdalene Bridge; it becomes Sidney Street, St. Andrew's Street, and finally Regent Street. Taxis are available at the train station; if you need one elsewhere in town, call **A1 Taxis** (© **01223/525-555**) or **Cabco** (© **01223/312-444**).

2 A Day in Cambridge

You won't have time to see all the colleges, and some are not of great architectural interest anyway. To see a nice swath of colleges from the outside and to get a sense of the university's grandeur, take a stroll along the Backs—the meadows between the colleges and the River Cam.

Start at ❶ **Market Square.** From there, follow King's Parade and take a right on Silver Street to ❷ **Queens' College** (© **01223/335-511**), founded in 1448 and named for Margaret of Anjou, the wife of Henry VI, and Elizabeth, wife of Edward IV. The college straddles both banks of the River Cam, which you cross using the famous wooden Mathematical Bridge—or infamous, as unfounded stories hold that students have taken it apart and been unable to reconstruct it. The bridge is one of many architectural landmarks at Queens' College that include the handsome brick 16th-century **President's Lodge,** and **The Tower,** where the great scholar, Erasmus, lived from 1510 to 1514. Hours vary, but the college is generally open to the public from October 20 to March 21, daily from 1:45 to 4:30pm; at other times, from 10 or 11am to 4:30pm—check at the porter's lodge. The entrance fee is £1.30 ($2).

Head back down King's Parade to ❸ **King's College** (© **01223/331-100,** or 01223/331-155 for the chapel), founded by Henry VI in 1441 and justifiably famous for its choir and the traditional Festival of Nine Lessons and Carols, which is broadcast every Christmas Eve. Even without the presence of these heavenly voices, the chapel is a fairly transcendental place, with its incredible fan vaulting, stained-glass windows and, behind the altar, Rubens's glorious *Adoration of the Magi,* painted in 1634. Step into the small exhibition room to read about the chapel's history.

Try to attend a choral service for the full experience. (You can normally hear Evensong Mon–Sat at 5:30pm and Sun at 10:30am and 3:30pm, but only during university terms and during the first half of July; call to check.) During term, the college (including the chapel) is open Monday through Friday from 9:30am to 3:30pm, Saturday from 9:30am to 3:15pm, and Sunday from 1:15 to 2:15pm. Out of term, the college is open Monday through Saturday from 9:30am to 4:30pm, and Sunday from 10am to 5pm. The chapel is closed December 26 through January 1, and often without notice for recording sessions and rehearsals. Admission is £4 ($6) for adults, £3 ($4.80) for students and children.

King's Parade turns into Trinity Street, which will lead you to ❹ **Trinity College** (✆ **01223/338-400**), the largest and wealthiest of Cambridge's colleges, founded by Henry VIII in 1546. (The king is irreverently commemorated in a statue on the Great Gate in which he clutches a chair leg instead of a sword—the alteration was a student prank.) Trinity has produced 31 Nobel Laureates. Famous alumni include former Indian prime minister Jawaharlal Nehru; the scientist Sir Isaac Newton; poets and writers Francis Bacon, Lord Tennyson, Lord Byron, Andrew Marvell, and John Dryden; and philosopher Bertrand Russell. The 2-acre (.8-hectare) Great Court—the largest enclosed courtyard in Europe—is the scene of the Great Court Run, the point of which is to run around the court in the time it takes the clock to strike noon, a scene you may remember from the movie *Chariots of Fire.* Pass through the hall at the west end of the court to Nevile's Cloister and the impressive **Wren Library,** designed by the 17th-century architect of St. Paul's cathedral in London. The college (not including the library) is open to the public daily from 10am to 5pm, but it closes during exams and at other periods, and certain parts may be closed the day you visit; ask at the porter's lodge before you pay admission, which is £2 ($3.20) for adults, £1 ($1.60) for seniors and students. The library is open free of charge to the public Monday to Friday from noon to 2pm and Saturday from 10:30am to 12:30pm.

From the library, head toward the Backs and follow the Cam up to ❺ **St. John's Bridge,** a replica of the Bridge of Sighs in Venice; the span joins the New Court of St. John's College with the older section

---

Fun Fact Mad, Bad & Dangerous to Know

According to legend, the poet Byron used to bathe naked in the large central fountain in Trinity College's Great Court. The famous description of Byron as "mad, bad, and dangerous to know" was given to him later in life by Lady Caroline Lamb, one of Byron's many conquests.

Apostles of Knowledge

Of the many learned societies that have flourished at Cambridge over the centuries, few have become better known than the Bloomsbury Group, named for the district of London around the British Museum where this salon of writers, artists, and thinkers lived and often met. Most of the male members—E. M. Forster, Lytton Strachey, John Maynard Keynes, and Leonard Woolf among them—studied at Cambridge, and many belonged to the Apostles, a club founded at the university in the 1820s that met to discuss intellectual and philosophical issues. In London the group branched out to include women, most notably Vanessa Bell and Virginia Woolf (sisters of Thoby Stephens, a Cambridge Apostle and group founder). The group flourished into the 1930s.

of the college. Take St. John's Street to Magdalene (pronounced "*maud*-len") Street. It leads to ❻ **Magdalene College** (✆ **01223/332-100**), where the Pepys Library houses the diarist's collection of 3,000 volumes (open to the public 2 hr. a day; check with the porter); and **Jesus College** (✆ **01223/339-339**), where the chapel's stained-glass windows were designed by Edward Burne-Jones and its ceiling by William Morris. (You can admire them during Evensong on Tues, Thurs, and Sat at 6:30pm.)

Continue up Magdalene until you reach the intersection of Castle and Northampton streets, where you'll find ❼ **Kettle's Yard** (✆ **01223/352-124;** www.kettlesyard.co.uk), a very different kettle of fish. Jim Ede was the curator at the Tate during the 1920s and 1930s. He and his wife Helen acquired this collection of artworks, furniture, and decorative objects, which are displayed as he arranged them in his home. You'll find work by Ben Nicholson, Christopher Wood, and Alfred Wallis; and sculptures by Henry Moore, Henri Gaudier-Brzeska, Brancusi, and Barbara Hepworth. The gallery, meanwhile, holds exhibitions of 20th-century art. The house is open Tuesday to Sunday and Bank Holiday Mondays from 1:30 to 4:30pm (2–4pm in winter), and the gallery Tuesday to Sunday and Bank Holiday Mondays from 11:30am to 5pm. Admission is free.

MORE THINGS TO SEE & DO

❽ **The Fitzwilliam Museum** This museum is an eclectic treasure house of Egyptian and Greek antiquities, Chinese jades and bronzes, pages from Books of Hours, and the first draft of Keats's "Ode to a

Moments **Picnic by the Cam**

If the weather's nice, go to Market Square for picnic provender (see "Shopping," below). Then head to the Backs for an idyllic stolen moment by the River Cam.

Nightingale," as well as china, glass, majolica, silver, and clocks. The paintings range from medieval and Renaissance works to contemporary canvases and include Titian's *Tarquin and Lucretia,* Rubens's *The Death of Hippolytus,* brilliant etchings by van Dyck, rare Hogarths, and 25 Turners, as well as works by William Blake, the Impressionists, and the more recent artists Paul Nash and Sir Stanley Spencer. Expect to see a few hard hats during your visit: The ongoing courtyard development will provide new exhibition, education, and shopping space.

Trumpington St. ✆ **01223/332-900.** www.fitzmuseum.cam.ac.uk. Free admission. Tues–Sat 10am–5pm; Sun 2:15–5pm.

9 Scott Polar Research Institute *Finds* One of Cambridge's hidden gems of historical memorabilia commemorates Sir Robert Scott and his team, who died at the South Pole in 1912. The gear, photos, and diaries are fascinating.

Lensfield Rd. ✆ **01223/336-540.** Free admission. Mon–Sat 2:30–4pm.

ORGANIZED TOURS

Walking tours leave from the Tourist Information Centre at least twice daily, at 11:30am and 1:30pm, from April to October—more frequently at the height of the summer, less frequently in the fall and winter. Tickets are £7 ($11) and include entrance to King's College Chapel or another college. For more info on guided tours, call ✆ **01223/457-574.**

OUTDOOR ACTIVITIES

"Punting," or pole-boating, is a Cambridge tradition. At the venerable **Scudamore's Punting Company** (✆ **01223/359-750;** www.scudamores.com), expect to pay £12 ($19) per hour on weekdays, £14 ($22) per hour on weekends, to hire a punt; you must leave a £50 ($80) refundable deposit. Scudamore's also organizes "chauffeured" punting tours of the college Backs and the riverside village of Granchester, with fees of about £10 to £12 ($16–$19) for adults, £10 ($16) for seniors and students, and £6 ($9.60) for children under 12. Punts are available at the **Mill Lane punting station,** next to Silver Street bridge (open daily 10am–dusk Feb–Mar and Oct–Nov; daily 9am–dusk Apr–Sept; weekends only 10am–dusk Dec–Jan); **Jesus**

Green, near the Chesterton Foot Bridge (open weekends Apr–May and Sept–Oct 10am–dusk; open daily June–Aug 10am–6pm); **Magdalene Bridge** (open daily 10am–dusk Feb–Mar and Oct–Nov; daily 9am–dusk Apr–Sept; weekends only 10am–dusk Dec–Jan); and the **Main Boatyard,** Mill Lane (open daily Apr–Sept 9am–dusk; weekends only Oct and Mar 10am–dusk).

You can join the rank and file of cycling students and rent a bike from **Geoff's Bike Hire** (near the train station at 65 Devonshire Rd.; ✆ **01223/365-629**). Rates are £7 ($11) for a day, £4 ($6.40) for half a day; ask for the free leaflet on suggested cycling itineraries around town and through the nearby countryside.

3 Shopping

Every Saturday a crafts market takes over All Saints Passage, opposite Trinity Hall. On Sunday you'll find a farmers' market in Market Square, plus an art, crafts, and antiques market. A general market, selling everything from fish to fruit to fripperies, is open every day but Sunday in Market Square.

Stop at the **King's College Chapel Shop** (✆ **01223/331-228**) for souvenirs, books, postcards, and recordings of the King's College Choir. It's open Monday to Saturday from 9:30am to 3:45pm during university term; out of term Monday to Saturday from 9:30am to 4:50pm and Sunday from 10am to 4:15pm (winter) or 5:15pm (summer). The store at the **Fitzwilliam Museum** (✆ **01223/470-474**) is also well worth a stop.

4 Where to Dine

The Anchor PUB Looking out on a raft of punts and the willow-fringed river, the Anchor is loaded with atmosphere—inside you'll find beams, sloping ceilings, and odds and ends like cider pots and prints. It serves traditional homemade English pub grub like battered cod and plaice; lamb-and-vegetable or leek-and-potato pies; or sausage, eggs, and chips. Come here for real ale, as well as the usual selection of lagers and bitters.

Silver St. ✆ **01223/353-554.** £1.95–£5.50 ($3.10–$9). MC, V. Food served Mon–Thurs noon–7:45pm; Fri–Sat noon–3:45pm; Sun noon–2:30pm.

Auntie's PUB This tearoom is as much a tradition as the market that transpires nearby, and dispenses sandwiches, soups, and pastries to an interesting mix of town and gown.

1 St. Mary's Passage, off Market Sq. ✆ **01223/315-641.** Most items £3–£5 ($4.80–$8). MC, V. Mon–Fri 9:30am–5:30pm; Sat 9:30am–6:30pm; Sun 11am–5:30pm.

5 Extending Your Trip

You may want to extend your exploration of Cambridge into the evening hours, when the medieval streets can seem especially welcoming and you can find plenty of diversion in a pub or at one of many performances staged throughout the year. The main venue for music and theater is **The Corn Exchange** on Wheeler Street (✆ **01223/357-851;** www.cornex.co.uk), which hosts visiting companies. The other place to see theater is the **University Amateur Dramatics Club** on Park Street near Jesus Lane (✆ **01223/503-333**), where two student productions are performed nightly Tuesday through Saturday; it is closed in August and September. For music, check out the schedule of the **Trinity College Music Society** (✆ **01223/304-922;** www.tcms.org.uk). It presents 20 concerts each term, ranging from Renaissance to modern music, in the college chapel, Wren Library, and other interesting venues.

If you want to spend the evening nursing a pint or two in atmospheric surroundings, check out the 600-year-old **Pickerel Inn,** 30 Magdalene St. (✆ **01223/355-068**), the oldest pub in Cambridge; and the **Eagle,** on Benet Street (✆ **01223/505-020**), where airmen who drank here during World War II carved their names into the darkened ceiling of the back room—and often stop by to relive old times.

De Vere University Arms The best hotel in Cambridge lies behind an unappealing modern entrance on Regent Street. The original wing, though, is charmingly Victorian and faces Parker's Piece through large windows. The best guest rooms are the high-ceilinged ones in this wing, but all accommodations are gracious and traditionally furnished, and all have well-equipped modern bathrooms.

Regent St. ✆ **01223/351-241.** www.devereonline.co.uk. £95–£120 ($152–$192) double. Rates include English breakfast. AE, DC, MC, V.

Trip 5

Canterbury

Spinning the stories immortalized in *The Canterbury Tales,* Chaucer's pilgrims made their way to Canterbury to visit the shrine of Thomas Becket in Canterbury Cathedral. For nearly 400 years, until Henry VIII had the shrine destroyed in 1538, the pilgrims flocked to this medieval mecca in search of miracles and a bit of adventure. Canterbury Cathedral remains one of England's greatest and most venerable glories. Its social and spiritual impact over the

Canterbury Highlights

- Exploring magnificent Canterbury Cathedral.
- Visiting the ancient grounds of St. Augustine's Abbey.
- Discovering the city's Roman past in the Roman Museum.

centuries has been so profound that UNESCO designated the cathedral a World Heritage Site.

Canterbury, on the River Stour in Kent, some 62 miles (99km) east of London, makes a perfect day trip. The cathedral is without a doubt the chief reason to visit, but there are also medieval buildings that will give you a glimpse into the pilgrim's world of 600 years ago, like the ruins of St. Augustine's Abbey, founded in the 6th century, and a host of small museums and attractions devoted to Canterbury's Roman and medieval past. If you're a history buff, you may want to spend more than a day here; see the hotel recommendations at the end of this chapter.

1 Essentials

VISITOR INFORMATION

The **Tourist Information Centre,** 12–13 Sun St. (© **01227/378-100;** www.canterbury.co.uk), is located opposite Christchurch Gate at the entrance to the cathedral precincts. Easter through October, the center is open Monday through Saturday from 9:30am to 5:30pm and Sunday from 10am to 4pm; November through Easter, it's open Monday through Saturday from 9:30am to 5pm.

SCHEDULING CONSIDERATIONS

You may want to time your visit so that you can hear Evensong sung in Canterbury Cathedral; it takes place at 5:30pm Monday through Friday, and at 3:15pm on Saturday.

GETTING THERE

BY TRAIN

Canterbury has two train stations, both within easy walking distance of the city center. From London's Victoria Station, starting at 7:05am, direct trains run about every half hour to **Canterbury East;** trains depart Canterbury for London until 9:18pm. Starting at 7:55am (later on weekends), hourly trains from London's Charing Cross stop

Canterbury

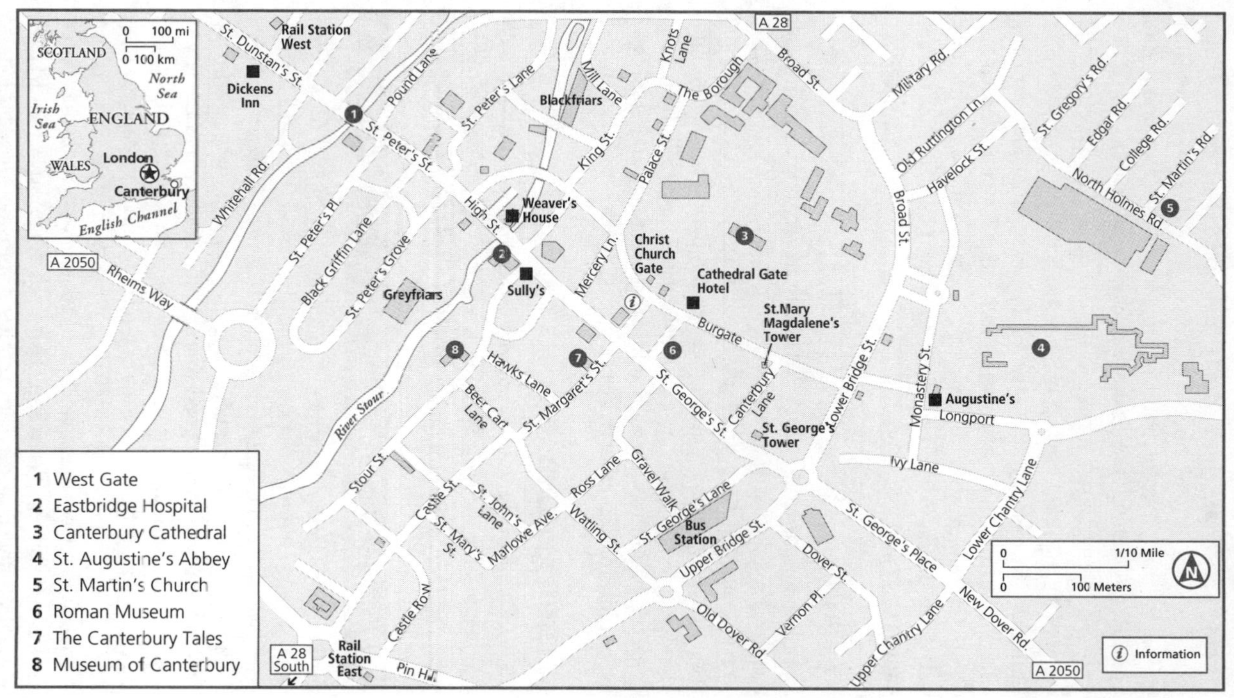

1 West Gate
2 Eastbridge Hospital
3 Canterbury Cathedral
4 St. Augustine's Abbey
5 St. Martin's Church
6 Roman Museum
7 The Canterbury Tales
8 Museum of Canterbury
Information
1/10 Mile
100 Meters
SCOTLAND
ENGLAND
WALES
London
Canterbury
North Sea
Irish Sea
English Channel
100 mi
100 km
Rail Station West
Dickens Inn
St. Dunstan's St.
Whitehall Rd.
Rheims Way
A 2050
Pound Lane
St. Peter's St.
St. Peter's Lane
St. Peter's Pl.
Black Griffin Lane
St. Peter's Grove
Greyfriars
River Stour
High St.
Weaver's House
Sully's
Blackfriars
Mill Lane
King St.
Knots Lane
The Borough
Palace St.
Mercery Ln.
Christ Church Gate
Cathedral Gate Hotel
Burgate
St.Mary Magdalene's Tower
Canterbury Lane
St. George's Tower
St. George's St.
Broad St.
A 28
Military Rd.
Old Ruttington Ln.
Havelock St.
St. Gregory's Rd.
Edgar Rd.
College Rd.
North Holmes Rd.
St. Martin's Rd.
Lower Bridge St.
Monastery St.
Augustine's
Longport
Ivy Lane
Lower Chantry Lane
New Dover Rd.
St. George's Place
Upper Chantry Lane
Dover St.
Vernon Pl.
Old Dover Rd.
Upper Bridge St.
Bus Station
St. George's Lane
Gravel Walk
Ross Lane
Watling St.
St. Margaret's St.
Hawks Lane
Beer Cart Lane
St. John's Lane
Marlowe Ave.
St. Mary's St.
Castle St.
Castle Row
Stour St.
Rail Station East
A 28 South

at **Canterbury West,** returning to London up until 8:15pm. The journey takes from 1½ to 2 hours and costs £17 ($26) for a cheap day return. For train schedules and information, contact **National Rail Enquiries** (✆ **08457/484-950;** www.nationalrail.co.uk).

BY BUS

National Express (✆ **0990/808-080;** www.nationalexpress.com) offers frequent, direct bus service from London's Victoria Coach Station to Canterbury's bus station on St. George's Lane, a few minutes' walk from the cathedral. The trip takes 1 hour and 50 minutes; day return fare is £11 ($17).

BY CAR

From London, take A2, then M2. The city center is closed to cars, but there are several parking areas close to the cathedral. The car parks in Sturry Road, Wincheap, and New Dover Road provide free Park and Ride service into Canterbury city center and back from 7am to 7pm Monday through Saturday. Parking vouchers, available from local shops and post offices, are needed for most on-street parking spots on the outskirts of Canterbury city center.

GETTING AROUND

Walking is the easiest way to get around Canterbury. Cabs are usually available outside the train stations, or you can order a taxi by calling **Lynx** (✆ **01227/464-232**) or **Cabwise** (✆ **01227/712-929**).

2 A Day in Canterbury

For a pilgrim's tour of Canterbury, enter the city through the ❶ **West Gate,** where St. Peter's Street crosses the River Stour. The gate has stood guard over the road to and from London for some 600 years, and hundreds of thousands of medieval pilgrims, on their way to visit St. Thomas Becket's shrine, passed through this gateway into the city. A spiral access stair leads up to the battlements for a panoramic view of the city and its cathedral. The tower is open Monday through Saturday from 11am to 12:30pm and 1:30 to 3:30pm. Admission is £1 ($1.65).

Follow St. Peter's Street, which becomes High Street, and take a few minutes to visit ❷ **Eastbridge Hospital,** High Street (✆ **01227/471688**), founded in the 12th century to provide overnight lodging to pilgrims visiting the shrine of Thomas Becket. It has an undercroft, two chapels, and a refectory. The hospital is open Monday through Saturday from 10am to 4:45pm. Admission is £1 ($1.65) for adults, 50p (80¢) for children.

Canterbury Cathedral

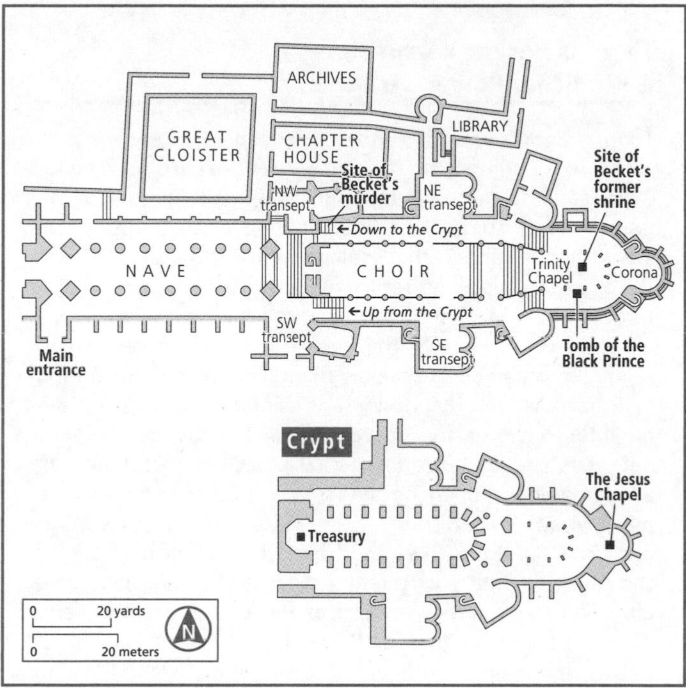

Turn north on Mercery Lane and follow it to Christ Church Gate, where you enter the precincts of venerable ❸ **Canterbury Cathedral** (✆ **01227/762-862;** www.canterbury-cathedral.org). The origins of this massive and magnificent structure date back to A.D. 597, when St. Augustine arrived on a mission from Rome. What stands on the site today is the first cathedral in England to be built in the Gothic style. The crypt dates from about 1100 and the cathedral itself from the 13th century, with a central bell tower (called Bell Harry) added in the 15th century. After Archbishop Thomas Becket was murdered in the cathedral in 1170, pilgrims from all over Europe began to flock to his shrine; its location is still marked in the Trinity Chapel near the high altar. Noteworthy features of the cathedral include panels of rare stained glass and the medieval royal tombs of Henry IV and Edward the Black Prince. The cathedral is open Monday through Saturday 9am to 5pm (Nov–Mar until 4:30pm); Sunday 12:30 to 2:30pm and 4:30 to 5:30pm. Admission is £4 ($6) for adults; £3 ($4.95) for seniors, students, and children. **King's School,** the oldest public school in England, is housed in several fine medieval buildings (not open to the public) around the cathedral.

Follow Burgate east, crossing Lower Bridge Street and Monastery Street, to Longport, where the atmospheric ruins of ❹ **St. Augustine's**

Thomas Becket Versus Henry II: A Medieval Power Struggle

Thomas Becket was born in Normandy in 1118, the son of a prosperous English merchant. He was sent to Paris for his education and from there to England, where he joined the household of Theobold, the archbishop of Canterbury. The archbishop, noting Becket's talents, sent him back to Paris to study law and upon his return made him archdeacon of Canterbury. In 1154 Theobold introduced Becket to the newly crowned king, Henry II. The two hit it off immediately, and Henry soon named Becket his chancellor. When Archbishop Theobold died in 1161, Henry saw the opportunity to increase his influence over the Church by naming his loyal advisor Becket to the highest ecclesiastical post in the land. Becket, who had never been ordained, was quickly invested as a priest, ordained a bishop, and made archbishop of Canterbury in 1162. But Becket and Henry clashed on the issue of the Church's right to try felonious clerics in their own religious courts of justice instead of those of the crown, and eventually, in royal disfavor, Becket fled to France.

The two former friends met again in Normandy in 1170, and Becket was allowed to return to his post as archbishop. But another power struggle broke out when Becket refused to absolve two English bishops whom he had excommunicated

Abbey (✆ **01227/767-345**) are set within a spacious park. (It's about a 15-min. walk from the cathedral.) Founded in A.D. 598, this is one of the oldest Anglo-Saxon monastic sites in the country and, like the cathedral, has been designated a World Heritage site by UNESCO. The grounds are open daily 10am to 6pm (until 4pm Nov–Mar). Admission is £3 ($4.95) for adults, £2.30 ($3.80) for seniors and students.

Walk another 5 minutes east from St. Augustine's Abbey to North Holmes Road and you find the oldest parish church in England. No one knows for sure who founded ❺ **St. Martin's Church** (✆ **01227/459-482**), but it was already in existence when Augustine arrived from Rome to convert the Anglo-Saxon natives in A.D. 597. The tiny church was given to Queen Bertha, the French (Christian) wife of (pagan) Saxon King Ethelbert of Kent, as part of her marriage contract. It's open daily from 9am to 5pm and admission is free.

Backtrack to Christchurch Gate on Burgate and follow Butchery Lane to the ❻ **Roman Museum** (✆ **01227/785-575**). Two millennia ago, following their conquest of England, Romans were living in for supporting the king. Henry, still in France, flew into a rage and purportedly shouted, "What sluggards, what cowards have I brought up in my court, who care nothing for their allegiance to their lord. Who will rid me of this meddlesome priest?" Henry's outrage inspired four knights to sail to England to rid the realm of this annoying prelate. They arrived at Canterbury during the afternoon of December 29 and immediately searched for the archbishop. Becket fled to the cathedral, where a service was in progress. The knights found him at the altar, drew their swords, and began hacking at their victim, finally splitting his skull.

The brutal act sent shock waves through medieval Europe and unnerved the king, who was blamed for inciting the murder. When miracles were reported at Becket's tomb, the former archbishop was canonized and hordes of pilgrims transformed Canterbury Cathedral into a shrine. Four years later, in an act of penance, the king donned sackcloth and walked barefoot through the streets of Canterbury while 80 monks flogged him with branches. Henry capped his atonement by spending the night in the martyr's crypt. St. Thomas remained a popular cult figure throughout the Middle Ages.

Canterbury, which they called *Durovernum Cantiacorum.* Their daily lives are chronicled in this small but fascinating museum in the excavated Roman levels of the city between the cathedral and High Street. It's open Monday through Saturday from 10am to 5pm year-round, and also on Sunday from 1:30 to 5pm June through October. Admission is £2.60 ($4.30) for adults; £1.65 ($2.75) for seniors, students, and children.

Take St. George's Street north to St. Margaret's Street and turn left.

❼ **The Canterbury Tales,** 23 St. Margaret's St., in St. Margaret's Church (✆ **01227/454-888**), is informative and entertaining even if you don't know a thing about Chaucer or *The Canterbury Tales,* his spirited and sometimes bawdy stories about a group of medieval pilgrims on their way to visit Becket's shrine at Canterbury Cathedral. The pilgrimages that were so popular in Chaucer's time are re-created here in tableaux. The attraction is open daily from 10am to 5pm March through June, September, and October; from 10am to 4:30pm November through February; and from 9:30am to 5:30pm July and

Moments **St. Thomas Becket's Shrine**

Only one burning candle now marks the spot where the shrine of St. Thomas Becket stood in Canterbury Cathedral. The shrine, the most popular pilgrimage spot in England for nearly 400 years, was destroyed by order of Henry VIII in 1538.

August. Admission is £6.50 ($11) for adults; £5 ($8) for seniors, students, and children.

Follow St. Margaret's Street to Hawks Lane and follow Hawks Lane to Stour Street. The 8 **Museum of Canterbury** (**© 01227/452-747**) is housed in the ancient Wool Priests' Hospital with its medieval interiors and soaring oak roofs. The museum features artifacts and interactive exhibits that shed light on Canterbury's long history. The museum is open Monday through Saturday from 10:30am to 5pm. Admission is £2.60 ($4.30) for adults; £1.65 ($2.75) for seniors, students, and children. Before you go, have a look at the collection of pilgrim badges from medieval souvenir shops—600 years ago, you might have bought one as a souvenir of your trip to Canterbury.

ORGANIZED TOURS

Guided walks of the city and cathedral leave from the Tourist Information Centre on Sun Street daily at 2pm. (Additional walks are held daily at 11:30am Easter to Oct.) The cost is £3.75 ($6) for adults; £3.25 ($5) for seniors, students, and children under 14. Buy your tickets at the Tourist Information Centre.

Canterbury Historic River Tours, Weaver's House, 1 St. Peter's St. (**© 07790/534-744**), offers half hour boat trips on the Stour River with commentary on the history of the buildings you pass. April through September, river conditions permitting, boats depart daily every half hour from 10am to 5pm. Tickets are £4.80 ($8). Umbrellas are available in case of rain. The boats leave from behind the 15th-century Weaver's House (access via the Weaver's restaurant garden).

The **Canterbury River Navigation Company,** Westgate Gardens (**© 01227/768-915**), offers punt trips along the River Stour by experienced boatmen. A choice of scenic trips, including city trips, picnic trips, and wine-and-dine trips are available seasonally. Boats leave from the slipway next to West Gate. The cost is £6 ($10) per person with a £15 ($25) minimum per boat.

OUTDOOR ACTIVITIES

The **Crab and Winkle Way** is an attractive, 7-mile (11km), one-way, nearly traffic-free walking and cycling route that follows part of the old Canterbury & Whitstable railway line. For a free detailed map covering the route and attractions along the way, ask for the Crab & Winkle Way brochure in the Canterbury Tourist Information Centre. **Downland Cycles** (© **01227/479-643**), located in Canterbury West train station, rents bikes for £10 ($16) per day; you must reserve in advance.

3 Shopping

Canterbury Farmers Market, located in the refurbished Victorian goods shed just outside Canterbury West train station, has more than 17 stalls where local farmers sell produce, including an enticing range of breads and homemade cakes. The market is open Tuesday through Saturday from 8am to 7pm and on Sunday from 10am to 4pm. Unique to Canterbury, the Farmer's Market also has a restaurant, **The Goods Shed** (© **01227/459-153**), with a menu that changes twice daily to reflect the best seasonal produce available at the market. Food is prepared by top London chef Blaise Vasseur. Hours are the same as market hours.

A market with stalls selling more general goods, from clothes to gewgaws, is held on Wednesday and Friday from 8am to 4pm in Canterbury's city center.

4 Where to Dine

Augustine's MODERN BRITISH This fun, informal restaurant in a Georgian house on the way to St Augustine's Abbey is a neighborhood favorite and can be depended upon to serve up good cooking, including vegetarian dishes, using fresh, local ingredients.

1 and 2 Longport. © **01227/453-063.** Main courses £12–£25 ($20–$41). Fixed-price lunch £8.95 ($15). MC, V. Tues–Sat noon–1:30pm and 6:30–9pm; Sun noon–2pm. Closed Jan.

Sully's TRADITIONAL BRITISH This restaurant in the County Hotel is one of the best in Canterbury. You can choose from a selection of traditional English dishes, try one of the more imaginatively conceived platters, or sample seasonal specialties such as grilled lemon sole or roasted breast of pheasant.

County Hotel, High St. © **01227/766-266.** Reservations recommended. Fixed-price lunch £17 ($27); fixed-price dinner £23–£28 ($37–$45). AE, DC, MC, V. Daily 12:30–2:30pm and 7–10pm.

5 Extending Your Trip

Cathedral Gate Hotel If you want to stay near the cathedral, like the pilgrims of yore, you can't get any closer than this 27-room hotel adjoining Christchurch Gate (one of the gates into the cathedral precincts). Dating from 1438, the hotel has comfortable and modestly furnished rooms and an overall ambience of sloping floors, massive oak beams, and winding corridors.

36 Burgate, Canterbury, Kent CT1 2HA. ✆ **01227/464-381.** Fax 01227/462-800. www.cathgate.co.uk. £47–£100 ($74–$160) double. Rates include continental breakfast. AE, DC, MC, V.

The Dickens Inn This half-timbered Tudor inn is close to the Canterbury West train station, a 5-minute walk to the center of town. The inn has nine comfortable rooms, all with private bathrooms and modern amenities. A good, on-site restaurant serves traditional English meals and afternoon teas.

71 St. Dunstan's St., Canterbury, Kent CT2 8BN. ✆ **01227/472-185.** Fax 01227/464-527. www.dickens-inn.co.uk. £55–£75 ($88–$120) double. DC, MC, V.

Dover Castle

The strategic importance of this spot atop the White Cliffs, facing the Continent from high above the English Channel, has been appreciated for more than 2,000 years. Within a mighty ring of walls, the oldest and most important fortification in England houses a Roman pharos (lighthouse), a magnificent keep built by Henry II, and secret tunnels burrowed into the chalky cliffs during World War II. An exploration of the compound provides a

Dover Castle

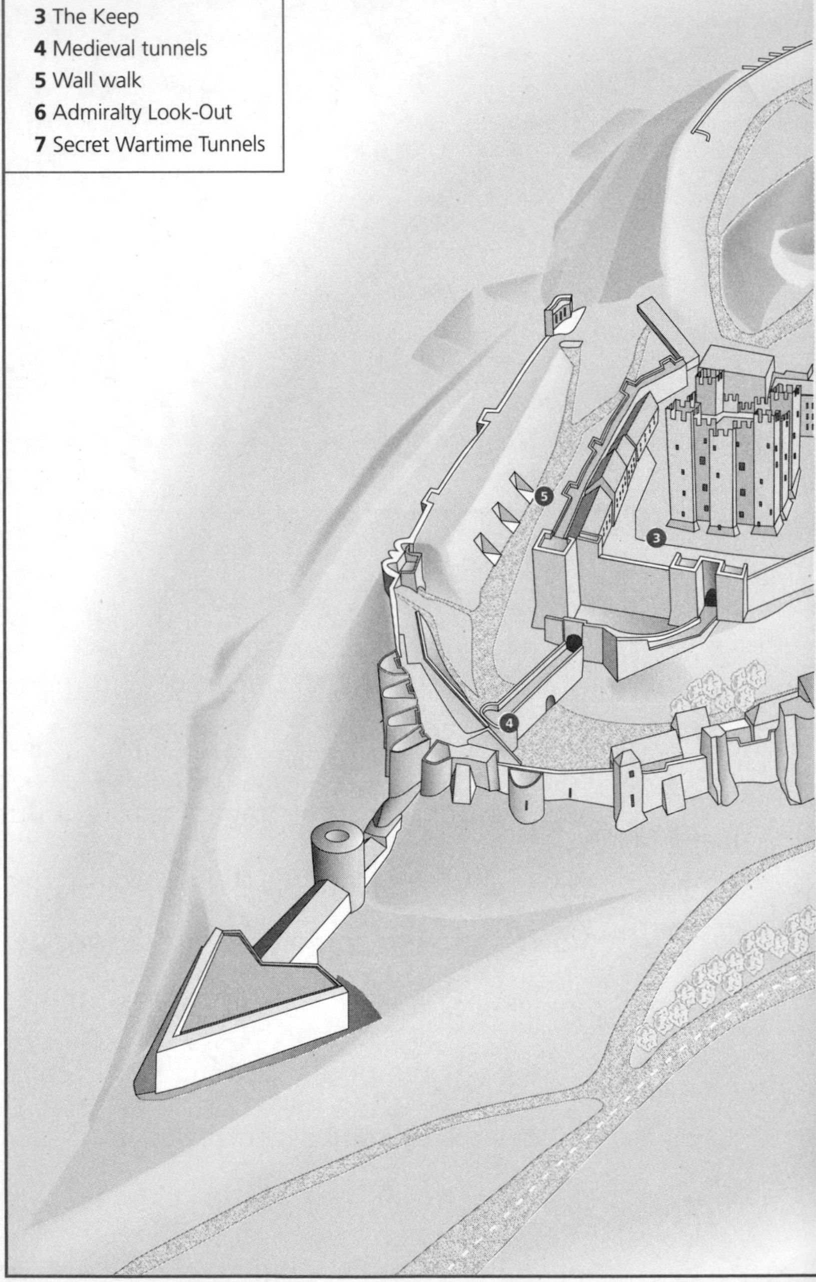

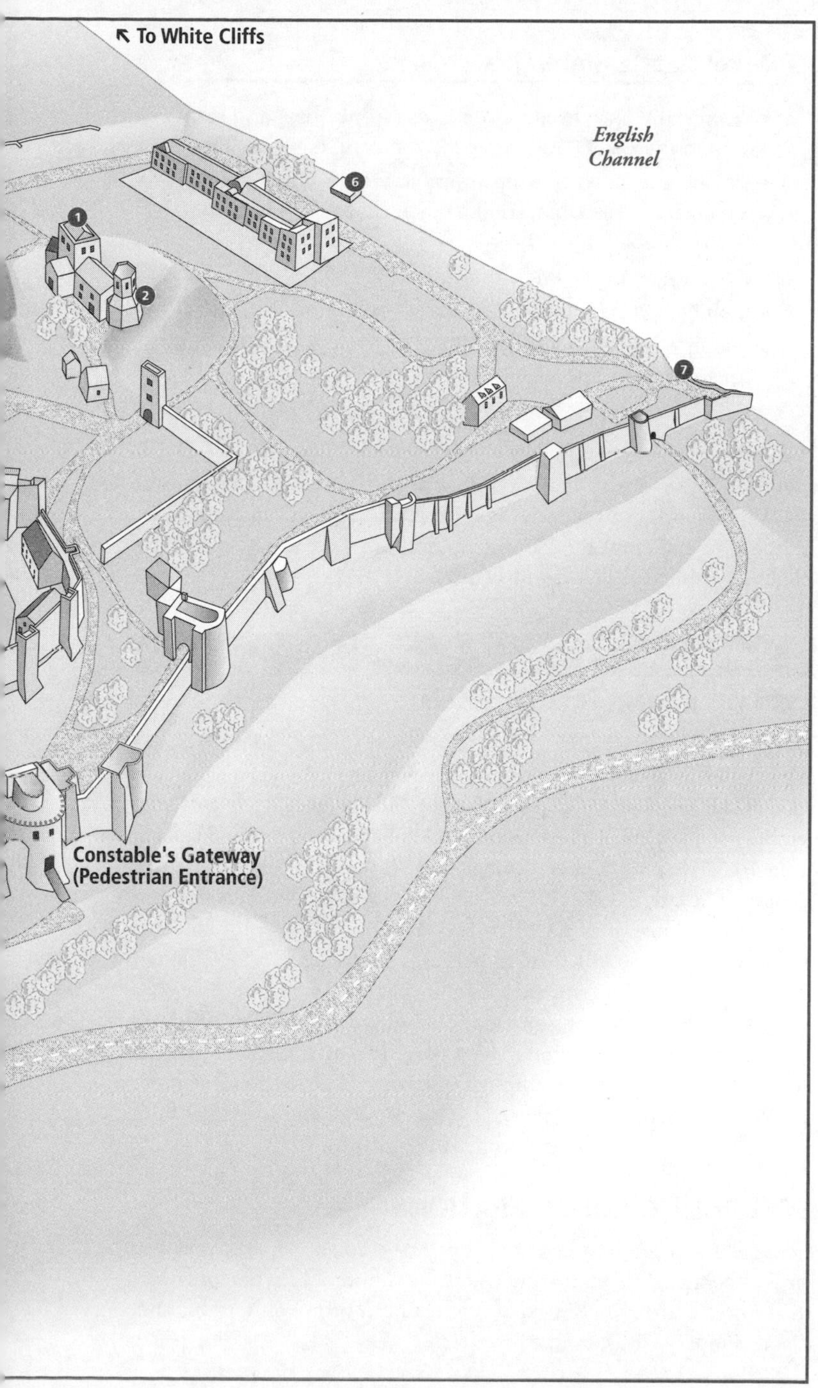
To White Cliffs
English Channel
1
2
6
7
Constable's Gateway (Pedestrian Entrance)

Dover Castle Highlights

- Visiting the ancient Roman pharos (lighthouse) and stepping inside the 1,000-year-old Saxon church.
- Visiting the Keep of King Henry II, where you'll see the remains of the Great Hall and a chapel dedicated to Thomas Becket.
- Walking along the walls that circle the castle.
- Taking in the view from Admiralty Look-Out.
- Taking a tour of the Secret Wartime Tunnels, which were constructed during World War II.

short course on British history—along with breathtaking views over the White Cliffs and the busy docks below (England's main port for shipping to and from the Continent) and, on a clear day, across the English Channel all the way to France.

1 Essentials

VISITOR INFORMATION

Dover is 78 miles (126km) southeast of London. **Dover Castle** (✆ **01304/201-628;** www.english-heritage.org.uk), at the eastern edge of the city atop the famous White Cliffs, is open April 1 to September 30, daily from 10am to 6pm; October 1 to October 31, daily from 10am to 5pm; and November 1 to March 31, daily from 10am to 4pm. The castle is closed December 24 through December 26 and January 1. Admission is £8 ($13) for adults, £6 ($9.60) for students and seniors, £4 ($6.40) for children ages 5 to 15, free for children under 5, and £20 ($32) for families of up to two adults and three children. The **Dover Visitor Information Centre** (✆ **01304/205-108;** www.whitecliffscountry.org.uk) is in the Old Town Gaol, on Biggin Street. It is open June 1 through August 31, daily from 9am to 5:30pm; and September 1 through May 31, Monday to Friday from 9am to 5:30pm and Saturday from 10am to 4pm.

SCHEDULING CONSIDERATIONS

Dover is not a place to save for a rainy day. You'll get soaked as you cross the vast castle compound, and the White Cliffs not only lose their luster in the rain, but exploring them can be uncomfortable and, due to slippery paths, even dangerous.

GETTING THERE

BY TRAIN

Trains run about every half hour throughout the day from both Victoria and Charing Cross stations in London to Dover Priory Station, with the first train leaving Victoria at 5:41am and the first train leaving Charing Cross at 6am; the last train for Victoria leaves Dover at 9:53pm and the last train for Charing Cross leaves Dover at 9:09pm. The trip takes about an hour and 45 minutes. The cheap day return fare is £20 ($32). For more information, contact **National Rail Enquiries** (✆ **08457/484-950;** www.nationalrail.co.uk).

BY BUS

National Express coaches run from London's Victoria Coach Station to Dover every hour between 8:30am and 6:30pm, with service every hour or hour and a half before and after those times; the first bus is at 7am and the last bus is at 11:30pm. The trip takes about 2½ to 3 hours and the day return fare is £11 ($18). For more information, call ✆ **08705/808-080** or go to www.nationalexpress.com.

BY CAR

The trip from London takes about an hour and a half, depending on traffic. Take the M25 to the M20 for the speedy drive down to Folkstone, then the A20 to Dover. As you approach Dover on the A20, there is a well-marked exit to the castle, where you'll find several free car parks.

Fun Fact **The Cinque Ports**

Beginning in the 11th century, the port towns of Dover, Hastings, Hythe, Romney, and Sandwich formed the Confederation of Cinque Ports to defend themselves against invasion from the Continent and to protect their lucrative trading routes on the Channel. Dover became the headquarters of the confederation in the 13th century, by which time the Cinque Ports was a formidable organization that enjoyed considerable privileges, including exemption from taxation. As the towns grew increasingly rich and powerful, the monarchy decided it was wise to keep a hand in the control of the Cinque Ports by appointing a warden to oversee them. Notable figures who have held this title include the duke of Wellington, Sir Winston Churchill, and H. M. Queen Elizabeth, the late queen mother.

GETTING AROUND

It's easy to reach the castle from the train station on foot; the route is well marked and takes about 15 minutes. Bus no. 113 makes the trip once an hour (at 20 past), leaving from the bus station in the town center on Pencester Road; the fare is £.80 ($1.30). The taxi fare is between £3 and £4 ($4.80 and $6), so if you're traveling with one or more companions, the cost per person will be the same or even less than it will be on the bus. There's a taxi stand outside the station, but to ensure that a car will be available when you arrive, arrange a pickup in advance by calling **Heritage Taxis** at ✆ **01304/225-522.**

2 A Day at Dover Castle

Dover Castle can easily overwhelm you: A lot of history has transpired within these massive walls, and the complex is vast (70 acres/28 hectares) and crowded with sites. The most satisfying way to see the castle is to let history be your guide and to tour the compound in chronological order. Begin at the highest point in the castle, a rise crowned with the rather humble-looking ❶ **pharos** (lighthouse) the Romans constructed to guide their ships across the Channel. Next to it stands a ❷ **small stone church** that, despite some clumsy restoration, is solidly Saxon, built a thousand years ago.

Between 1160 and 1180, Henry II transformed Dover into one of the mightiest fortifications in Europe—the castle came to be known as the "key of England" because to take it would have meant to take the rest of the country. At the heart of Henry's medieval defenses is the ❸ **Keep,** where you can step into the hulking remains of the Great Hall and a small, graceful stone chapel dedicated to Thomas Becket, who Henry's knights murdered in 1170. The Keep is still the social center of the castle, and houses a restaurant, a shop, and a theater that stages "The 1216 Siege Experience," a sound-and-light show that dramatizes the French attempt to seize the castle (included in the admission fee).

Just south of the Keep is an ingenious series of ❹ **medieval underground tunnels** that allowed soldiers to get from one part of the castle to another during a siege. The castle's greatest strength, though, is the ❺ **series of walls** that completely encircle the compound. You can

---

Moments **A Perch with a View**

Climb up to Admiralty Look-Out and enjoy the view. The vista of the White Cliffs, often shrouded in a light mist, rising above the choppy seas of the Channel is exhilarating every time you see it.

---

make a complete circuit of the castle on them, stopping to enjoy the view of the port and the Channel from ❻ **Admiralty Look-Out** and to tour the ❼ **Secret Wartime Tunnels.** To create this amazing labyrinth, in 1942 the British War Cabinet began to expand an 18th-century tunnel system. By war's end the tunnels comprised an underground city and housed barracks, military headquarters, a communications center, and a hospital. You can view the complex only on hour-long guided tours, with the last one departing an hour before the castle closes.

MORE THINGS TO SEE & DO

There's not much to capture your interest in Dover, as the old town was leveled by World War II bombers and assaulted again by ugly postwar rebuilding. But before you board the train for the trip back to London, you might want to take a short walk around the small town center. The **Maison Dieu** (in the town hall on Biggin St.; Tues–Sat 10am–4:30pm and Sun 2–4:30pm) dates to 1221 and was built as a hostel for pilgrims traveling from the Continent to Canterbury. Admission is free. In the **Roman Painted House** (New St.; ✆ **01304/203-279;** Apr–June Tues–Sun 10am–5pm; July–Aug daily 10am–5pm; Sept Tues–Sun 10am–5pm), frescoes and a heating system beneath the floor are remarkably well preserved. Admission is £2 ($3.20) adults, £.80 ($1.28) seniors and children.

ORGANIZED TOURS

A **Guide Friday** sightseeing bus operates in Dover from May 3 to September 28 (✆ **01708/866-000;** www.guidefriday.com). You can get off the bus at selected stops—so, you can board the bus at Dover Priory train station or in Market Square, take it to Dover Castle, get off, then board it again at your convenience for the trip up to the White Cliffs, then return to the station. The tour also provides a look at Dover's extensive docks. Buses operate daily from 10am to 4pm, and the fees are £6 ($9.60) for adults, £5 ($8) for seniors and students, £2.50 ($4) for children 5 to 15, and £15 ($23) for families of up to two adults and four children. Unless you're traveling alone, you can probably see what you want to see and get where you want to go in Dover for less by taxi.

OUTDOOR ACTIVITIES

One of the most exhilarating walks you're going to enjoy in England is atop the famous White Cliffs of Dover (✆ **01304/202-756;** www.nationaltrust.org.uk). From a parking area about a quarter of a mile (.5km) beyond the castle (follow the signs from the castle entrance), a

Start Walking!

If you want some bracing exercise in the sea air, approach your day in Dover as a good hike: Climb the mile or so from the station to the castle, cover the 70-acre (28-hectare) castle compound on foot, walk the half mile or so to the White Cliffs, and follow the trails across the top for several miles. Wear good walking shoes, carry water, and dress appropriately for the season—that means layered clothing for warmth for much of the year, rain gear just about any time, and light clothing and sunscreen for rare but memorable warm summer days.

2½-mile (4km) path follows the top of the chalk cliffs, rendered white by fossilized marine life that millennia ago floated in a tropical sea, to South Foreland Lighthouse. In 1898, Guglielmo Marconi made the first shore-to-ship radio transmissions from the top of the lighthouse, which is open daily in July and August, and Thursday through Monday from March 1 to June 30, from 11am to 5:30pm. Admission is £2 ($3.20) for adults, £1 ($1.60) for children under 16, and £5 ($8) for families of up to two adults and three children. The bracing sea air, the looming presence of the mighty castle, the busy traffic in the shipping lanes far below, and the views 17 miles (27km) across the English Channel to France make this a walk you will long remember.

3 Where to Dine

White Cliffs Teashop CAFETERIA/LIGHT FARE This simple cafeteria in a handsome glass pavilion at the entrance to the National Trust's White Cliffs walk is a delightful place for a snack or light meal. Sandwiches, a few hot dishes, desserts, and beverages can be enjoyed in the airy dining room or on the terrace.

White Cliff Visitors Centre. ✆ **01304/202-754.** Most items £3–£7 ($4.80–$11). DC, MC, V. Mar 1–Oct 31 daily 10am–5pm; Nov 1–Feb 28 daily 11am–4pm.

Trip 7

Greenwich

Time is of the essencc in Greenwich, a town and borough of Greater London, about 4 miles (6.5km) east of the city center. The world's clocks are set according to Greenwich Mean Time, and visitors from around the globe flock here to stand on the Prime Meridian, the line from which the world's longitude is measured. The main attractions in Greenwich, parts of which have been designated a World Heritage Site by UNESCO, are the Old Royal

Greenwich Highlights

- Climbing aboard the clipper ship *Cutty Sark.*
- Visiting the Old Royal Observatory.
- Exploring Greenwich Park, home of the National Maritime Museum and Queen's House.
- Enjoying the heroic architecture of the Royal Naval College.

Observatory, the Queen's House, and the National Maritime Museum, all located in Greenwich Park, and the Royal Naval College, a grouping of historic buildings on the Thames. The *Cutty Sark,* a 19th-century clipper ship, is another popular attraction. Greenwich offers enough to keep you fully occupied for a day and is a great outing for kids.

1 Essentials

VISITOR INFORMATION

The **Greenwich Tourist Information Centre,** Pepys House, Cutty Sark Gardens (✆ **0870/608-2000**), is open daily from 10am to 5pm.

SCHEDULING CONSIDERATIONS

All the main sights in Greenwich are open daily from 10am to 5pm.

GETTING THERE

BY LIGHT RAIL

The most interesting route to Greenwich is by **Docklands Light Rail** from Tower Hill Gateway (the Docklands Station near the Tower of London), which takes you past Canary Wharf and all the new Docklands development. Take the light rail to Island Gardens, the last stop, and then walk through the Victorian foot tunnel beneath the Thames to Greenwich. You come out next to the *Cutty Sark.* The fare is £1.60 ($2.55) adults, 60p (95¢) children.

BY UNDERGROUND

North Greenwich is a stop on the Jubilee Underground line, but it's too far to walk into town from the Tube station. Bus no. 188, which stops right outside the Tube station, will take you into Greenwich for 70p ($1.15); ask the driver to let you off near the *Cutty Sark.*

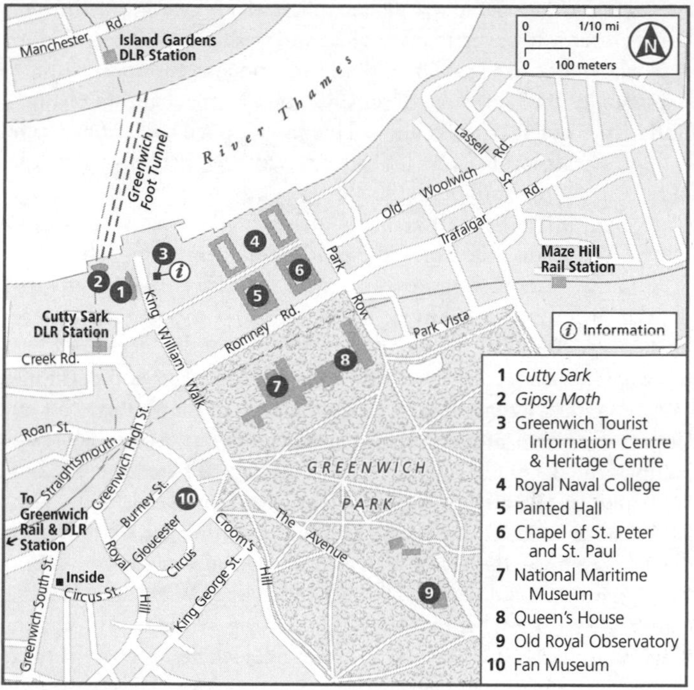

BY FERRY

Regular services are provided from Tower Pier, Embankment Pier, and Westminster Pier to Greenwich. **Thames River Services** (✆ **020/7930-1616;** www.westminsterpier.co.uk) runs a year-round fleet of boats from Westminster Pier to Greenwich Pier; the journey takes about 1 hour. A return ticket is £7.80 ($12) adults, £6.30 ($10) seniors, £3.90 ($6) children, and £20 ($32) families (two adults/two children). The boat landing is next to the *Cutty Sark.*

GETTING AROUND

All the attractions in Greenwich are signposted, and you can easily reach them on foot. The Old Royal Observatory, Royal Maritime Museum, and Queen's House are located in Greenwich Park.

2 A Day in Greenwich

Start your day in Greenwich at the ❶ ***Cutty Sark,*** berthed on King William Walk next to the Thames (✆ **020/8858-3445**). Last of the tea-clipper sailing ships, the *Cutty Sark* was launched in 1869 and used for the lucrative tea trade in the China Sea. Designed for speed, the vessel could cover almost 400 sea miles a day. Later, it carried wool from Australia. It was restored in 1922 and was used as a training ship until the end of World War II. The ship contains historic maritime memorabilia; the Long John Silver Collection of merchant ship figureheads is the largest in the country. The vessel is open daily from 10am to 5pm. Admission is £3.95 ($6) adults, £2.95 ($5) children 5 to 15, and £9.80 ($16) families. Berthed a few yards away is the ❷ ***Gipsy Moth,*** built in 1966 for Sir Francis Chichester and sailed single-handedly by him around the world; the boat is not open to the public.

From the *Cutty Sark,* make your way to the adjacent ❸ **Greenwich Tourist Information Centre,** Pepys House, Cutty Sark Gardens (✆ **0870/608-2000**), and spend a few minutes in the **Heritage Centre,** where you can learn more about Greenwich's royal and maritime past. From the Heritage Centre it's a short walk to the ❹ **Royal Naval College** (✆ **0800/389-3341**), a majestic grouping of buildings that occupies the site of Greenwich Palace, which stood here from 1422 to 1620 and was the birthplace of Henry VIII, Mary I, and Elizabeth I. Badly damaged by Oliver Cromwell's troops during the Civil War in the 17th century, the palace was torn down and replaced, in 1696, with a naval hospital designed by Sir Christopher Wren. Its 4 blocks, named after King Charles, Queen Anne, King William, and Queen Mary, are split into two sections so as not to block the view of the river from Queen's House in Greenwich Park (see below). UNESCO recognized the architectural and historic importance of the college by naming it a World Heritage Site. The Navy moved out of the college in 1998, and the various buildings are now home to the University of Greenwich and other public organizations. Stop in to see the magnificent ❺ **Painted Hall,** designed by Wren and completed in 1704, and the neoclassical ❻ **Chapel of St. Peter and St. Paul,** with an altarpiece painted by the American-born artist Benjamin West. The rooms are open daily from 10am to 5pm and admission is free.

From the Royal Naval College, cross Romney Road and take the pathway to the ❼ **National Maritime Museum** (✆ **020/8312-6608**), where Britain's seafaring past is charted in recently revamped galleries. Highlights include Prince Frederick's amazing gilded barge, built in 1732 for the eldest son of George II; Queen Mary's royal barge from 1689; and a collection of intricate ship models. An enormous collection of Lord Nelson memorabilia is also on display, including the bullet-pierced coat he was wearing when he died. The museum is open daily from 10am to 5pm and admission is free.

Adjacent to the National Maritime Museum is the splendidly restored ❽ **Queen's House** (✆ **020/8858-4422**), designed by the innovative Inigo Jones in 1616 and later used as a model for the White House. The first classical building in England, Queen's House was

The Four Corners of the World

In the Painted Hall of the Royal Naval College, have a look at the paintings beyond the arch in the upper hall. They are meant to reflect Britain's triumph as a maritime power, with figures representing Europe, Africa, Asia, and America (the four corners of the world) acclaiming Queen Anne and her husband Prince George of Denmark. America is dressed in the regalia of an Indian chief, while Asia has a camel, Africa a lion, and Europe a white horse.

commissioned by Anne of Denmark, the wife of James I, and completed in 1635 (with later modifications). You can visit the royal apartments on a self-guided tour; the house has become a kind of art gallery with many fine paintings. Queen's House is open daily from 10am to 5pm and admission is free.

The vast expanse of Greenwich Great Park, the first Royal Park to be enclosed (1433), begins directly behind the Maritime Museum and Queen's House. There have been deer in the park since the 15th century. After leaving Queen's House, make your way up the park's hill to explore the ⑨ **Old Royal Observatory** (✆ **020/8312-6608**), founded in 1675 by Charles II as part of his quest to determine longitude at sea by time instead of by the stars. Clockmaker John Harrison eventually solved the problem in 1763, and received £20,000 for his pains. Of particular interest inside the observatory is the collection of Harrison's original 18th-century chronometers (marked H1, H2, H3, and H4). All time is measured from the Prime Meridian Line (longitude 0°), marked outside the observatory. You can stand astride the meridian (with a foot in each hemisphere) and set your watch precisely by the falling time-ball, which is how shipmasters have set their chronometers from 1833. The observatory is open daily from 10am to 5pm; admission is free.

MORE THINGS TO SEE & DO

⑩ **Fan Museum** The Fan Museum is the only museum in the world devoted entirely to every aspect of fans and fan making. Home to more than 3,500 predominantly antique fans from around the world dating from the 11th century to the present day, its collections are displayed in changing exhibitions that present fans in their historical, sociological, and economic contexts. Afternoon tea is served on Tuesday and Sunday from 3 to 4:30pm for £3.50 and £4.50 ($6 and $7). 12 Crooms Hill. ✆ **020/8305-1441.** Admission £3.50 ($6). Tues–Sat 11am–5pm; Sun noon–5pm.

ORGANIZED TOURS

The Tourist Information Centre in Greenwich (see "Visitor Information," above) offers daily 1½-hour walking tours of the town's principal sights at 12:15pm and 2:15pm. Walks leave from the information center and cost £4 ($6). Reservations aren't necessary, but it's a good idea to call first to verify the schedule.

3 Shopping

Greenwich Market is an essential part of a weekend visit to this historic maritime borough. Greenwich's upscale character is reflected in the quality of goods for sale: from fine antiques to collectors' oddities, old and new. The **Central Market,** which is a treasure trove of antiques, vintage clothing, and music stalls (Sat–Sun 9am–5pm), and the **Food Market** (Sat 10am–4pm) are on Stockwell Street, just off Greenwich High Road, opposite St. Alfege's Church. The **Craft Market** (Thurs 7:30am–5pm and Fri–Sun 9:30am–5:30pm) is in College Approach.

4 Where to Dine

Inside MODERN BRITISH The menu changes weekly at this contemporary restaurant serving Modern British cuisine. For starters you might try the spinach soup with crème fraiche or the wok-fried Szechuan pepper squid. Main courses generally include dishes such as roast chicken or lamb, fresh fish, and vegetarian options like truffle button-mushroom risotto.

19 Greenwich S. St., SE 10. ✆ **020/8265-5060.** Main courses £11–£17 ($18–$27); set-price meals £15–£18 ($24–$29). MC, V. Wed–Fri noon–2:30pm; Tues–Sat 6:30–11pm; Sat–Sun brunch 11am–1pm.

Trip 8

Hampstead

Hampstead is an attractive village that has attracted many writers, artists, architects, musicians, and scientists over the years. John Keats, Robert Louis Stevenson, the painter John Constable, D. H. Lawrence, Karl Marx, Sigmund Freud, and John Le Carré have all called Hampstead home. The Oscar-winning actress *(Women in Love)* Glenda Jackson is currently Hampstead's Member of Parliament. The original village, just 20 minutes by Tube from

Hampstead Highlights

- Visiting Fenton House, with its air of 18th-century gentility, and 2 Willow Rd., the architect Erno Goldfinger's 1939 International Style house.
- Rambling through Hampstead Heath.
- Viewing the Regency-era library and the Rembrandt and Vermeer paintings in Kenwood House.

central London, is a picturesque place to explore, loaded with charming Regency and Georgian houses, old roads, alleys, steps, and courts. Many people come for weekend jaunts on Hampstead Heath, an 800-acre (320-hectare) expanse of high heathland that serves as one of London's most popular and picturesque parks.

1 Essentials

VISITOR INFORMATION

Hampstead is part of Greater London and does not have its own tourist information center. The main London Tourist Information Centre, run by the London Tourist Board, is in the forecourt of Victoria Station and is open daily from 8am to 7pm.

SCHEDULING CONSIDERATIONS

Fenton House is closed between November and March. The old western cemetery at Highgate is open only to guided tours. (See tour times below.)

GETTING THERE

BY UNDERGROUND

The fastest and easiest way to get to Hampstead is by Underground. Ride the Northern Line to Hampstead Station; the trip takes about 20 minutes from central London.

GETTING AROUND

The pleasures of Hampstead village and Heath can only be appreciated on foot. To reach Kenwood House and Highgate Cemetery, both described below, you can take bus no. 210, which runs from the Archway, Golders Green, Hampstead, and Highgate Underground stations.

Hampstead

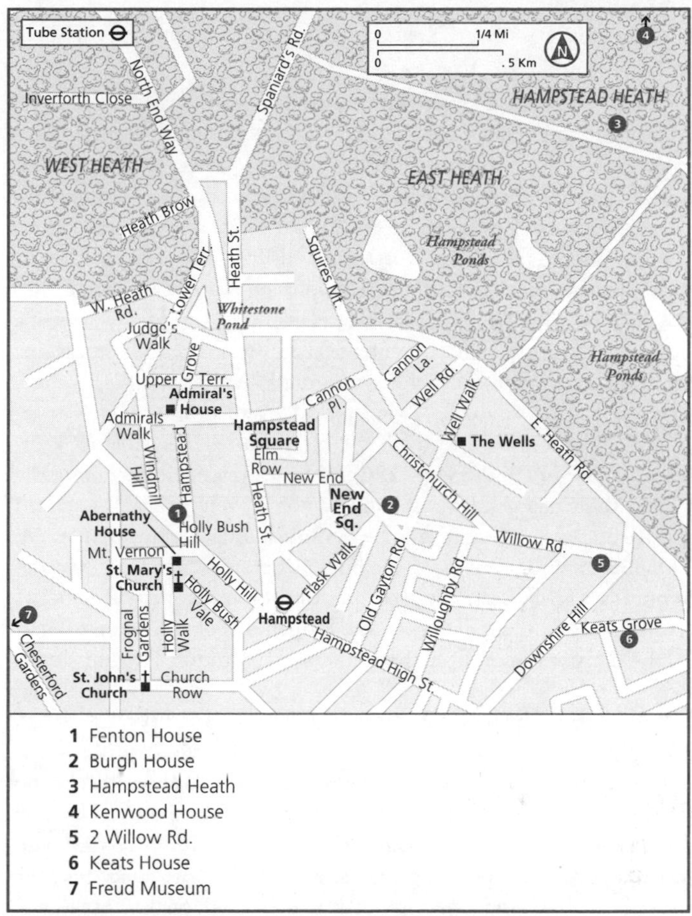

2 A Day in Hampstead

From the Hampstead Underground station, walk north on Holly Hill to Hampstead Grove. ❶ **Fenton House** (✆ **020/7435-3471**), set in a walled garden on the west side of Hampstead Grove, was built in 1693 and is one of the earliest, largest, and finest houses in Hampstead. Displayed within are fine collections of Asian and European porcelain, needlework, and furniture, and an important collection of early keyboard instruments, including a 1612 harpsichord that Handel probably played. Fenton House is open April through October, Wednesday to Friday from 2 to 5pm, and Saturday and Sunday from 11am to 5pm. Admission is £4.40 ($7) for adults, £2.20 ($3.50) for children 16 and under.

Backtrack to the Underground station and take Flask Walk north to New End Square. Here you'll find ❷ **Burgh House** (✆ **020/7431-0144**), a handsome Queen Anne house that serves as Hampstead's center for meetings, concerts, and art exhibitions. It's also home to the local history museum, with a permanent display about the great landscape artist John Constable, who lived and worked in Hampstead. Burgh House is open Wednesday to Sunday from noon to 5pm. (It's closed 2 weeks at Christmas.) Admission is free.

From Burgh House, walk north on Well Walk and enter ❸ **Hampstead Heath,** 800 acres (320 hectares) of high heath, park, wood, and grassland that separate the villages of Hampstead and Highgate. On a clear day, from the highest point on Hampstead Heath, you can see St. Paul's and even the hills of Kent south of the Thames. People come to walk, fly kites, sunbathe, swim, picnic, or jog.

Follow the footpaths through the Heath to reach palatial ❹ **Kenwood House** (✆ **020/8348-1286**) in the northwestern section of the Heath. Built as a gentleman's country home, Kenwood was enlarged and decorated in neoclassical style by Robert Adam, starting in 1764. The impressive art collection includes a Rembrandt self-portrait and Vermeer's *The Guitar Player.* During the summer, open-air concerts are given beside the lake. The house is open daily from 10am to 6pm (Nov–Mar until 4pm, from 10:30am on Wed and Fri). Admission is free.

Backtrack through the Heath and follow Heath Road southeast, exiting near the eastern end of Willow Road. ❺ **2 Willow Rd.** (✆ **01494/755-570**), the home of Hungarian architect Erno Goldfinger and his wife, the artist Ursula Blackwell, is now a National Trust property and can be visited. Built by Goldfinger in 1939 and still filled with his furniture, books, and modern art collection, the house is a fascinating example of the sleekly functional International Style. The house is open in March and from November 8 to 22 on Saturday only, from noon to 5pm; April through October, it's open Thursday through Saturday from noon to 5pm. Admission is £4.50 ($7). It was from Goldfinger, by the way, that Ian Fleming got the name for one of his most famous James Bond novels.

From Willow Road, head south on Downshire Hill and east on Keats Grove to reach ❻ **Keats House,** Wentworth Place (✆ **020/7435-2062**). The Romantic poet John Keats lived in this charming Regency cottage for only 2 years (1818–20) of his short life, but it was here that he wrote one of his most celebrated poems, "Ode to a Nightingale," and fell in love with Fanny Brawne, his neighbor's daughter. On display are manuscripts, including his last sonnet ("Bright star, would I were steadfast as thou art"), first editions, diaries, letters, and memorabilia. The house is open Tuesday through

Moments An Inspiring Stroll

A snowy walk on Hampstead Heath inspired C. S. Lewis to write *The Lion, the Witch and the Wardrobe.* They do feel like a parallel universe, these 800 acres (320 hectares) of half-wild, half-manicured green in northwest London. Sundays are like a fiesta: Lie back and listen to the bandstand concerts on Parliament Hill, with its unparalleled view across the capital. People fly kites or wield a mean Frisbee. Others fish, swim, or race model boats in the ponds.

Sunday from noon to 5pm (Nov–Mar until 4pm). Admission is £3 ($4.95) for adults, £1.50 ($2.50) for seniors and students.

MORE THINGS TO SEE & DO

7 **Freud Museum** After he and his family left Nazi-occupied Vienna as refugees, Sigmund Freud lived, worked, and died in this spacious three-story redbrick house. Rooms on view contain original furniture, letters, photographs, paintings, and personal effects of Freud and his daughter, Anna. In the study and library, you can see the famous couch and his large collection of Egyptian, Roman, and Asian antiquities. From the Hampstead Underground station, walk south along Fitzjohn's Avenue, turning west on Nutley Terrace and south on Maresfield Gardens; the walk takes about 15 minutes.

20 Maresfield Gardens. ✆ **020/7435-2002.** Admission £5 ($8) adults, £2 ($3.30) students. Wed–Sun noon–5pm.

ORGANIZED TOURS

The **Heath & Hampstead Society** (www.heathandhampsteadsociety.org.uk) organizes a 2-hour walk on the first Sunday afternoon of every month except January. The walks start from Burgh House, New End Square, and are open to the public; there is a suggested donation of £1 ($1.60). Times are either 10:30am or 2:30pm. For further information, contact Michael Welbank at ✆ **020/7435-0553.**

OUTDOOR ACTIVITIES

The **Highgate Men's Pond** in Hampstead Heath is the closest thing London has to a beach; it has an enclosed sun deck for sunbathing, and swimmers share the water with lots of quacking ducks and algae. The nearby **Kenwood Ladies' Pond** is for women only. These outdoor ponds are open year-round from dawn to dusk. Admission is free.

3 Where to Dine

The Wells MODERN BRITISH/FRENCH/MEDITERRANEAN A stylish new bar-restaurant in an old house between High Street and the Heath, The Wells is Hampstead at its gentrified best. The menu changes often, but you'll find main courses such as roast lamb, pan-fried salmon with tomato and paprika couscous, fresh crab and black olive risotto, and deep-fried fishcakes.

30 Well Walk. ✆ **020/7794-3785.** Main courses £10–£15 ($16–$25); fixed-price lunch £13 ($21). Daily noon–2:30pm and 6–10pm (Fri–Sat until 10:30pm). MC, V.

Hampton Court

Cardinal Thomas Wolsey, Henry VIII's lord chancellor, began building Hampton Court in 1514. But the cardinal got on Henry's bad side when he opposed the king's request for a divorce from Catherine of Aragon. This provided a convenient excuse for the greedy Tudor monarch to nab Hampton Court for himself and make the property a royal residence, a status it held from 1525 until 1760. Henry's fifth wife, Katherine Howard, supposedly haunts

Hampton Court Highlights

- Wandering through the enormous palace.
- Exploring the riverside gardens and Maze.

the place to this day. Located in East Moseley, Surrey, 13 miles (21km) west of London on the north side of the Thames, Hampton Court is one of the easiest and most rewarding day trips from London.

1 Essentials

VISITOR INFORMATION

The **Information Centre** (✆ **0870/752-7777**) in Clock Court is open the same hours as the palace: mid-March through mid-October, Monday from 10:15am to 6pm and Tuesday through Sunday from 9:30am to 6pm; mid-October through mid-March, Monday from 10:15am to 4:15pm, Tuesday through Sunday from 9:30am to 4:30pm. It's closed December 24 to 26. Admission to the palace is £11 ($18) for adults, £8.25 ($13) for seniors and students, and £7.25 ($12) for children 5 to15.

SCHEDULING CONSIDERATIONS

The last admission to the palace is at 5:15pm in summer, 3:45pm in winter. On Sunday, visitors are welcome to attend choir services in The Chapel Royal at 11am and 3:30pm.

GETTING THERE

BY TRAIN

The fastest, easiest, and most direct route to Hampton Court is by train. **South West Trains** (✆ **0845/6000-650;** www.swtrains.co.uk) run at 26 and 56 minutes past each hour direct from London Waterloo to Hampton Court, and return to London from Hampton Court throughout the day and into the evening at 9 and 39 minutes past the hour. The journey takes 30 minutes, and the standard day return fare is £7.70 ($12). For more information, call **National Rail Enquiries** (✆ **08457/484950;** www.nationalrail.co.uk). The palace entrance is a 5-minute walk from the station.

BY BOAT

If you have plenty of time, you can take a boat from Westminster Pier to Hampton Court; the journey takes almost 4 hours. From April to

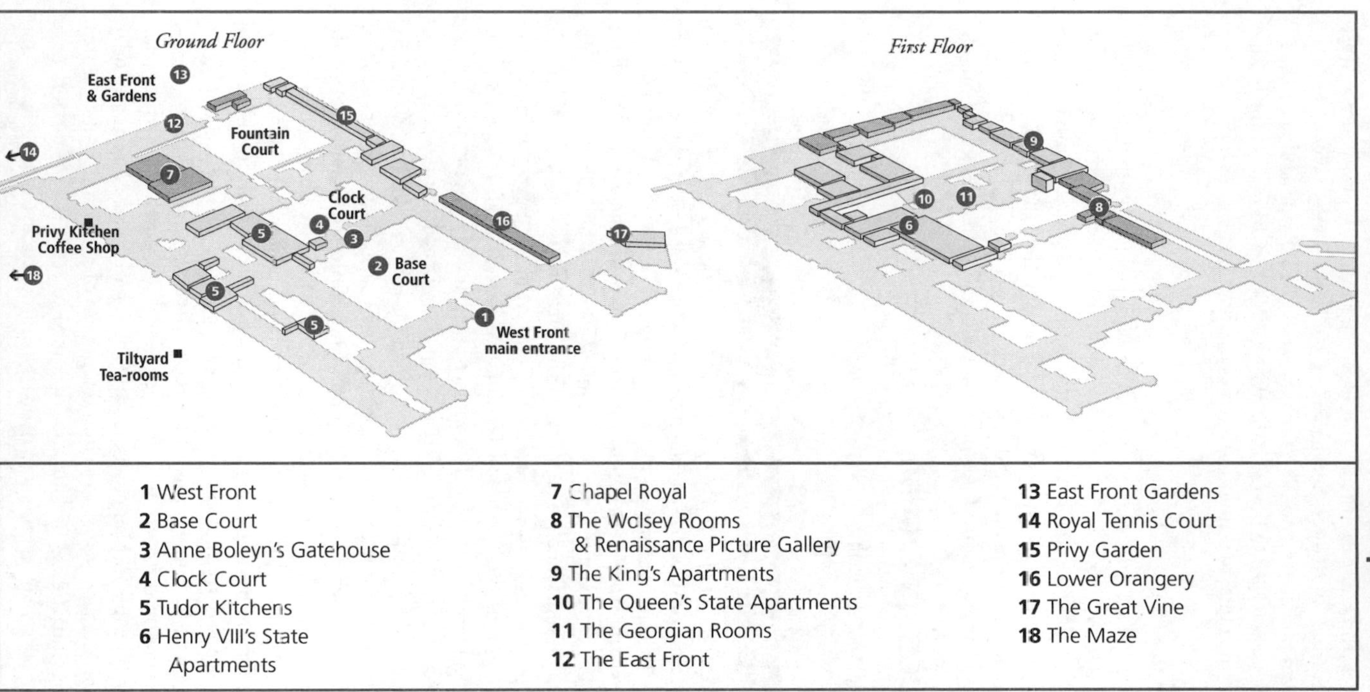
Ground Floor
East Front & Gardens
Fountain Court
Privy Kitchen Coffee Shop
Clock Court
Base Court
West Front main entrance
Tiltyard Tea-rooms
First Floor
1 West Front
2 Base Court
3 Anne Boleyn's Gatehouse
4 Clock Court
5 Tudor Kitchens
6 Henry VIII's State Apartments
7 Chapel Royal
8 The Wolsey Rooms & Renaissance Picture Gallery
9 The King's Apartments
10 The Queen's State Apartments
11 The Georgian Rooms
12 The East Front
13 East Front Gardens
14 Royal Tennis Court
15 Privy Garden
16 Lower Orangery
17 The Great Vine
18 The Maze

September, boats usually run at 10am and 12:45pm; contact **Westminster Passenger Service** (✆ **020/7930-2062;** www.wpsa.co.uk) for more information. Return fares are £18 ($29) for adults, £12 ($19) for seniors, £9 ($14) for children 5 to 15, and £45 ($72) for families (two adults, two children).

BY CAR

The palace is located on the A308 and is well signposted from all the major local roads; follow the brown tourist attraction road signs. From the M25, take either exit 10 onto the A307, or exit 12 onto the A308. The palace is also accessible via the A3 and then the A309. Parking is available on-site for £3.50 ($6). Alternative parking is available nearby at Hampton Court Green, Bushy Park, and Hampton Court Station.

GETTING AROUND

The entrance to Hampton Court is a 5-minute walk from the train station.

2 A Day in Hampton Court

Henry VIII (1491–1547) is the dominant personality associated with **Hampton Court,** but much of his palace was lost at the end of the 17th century when William III (reigned 1689–1702) and Mary II (reigned 1689–94) commissioned Sir Christopher Wren to rebuild Hampton Court. From the time it was first built until the 1660s, Hampton Court, like most of the great houses near London, was approached by water. ❶ **The West Front** of the palace, where visitors enter today, was begun by Cardinal Wolsey (ca.1475–1530) and completed for Henry VIII. The wings to the left and right of the gatehouse were added by Henry VIII and once contained the Great House of Easement (communal lavatories) and the kitchens. ❷ **Base Court,** the first courtyard, contained lodgings for Cardinal Wolsey's guests and large household. Pass through ❸ **Anne Boleyn's Gatehouse,** on the far side of Base Court, and you enter ❹ **Clock Court,** the principal Tudor courtyard and the heart of both Wolsey's and Henry VIII's palaces. Over the gateway you can see Wolsey's coat of arms and the famous **Astronomical Clock** made for Henry VIII in 1540.

Start your tour in ❺ **The Tudor Kitchens,** a complex of some 50 rooms on the north side of Clock Court. Cardinal Wolsey had about 600 people in his household, and Henry VIII had twice that. Today, the kitchens are set up as if in the process of preparing food for a great feast in 1542. The kitchens continued to serve the royal court until 1660, when servants lost their right to be fed at the king's table and were put on wages instead.

From Clock Court, make your way to ❻ **Henry VIII's State Apartments. The Horn Room,** originally a waiting place for servants bringing food to The Great Hall next door, is decorated with elk horns, including the large fossilized antlers of a prehistoric great elk found in Ireland and presented to Charles II (reigned 1660–85). In **The Great Watching Chamber,** the Yeomen of the Guard were stationed to control access to the king. The room's decorated ceiling incorporates the arms and badges of Henry VIII and his third and favorite wife, Jane Seymour. Probably the most famous room in Hampton Court is **The Haunted Gallery,** which tradition holds is haunted by the ghost of Katherine Howard, Henry VIII's fifth wife. Only 15 months after her marriage in 1540, the young queen was charged with adultery and arrested. According to legend, she managed to escape from her rooms and run along the gallery towards the chapel, where the king was at Mass. Guards seized her and dragged her screaming back to her rooms; she was later executed at the Tower of London.

❼ **The Chapel Royal,** built by Wolsey and in use for over 450 years, still has the Royal Pew, where the monarch and his companions would sit, and a magnificent vaulted ceiling installed in 1536. The vast oak screen was carved by Grinling Gibbons and installed in the 18th century by Sir Christopher Wren when the chapel was refitted for Queen Anne (1702–14).

❽ **The Wolsey Rooms,** on the south side of the palace, were part of Cardinal Wolsey's private lodgings in the 1520s. The two small rooms in this suite are lined with 16th-century linenfold paneling, so-called because it was intended to reproduce the effect of draped fabric on the walls. The plain Tudor-style fireplaces also date from Cardinal Wolsey's time. These rooms, and the adjacent **Renaissance Picture Gallery,** are now used to display 16th- and early 17th-century paintings from the Royal Collection, including works by Lucas Cranach, Pieter Bruegel, Correggio, Agnolo Bronzino, Lorenzo Lotto, Parmigianino, and Titian.

From The Wolsey Rooms, follow signs to ❾ **The King's Apartments,** built for William III (reigned 1689–1702) at the end of the 17th century by Sir Christopher Wren. **The King's Staircase,** the most spectacular in the palace, was decorated in about 1700 by the Italian painter, Antonio Verrio. The former **Guard Chamber** is decorated with a display of more than 3,000 arms, mostly muskets, pistols, bayonets, and swords. Even when the king was not present, courtiers would show their respect by bowing to the empty throne beneath its canopy in **The King's Presence Chamber.** The principal ceremonial room in the palace was **The King's Privy Chamber,** where ambassadors were received and court functions held. The increasing magnificence of William's apartments is apparent in **The Great Bedchamber,** with its gilded furniture, mirrors, painted ceiling, and carvings. **The**

Moments **Real Tennis**

Make sure your visit to the gardens includes a look at The Royal Tennis Court built for James I in 1626. It's still in use, and if you're lucky you'll see players engrossed in a match of Real Tennis, a complex game that's quite different from modern lawn tennis and makes use of the court's side walls and roof.

King's Backstairs lead down to a series of smaller, more intimate rooms that formed **The King's Private Apartments.**

From The King's Apartments, make your way to ⑩ **The Queen's State Apartments.** These rooms were begun by Sir Christopher Wren at the end of the 17th century for William III's wife, Mary II (reigned 1688–94), but were completed in succeeding reigns. The Queen's State Apartments that you see today were used by Queen Caroline between 1716 and 1737 for entertaining important visitors, receiving petitions, and holding court entertainments. **The Queen's State Bedchamber** is still furnished with its original state bed (complete with 18th-c. mattresses). The magnificent **Queen's Gallery** was built as Queen Mary's private gallery and later adopted by King William as his private gallery.

⑪ **The Georgian Rooms** were used by Caroline, wife of George II (reigned 1727–60) and are displayed as they were during the last visit of the full court to the palace in 1737. **The Communication Gallery** linking the King's and Queen's apartments is hung with portraits known as The Windsor Beauties, painted by Sir Peter Lely between 1662 and 1665 and representing the most beautiful women at the court of Charles II (reigned 1660–85). **The Cartoon Gallery,** one of the first picture galleries in Britain, was built for William III by Sir Christopher Wren to display Raphael's large drawings of the Acts of the Apostles. The original cartoons were lent by Queen Victoria to the Victoria and Albert Museum in 1865; today you see a set of copies painted in 1697.

As you leave the palace to enter the gardens behind, have a look at the palace's magnificent ⑫ **East Front.** The exterior of Sir Christopher Wren's building at Hampton Court is probably the best and most famous expression of the baroque style in England, and was intended to rival Louis XIV's palace of Versailles.

The Hampton Court **gardens** are a delightful mix of 500 years of royal gardening history. In Henry VIII's time, ⑬ **The East Front Gardens** area was parkland but was gradually enclosed and laid out as a great semicircular parterre with 12 marble fountains. Queen Anne (reigned 1702–14) added the surrounding semicircular canals in 1710. At the north end of the Broad Walk is ⑭ **The Royal Tennis**

Court, built in the 1620s and still in use today. ⓯ **The Privy Garden,** the king's private garden on the south side of the palace facing the river, has been restored to the way it appeared when it was completed for William III in 1702. ⓰ **The Lower Orangery,** originally built to house Mary II's collection of botanical specimens, was later converted into a gallery to display Andrea Mantegna's ***Triumphs of Caesar,*** a sequence of nine paintings that depict the triumphs of the Roman emperor Julius Caesar (104–44 B.C.). Painted at the Italian court of the Gonzagas in Mantua between 1484 and 1505, the paintings were acquired by Charles I in 1629 and probably arrived at Hampton Court in 1630, where they have been ever since. ⓱ **The Great Vine,** planted in 1768 by Lancelot "Capability" Brown, is the oldest known vine in the world and still produces 500 pounds to 700 pounds (230kg–320kg) of grapes each year. The grapes are harvested at the end of August and sold in the palace shops. ⓲ **The Maze,** made up of a thousand yews planted in 1702 on the north side of the palace, covers a third of an acre and is one of the most popular attractions at Hampton Court. You can climb the tower in the center of the maze for a view of the grounds.

ORGANIZED TOURS

Throughout the day, costumed guides give free tours of the State Apartments. These tours must be booked in advance at the Information Centre in Clock Court upon your arrival. An **audio guide,** available free from the Information Centre, provides a wealth of information and anecdotes about the history and contents of the building and the monarchs who lived there.

OUTDOOR ACTIVITIES

Daily (except Christmas) from December 6 to January 18, you can rent ice skates and cut figure eights on the **Hampton Court Palace Outdoor Ice Rink** set up near the West Front of the palace. Tickets for timed-entry 1-hour sessions, including skate rental, cost £8.50 ($14) and can be reserved in person at the Hampton Court box office or in advance by contacting **Ticketmaster** (✆ **0870/0601778;** www.ticketmaster.co.uk).

3 Shopping

The Barrack Block Shop, located in the former palace barracks, sells an extensive range of gifts from china to children's stationery as well as guidebooks and postcards. **The Garden Shop,** overlooking the gardens on the East Front of the palace, has a selection of garden-themed merchandise including books and garden accessories. **The Tudor Kitchens Shop,** next to The Tudor Wine Cellar, offers specialty food products and traditional kitchen equipment.

4 Where to Dine

Pop into the **Privy Kitchen Coffee Shop** near The Tudor Kitchens for tea, coffee, pastries, or a light lunch. The coffee shop is open from 10am to 5pm (Nov–Mar until 4pm). **The Tiltyard Tea-rooms** (**© 020/8943 3666**) in the palace gardens has a coffee bar and a buffet cafe-restaurant that serves hot and cold drinks, sandwiches, salad lunches, and hot meals. It's open 10am to 5.30pm (Nov–Mar until 4:30pm).

Trip 10

Hever Castle

With its time-mellowed stone, towers, moat, and drawbridge, Hever looks exactly what it is—a medieval castle that's played a colorful part British history for more than 800 years. Hever was the childhood home of Anne Boleyn, the second wife of Henry VIII, who later gave the house to his fourth wife, Anne of Cleves. An American, William Waldorf Astor, played a role in the castle's heritage, too: He bought Hever in 1903, restored it,

Hever Castle Highlights

- The library and other comfortable rooms created for Viscount Astor.
- Seeing what Anne Boleyn wrote in her Book of Hours.
- Strolling through the Italian Gardens, which took 1,800 workers and 2 years to create.
- The breathtaking view of the castle, with its moat and towers, as you approach.

filled the castle with acres of luxurious paneling, and created the stunning classical and natural gardens. Warm, welcoming, and with a painting, piece of statuary, or stunning vista to be enjoyed around every corner and along every garden path, Hever is a pleasure to visit. Plus, you can combine a visit here with a walk in the country or a visit to another fascinating noble dwelling nearby, Penshurst Place.

1 Essentials

VISITOR INFORMATION

Hever Castle (© **01732/866-5224**) is 30 miles (48km) southeast of London, in the Kent countryside between the towns of East Grinstead and Sevenoaks. The castle is off B2026, a small country lane, about 3 miles (5km) southeast of the village of Edenbridge. It is open March through October daily from noon to 6pm (grounds open at 11am and last admission is at 5pm), and in November daily from noon to 5pm (grounds open at 11am and last admission is at 4pm); and late April to late October, daily from noon to 6pm (grounds open at 11am and last admission is at 5pm). Admission to the castle and gardens is £8.40 ($13) for adults, £7.10 ($11) for seniors, £4.60 ($7) for children 5 to 14, and £21 ($34) for families of up to two adults and two children. Admission to the gardens only is £6.70 ($11) for adults, £5.70 ($9) for seniors, £4.40 ($7) for children 5 to 14, and £18 ($28) for families of up to two adults and two children.

SCHEDULING CONSIDERATIONS

Especially nice times to visit Hever are Spring Garden Week in mid-March, Rose Week in late June, and Autumn Color Week in mid-October. During these weeks the castle gardeners are on hand to point out seasonal highlights on the grounds, where gardens bloom in full

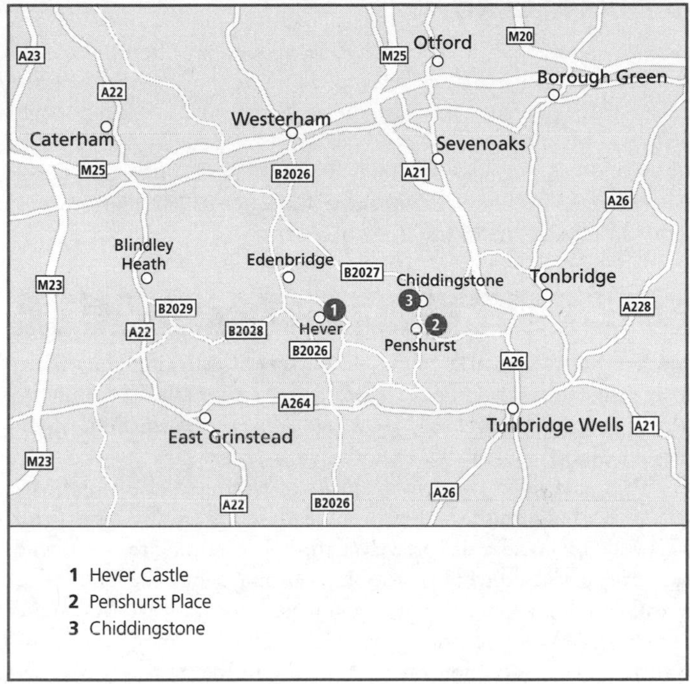

color. If you're planning a visit to Penshurst Place as well, keep in mind that it's closed in winter. (See below for more information.)

GETTING THERE

BY TRAIN

From London's Victoria Station, trains depart hourly throughout the day for Hever Station. The trip takes 50 minutes and requires a change at East Croydon, East Grimstead, or Hurst Green. (Be sure to ask where to transfer before you board the train at Victoria.) The first train leaves London at about 7:23am and the last train returns from Hever to London at 10:32pm; the fare is £14 ($22) standard day return.

BY CAR

The trip from London takes under an hour, depending on traffic. From the M25, take Junction 5 and follow A22 about 5 miles (8km) south to Bindley Heath; from there you will follow small country lanes (B2029, B2028, and B2026) east for about 8 miles (13km) to Hever Castle. (The route from A22 is well marked with signs.)

GETTING AROUND

Hever train station is in the countryside, about a mile from the castle. You can walk along country lanes to the castle, but in good weather it's far more pleasant to follow the well-marked footpath through fields and woods. You can also take a taxi, but make arrangements in advance from London because there is no taxi stand at the station, and cabs are often busy; call **Edenbridge Cars** (✆ **01732/864-009**) or **Rely On Cars** (✆ **01732/863-800**).

2 A Day at Hever Castle

You must follow a set route through ❶ **Hever Castle,** but you can do so at your own pace. Guides are posted in every room—take advantage of their knowledge; they are a gold mine of information, which they are pleased to share with inquisitive visitors.

The ground floor, where William Astor fashioned his living quarters, is lavishly furnished in exquisite early-20th-century taste—you will wish you could cross the velvet ropes and settle into one of the deep armchairs in the drawing room, morning room, or library. The next floor is less appealing, but as you make your way through a maze of rooms filled with historic bric-a-brac, you'll come upon some treasures. In a small exhibition room at the top of the stairs is a Book of Hours signed by Anne Boleyn, in which the young and ill-fated queen prophetically wrote, *"Le temps viendra"* ("The time will come"). When Anne, the mother of Queen Elizabeth I, failed to produce a male heir, Henry trumped up charges of an incestuous affair with her brother and had the siblings beheaded. Henry's bedroom is richly paneled and furnished as it was during his rare visits to the castle. In it hangs a much-reproduced portrait of the king attributed to Hans Holbein.

You can trace the history of Henry's marriages in the Long Gallery, peopled with mannequins of the monarch's six wives, beginning with his first queen, Catherine of Aragon. When the pope refused Henry's request to divorce Catherine and marry Anne Boleyn, Henry broke with the Catholic Church and formed the Church of England, with himself as head. Anne of Cleves, Henry's fourth wife, lived at Hever after the king divorced her and married Katherine Howard. The 13th-centuy Gatehouse, the last stop on the tour, is filled with a grisly collection of torture devices and explicit diagrams showing how defenders once poured boiling oil onto invaders through "murder holes" in the floor.

William Astor employed as many as 1,800 workers, who toiled for more than 2 years creating the gardens. (Clearly, the wealthy heir, who became a viscount, was not without feudal ideas—he housed his staff in a mock Tudor village that you can't visit but you can see across the

Moments Garden Idylls

After touring the castle, find a corner of the Italian Garden—all the better if the spot is next to one of the ponds—and relax for a while. You'll feel like the lord or lady of the manor.

lawns to the rear the castle.) It's hard not to feel rather grandiose as you stroll through the Italian Gardens, which surround a 35-acre (14-hectare) lake and are appointed with a stunning collection of classical sculpture and portions of the triumphal arch that the Roman emperor Claudius erected on the nearby coast in A.D. 52. If you have children in tow and want to enjoy these formal but welcoming gardens in peace, send them off to amuse themselves in the Yew Maze and the Water Maze, in which a misstep will get them doused in a spray of water.

MORE THINGS TO SEE & DO

❷ **Penshurst Place** This remarkably intact medieval manor house dates from the 13th century, and has at its heart the Baron's Hall. Stone-floored, with a chestnut-paneled ceiling and built around a massive octagonal hearth, the hall is considered one of the finest interiors remaining from the Middle Ages. Many of the grander staterooms and the Long Gallery upstairs date from the 16th century, when King Edward VI presented the house to the Sydney family. The most famous member of this clan is Sir Philip Sidney, soldier, courtier, poet, and personification of an Elizabethan gentleman, and his descendants live here still. The walled and terraced gardens are perfect places in which to spend part of a warm afternoon.

You won't be able to get from Hever to Penshurst easily via public transportation. If you are not driving, you can arrange for a taxi or you can walk, following public footpaths; see "Outdoor Activities," below. From Penshurst, you can return directly to London's Victoria Station by train. The trip takes about an hour and 10 minutes. There is a train every hour, and the last departure is at 11:22pm. The cheap day single ticket (one-way from Penshurst to London) is £8.70 ($14).

In the village of Penshurst, 5 miles (8km) southeast of Hever, on B2176. ✆ **01892/870-307.** House and grounds: £6.50 ($10) adults, £6 ($10) seniors and students, £4.50 ($7) children, £18 ($29) families. Grounds only: £5 ($8) adults, £4.50 ($7) seniors and students, £4 ($6) children, £15 ($24) families. Mar 1–28 grounds open weekends 10:30am–6pm, house open weekends noon–5:30pm; Mar 29–Nov 2 grounds open daily 10:30am–6pm; house open daily noon–5:30pm.

OUTDOOR ACTIVITIES

Well-maintained public footpaths crisscross the countryside all around Hever. One of the most pleasant walks takes you through

The Six Wives of Henry VIII

Among the lures of Hever Castle is its connection with King Henry VIII and his many marriages. Wax figures of Henry's queens are lined up in the Long Gallery, and they provide an illuminating lesson in a juicy episode in English history. **Catherine of Aragon** (1485–1536), the daughter of King Ferdinand and Queen Isabella of Spain, had been married to Henry's brother Arthur, and upon his death a year after the marriage, Catherine became betrothed to Henry, who was then too young to marry. After 20 years of marriage, Catherine failed to produce a male heir (she had one daughter, who would later reign as Mary I, or "Bloody Mary"), and Henry sought to annul the union. The pope refused, so Henry installed a new archbishop of Canterbury, Thomas Crammer, to carry out his wishes, thereby creating the Church of England. Henry then married **Anne Boleyn** (1500–36), whose family lived at Hever. The young queen produced a daughter (who would become Elizabeth I) but no male heir, and Henry became convinced the union was doomed. He had Anne executed on grounds of adultery and 11 days later married **Jane Seymour** (1509–37), who within the year finally gave Henry a son (the future Edward VI) but died in childbirth. Henry next married **Anne of Cleves** (1515–57) to further his alliances with Germany, but was dissatisfied with this queen (whom he thought was horse-faced) and soon arranged for a divorce; Hever was part of Anne's settlement. Sixteen days after freeing himself of Anne, Henry married **Katherine Howard** (1521–42), more than 30 years his junior. The king had his young queen, who was a first cousin of Anne Boleyn, executed when he discovered she was taking lovers. In 1543 Henry married **Catherine Parr** (1512–48), who outlived the king by only a year—but long enough to marry Thomas Seymour, brother of Henry's third queen.

woods and fields from the church near the castle gate for about 1½ miles (2.5km) to ❸ **Chiddingstone,** a charming village of half-timbered houses that looks so perfectly English you expect to see Miss Marple or another character from British fiction step out of a doorway. There's a castle, complete with banner flying from a turret, but it's ersatz 19th century (open to the public some days during the summer). If you're feeling energetic, you can continue to Penshurst (see above), but stop at the post office or a shop on the main street and ask for detailed directions; it can be really hard to find your way on the intersecting footpaths.

3 Where to Dine

King Henry VIII PUB Named for the monarch who's rather infamously linked with Hever Castle just up the road, this handsome, paneled pub serves sandwiches and meat pies, along with curries and other daily specials. The satisfying Sunday-roast lunch, when you can enjoy lamb, beef, or other substantial fare in front of a fire, adds a very nice touch to a day's outing from London.

Hever Rd., near castle entrance. ✆ **01732/862-457.** Main courses £4–£8 ($6–$13) DC, MC, V. Food served Mon–Sat noon–2:30pm and 6:30–9:30pm; Sun noon–3pm and 6–9pm.

Trip 11

Kew Gardens

Located 9 miles (14km) southwest of central London, the **Royal Botanic Gardens, Kew**—more familiarly known as Kew Gardens—are a feast for the eyes (and noses) of garden lovers. Kew's connections with royalty began with Frederick, prince of Wales, who leased the property in 1730 and had a hand in laying out the grounds. But it was Frederick's widow, Augusta, and his son, George III, who really developed Kew. Their work was aided by botanists

Kew Gardens

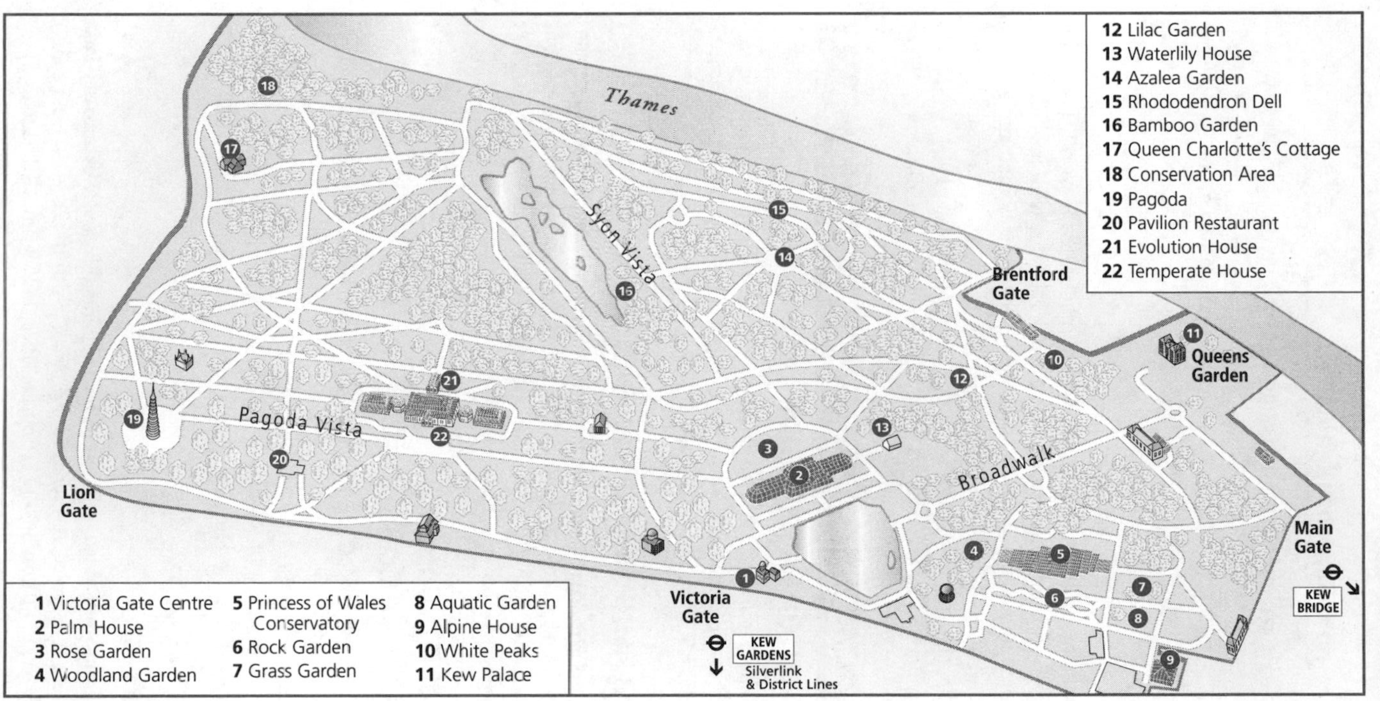

Thames
Syon Vista
Pagoda Vista
Broadwalk
Brentford Gate
Queens Garden
Lion Gate
Victoria Gate
KEW GARDENS
Silverlink & District Lines
Main Gate
KEW BRIDGE
12 Lilac Garden
13 Waterlily House
14 Azalea Garden
15 Rhododendron Dell
16 Bamboo Garden
17 Queen Charlotte's Cottage
18 Conservation Area
19 Pagoda
20 Pavilion Restaurant
21 Evolution House
22 Temperate House
1 Victoria Gate Centre
2 Palm House
3 Rose Garden
4 Woodland Garden
5 Princess of Wales Conservatory
6 Rock Garden
7 Grass Garden
8 Aquatic Garden
9 Alpine House
10 White Peaks
11 Kew Palace

Kew Gardens Highlights

- Exploring the world-famous plant collections in the Royal Botanic Gardens.
- Visiting the glasshouse conservatories, some new, some dating back to the Victorian era.

who began to bring plants to Kew from all over the world. The architect William Chambers decorated the royal estate with pavilions, temples, and even a pagoda. Capability Brown redesigned the gardens, and in 1840 the Royal Botanic Gardens were taken over by the nation. Recognizing the historic importance of the gardens, UNESCO appointed Kew Gardens a World Heritage Site in 2003.

1 Essentials

VISITOR INFORMATION

The **Victoria Gate Visitor Centre** on Kew Road provides information and remains open the same hours as the Royal Botanic Gardens, daily 9:30am to dusk.

SCHEDULING CONSIDERATIONS

The gardens are open daily from 9:30am to dusk, but the glass conservatories close an hour before the gardens themselves. The gardens are interesting year-round, but for overall peak blooming, visit between April and July.

GETTING THERE

BY UNDERGROUND

By far the easiest way to get to Kew is to take the District Line Underground to Kew Gardens. (Take a train marked RICHMOND, not one marked EALING BROADWAY or WIMBLEDON.) From the Kew station it's a 5-minute walk west on Lichfield Street to the garden entrance on Kew Road. For **London Transport** information, call © **020/7222-1234.**

BY BOAT

From April to late September, boats operated by the **Westminster Passenger Service Association** (© **020/7930-2062;** www.wpsa.co.uk) leave from London's Westminster Pier daily from 10:15am to 2pm.

Return fares for the 90-minute journey are £15 ($24) for adults, £10 ($16) for seniors, £7.50 ($12) for children 5 to 15, and £38 ($60) for families (two adults, two children). The last boat from Kew back to London usually departs around 5:30pm (depending on the tide).

BY CAR

Kew Gardens is well signposted from all the major local roads. The South Circular (A205) passes the northeast corner of Kew Gardens; and Kew Road (A307) forms the eastern border. There is a car park near the Brentford Gate, reached via Ferry Lane off Kew Green near the Main Gate; parking costs £3 ($4.80) for a full day. Free parking is available on Kew Road (A307) after 10am every morning; this provides easy access to the garden's principal entrance at Victoria Gate.

GETTING AROUND

Exploring the nooks and crannies of the Royal Botanic Gardens is best done on foot. You can get a 40-minute overview of the 300-acre (120-hectare) gardens by taking the **Kew Explorer** (✆ **020 8332 5615**), a hop-on/hop-off people-mover that makes eight stops within the gardens. Tickets are £3 ($4.80) for adults, £1.50 ($2.40) for children. You can purchase a ticket at any of the garden's ticket gates or from the driver of the vehicle. The main boarding point is close to the Victoria Gate Visitor Centre and the Palm House.

2 A Day in Kew

There are four entrances to the **Royal Botanic Gardens, Kew** (✆ **020/8332-5622;** www.rbgkew.org.uk). **Victoria Gate** on Kew Road is the largest entrance and nearest to the Kew Gardens Underground station. The **Main Gate** on Kew Green is the nearest entrance to the Kew Bridge train station and Kew Pier riverboat stop. The **Brentford Gate** is adjacent to the car park and a 10-minute walk along the riverbank from Kew Pier. **Lion Gate,** the southernmost gate on Kew Road, is nearest to the Pagoda and the Pavilion Restaurant. Admission to the gardens is £7.50 ($12) for adults, £5.50 ($9) for seniors and students. The gardens are open daily from 9:30am to dusk.

For a good and fairly complete walk encompassing the main garden areas and glasshouse conservatories, you'll need 3 to 4 hours. Start at ❶ **Victoria Gate Visitor Centre,** where you can pick up detailed maps and information. Then head west to the famous ❷ **Palm House,** which acts as a centerpiece to the gardens. Dramatic and elegant, this curvilinear structure is a classic example of Victorian design. Built between 1844 and 1848, it was constructed to house tropical trees, shrubs, and palms. Beneath the Palm House is the Marine Display with tanks containing fish, coral, and algae: the beginnings of plant life on earth. To one side of the Palm House is the ❸ **Rose Garden,** created in 1923 and a major focal point for visitors, especially June through September, the peak flowering months. The garden houses 54 rose beds, each containing a different variety of rose.

From the Rose Garden, make your way north to the ❹ **Woodland Garden.** This area illustrates the change in vegetation between forest and alpine zones. A deciduous tree canopy of oaks and birches supports climbing plants and provides shade for deciduous shrubs such as rhododendrons, which in turn protect ground-cover plants, including hellebores, primulas, Himalayan blue poppies, and North American trilliums. A short walk to the northwest brings you to the ❺ **Princess of Wales Conservatory,** named in honor of the garden's founder, Augusta, the princess of Wales, and Diana, Princess of Wales, who opened the Conservatory in July 1987. This contemporary glasshouse has 10 climatic zones, ranging from arid to moist tropical. The hot and humid area contains swamp and riverine habitats and displays giant Amazonian waterlilies. In contrast, the arid zone houses plants tolerant of desert conditions, particularly cacti and other succulents.

Just east of the conservatory is the ❻ **Rock Garden,** originally built in 1882 and designed to resemble a mountain valley in the Pyrenees. The site was recently redesigned to include moist gullies, water features, and other special environments that allow for the cultivation of a variety of alpine, Mediterranean, and woodland plants. Adjacent, to the north, is the ❼ **Grass Garden,** designed in 1982 and displaying some 550 species of grasses. Continue towards the northeast corner of the gardens and you'll reach the ❽ **Aquatic Garden,** which opened in 1909 and is famous for its 40 different varieties of waterlily. Nearby, in the northeastern corner of the gardens, is the ❾ **Alpine House,** built in 1981 to display Kew's collection of alpine plants. From late winter to May, corresponding with the flowering season of the plants being displayed, you'll see collections of crocus, fritillaria, narcissus, primula, and saxifrage. (***Note:*** At press time, the Alpine House was closed for major reconstruction, and a reopening date had not yet been set.)

Heading west across the park toward the Thames, you come to ❿ **White Peaks,** a restaurant and gift shop (see "Where to Dine," below). Immediately to the west is ⓫ **Kew Palace,** George III's family home and used by the royal family between 1729 and 1818. The small redbrick palace is the last survivor of several important royal residences at Kew; it is currently not open to the public. The **Queen's Garden,** behind Kew Palace, is a 17th-century-style garden with parterres of low boxwood hedges enclosing plantings of lavender, sage, and rosemary. Next to the parterres is a sunken nosegay garden planted with the fragrant flowers used to make posies or nosegays in the 17th century.

From the palace, backtrack to White Peaks and continue southeast to the ⓬ **Lilac Garden,** at its fragrant best in May. Completely renovated in 1993, the new garden has 105 specimens of hardy lilacs ranging from the oldest species to modern cultivars and hybrids. Just east of the Lilac Garden you'll find the ⓭ **Waterlily House,** the hottest and most humid glasshouse at Kew. In summer it houses tropical ornamental aquatic plants and giant waterlilies; it's closed in winter.

South of the Waterlily House is the ⓮ **Azalea Garden,** with its profusion of hardy azaleas that provide a blaze of springtime color. Zigzagging back towards the Thames, you reach the famous ⓯ **Rhododendron Dell,** planted with over 700 specimens of hardy, spring-flowering, shade-loving rhododendrons, some of them unique hybrids found only at Kew. The Rhododendron Dell was carved out of a riverside flood plain by the great landscaper Capability Brown in 1773. It became the Rhododendron Dell when Sir Joseph Hooker began bringing back rhododendrons from his Himalayan expeditions in the 1850s. The best time to visit is during late May, when the majority of rhododendrons are in flower.

In the neighboring ⓰ **Bamboo Garden,** over 120 individual specimens of hardy bamboo have been brought together from regions all over the world. From here, continue south past Kew's artificial lake to ⓱ **Queen Charlotte's Cottage.** This cottage began as a small, single-story building within the grounds of Richmond Lodge, which Queen Charlotte received as a wedding gift when she married George III in 1761. It was used as a summer house. Queen Charlotte's Cottage is not open to the public except once a year on the May Day Bank Holiday. The nearby ⓲ **Conservation Area** contains one of the finest spring-flowering bluebell woods in the London area. The woods are managed as a nature reserve.

Walk east from Queen Charlotte's Cottage and you'll reach the ⓳ **Pagoda,** completed in 1762 and a charming reminder of the passion for Chinoiserie in English garden design in the mid–18th century. Close by is the ⓴ **Pavilion Restaurant.** (See "Where to Dine," below.) North and slightly west of the restaurant, you come to ㉑ **Evolution**

Fun Fact The Chinese Pagoda

The Chinese Pagoda in Kew Gardens is a strange but oddly endearing sight. In 1761, when it was built, the Pagoda was the most accurate reconstruction of a Chinese building in Europe. It is 163 feet (49m) high and contains nothing but a staircase. Unfortunately, it's closed to the public.

House, a walk-through exhibition of plant evolution over 3,500 million years. ㉒ **Temperate House,** just east of Evolution House, is the world's largest ornamental glasshouse, and holds a collection of subtropical plants. The main center block and the octagons at each end were built between 1860 and 1862; the end blocks were added between 1860 and 1899. The world's largest indoor plant, the Chilean wine-palm, is displayed within.

From Temperate House you can walk back to Victoria Gate in about 5 minutes.

ORGANIZED TOURS

Free, hour-long guided walking tours of the gardens leave year-round (except Christmas and New Year's Day) at 11am and 2pm from the Guides' desk, just inside the Victoria Gate Visitor Centre. Tour groups are limited to 20 people on a first-come, first-served basis; register with the guide 15 minutes before the tour.

3 Shopping

The shops at **Victoria Gate** and **White Peaks** (✆ **020/8332-5653** for both) sell many exclusive products, including kitchenware and stationery lines designed for the Royal Botanic Gardens using illustrations from the Kew archives. There is also a comprehensive selection of horticultural books. The **Garden Shop** (✆ **01444/894-073**), at the entrance to the garden, is open from March to October and sells a wide range of interesting and unusual plants and garden items. (***Note:*** Live plants cannot be brought into the U.S.)

4 Where to Dine

The **Orangery Restaurant** (✆ **020/8332-5186**), located close to the Main Gate, with pretty views of the gardens, offers morning coffees, lunches, and afternoon teas. **White Peaks** is Kew's newest venue for snacks and drinks. The **Victoria Gate Coffee Shop,** in the Victoria Gate Visitor Centre, serves cappuccino and espresso, handmade pastries and cakes, ice cream, sandwiches, and baguettes. All three venues are open from 10am until 1 hour before the gardens close. The **Pavilion Restaurant** (✆ **020/8332-5186**), located near the Pagoda, is the garden's largest restaurant; in it you'll find a self-service cafeteria offering hot meals, snacks, salads, desserts, and hot and cold drinks. It's open the same hours as the restaurants above, but closes during the winter months.

Trip 12

Knole

One of Britain's largest and grandest houses covers 4.5 acres (1.8 hectares) and has 365 rooms, as well as a courtyard for every day of the week and a staircase for every week of the year. Large, yes, but Knole is certainly not homey—indeed, the house has always been meant to impress rather than charm, and its labyrinthine rooms and galleries are a treasure trove of furniture, textiles, and portraits by such masters as Anthony van Dyck and Sir Joshua

Knole Highlights

- A walk through the Deer Park.
- The Great Hall, with its embellished staircase and minstrels' gallery.
- The Count Ugolino painting and other works by Reynolds in the Reynolds Room.
- The rare silver furniture in the King's Room.

Reynolds. Since you can board a train in London and find yourself standing in the Great Hall at Knole in less than an hour, you can easily do this day trip in half a day—unless, that is, you want to explore more of British history on a visit to one or two other, nearby houses.

1 Essentials

VISITOR INFORMATION

Knole is in the town of Sevenoaks, about 30 miles (48km) southeast of London. The house (© **01732/450-608;** www.nationaltrust.org.uk), in a large deer park at the south end of town, is open March 22 to November 2, Wednesday to Sunday from 11am to 4pm; the last entry is at 3:30pm. The Deer Park is open year-round. Admission is £5.50 ($9) for adults, £2.75 ($4.40) for children, and £14 ($22) for families of up to two adults and three children.

SCHEDULING CONSIDERATIONS

On the first Wednesday of the month from May to September, the private gardens of the Sackville family are open to the public from 11am to 4pm. A walk through these large gardens adds a nice perk to a visit.

GETTING THERE

BY TRAIN

Trains run about every 15 minutes throughout the day from London's Charing Cross Station to Sevenoaks, with the first train leaving London at 5:30am and the last train returning from Sevenoaks at 11:22pm. The trip takes about 35 minutes. The standard day return fare is £8.90 ($14). For more information, call **National Rail Enquiries** (© **08457/484-950;** www.nationalrail.co.uk).

Knole

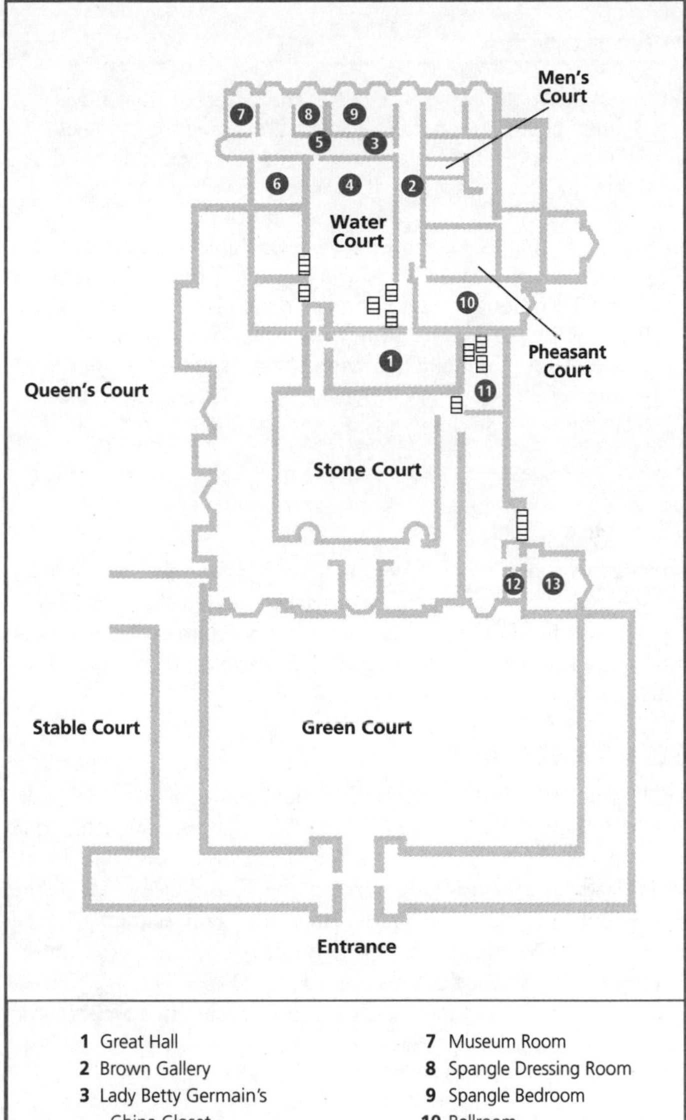

1 Great Hall
2 Brown Gallery
3 Lady Betty Germain's China Closet
4 Water Court
5 Leicester Gallery
6 Venetian Ambassador's Room
7 Museum Room
8 Spangle Dressing Room
9 Spangle Bedroom
10 Ballroom
11 Reynolds Room
12 King's Closet
13 King's Room

From *Orlando*

Virginia Woolf based the title character of her novel *Orlando* on her friend Vita Sackville-West, and she modeled Orlando's home in Kent on Knole, Vita's beloved childhood home. In Woolf's words, "It looked a town rather than a house, but a town built, not hither and thither, as this man wished or that, but circumspectly, by a single architect with one idea in his head. Courts and buildings, grey, red, plum colour, lay orderly and symmetrical; the courts were some of them oblong and some square; in this was a fountain; in that a statue; the buildings were some of them low, some pointed; here was chapel, there a belfry . . . while smoke from innumerable chimneys curled perpetually into the air."

BY CAR

Sevenoaks is about 3 miles (4.8km) off M25, the London ring road, and the trip from the center of the city takes about half an hour. Leave the M25 at Junction 5 and follow the signs into Sevenoaks. The entrance to Knole is at the south end of the town center off A225 Tonbridge Road.

GETTING AROUND

Knole is about a mile from the train station, and can be reached by an easy walk through the center of Sevenoaks. An especially picturesque way to approach the house is to follow Webb's Alley off High Street, which leads to a footpath that crosses the Knole Deer Park to the house. Bus no. 402 runs hourly from the train station past the entrance to Knole; the fare is 80p ($1.30). For additional bus information, call the Sevenoaks bus station at ✆ **01732/743-040.** There's a taxi stand outside the train station, but to ensure that a car will be available when you arrive, arrange a pickup in advance by calling **Beeline Radio Taxis** at ✆ **01732/456-214.**

2 A Day at Knole

The self-guided tour of the immense house includes only 13 rooms, but even so, you'll feel as though you're covering acres. After approaching the house through the enormous Deer Park, you'll pass into the ❶ **Great Hall** through two courtyards. (Part of this entrance wing was added by Henry VIII, who acquired Knole in 1538.) Thomas Bouchier, archbishop of Canterbury, who built the house between 1456 and

1480, used to dine on the dais at the far end of the cavernous hall. When Thomas Sackville took possession of Knole in 1603, he enhanced the dining experience by adding a gallery where his private orchestra would play throughout the meal. He also embellished the Great Staircase with carvings and murals to impress his guests as they climbed to the first-floor staterooms.

One of Thomas Sackville's most accomplished descendants was Vita Sackville-West, the 20th-century poet and novelist. She grew up at Knole and loved the house, but as a woman could not inherit it. Instead she bought nearby Sissinghurst and created one of the England's most famous gardens (see trip 21). Vita's friend and fellow novelist Virginia Woolf set her novel *Orlando* at Knole and you'll find the novel especially evocative after visiting the house; you can read a page or two in the facsimile edition on view in the Great Hall.

The staterooms at Knole are laid out as apartments comprising long galleries, bedchambers, and dressing rooms. As you pass through the first of these arrangements, the ❷ **Brown Gallery** and the adjoining ❸ **Lady Betty Germain's China Closet** (which houses a notable collection of Delft), look out the window into the ❹ **Water Court**—this half-timbered courtyard surrounded by bow windows is one of the few charming nooks and crannies at Knole.

In the nearby ❺ **Leicester Gallery** (named for the Earl of Leicester, a 16th-century owner of Knole who was a favorite of Elizabeth I), pay close attention to the full-length portrait of James I; the king is sitting on an X-framed chair exactly like the one beneath the painting. Another piece of notable furniture is in the ❻ **Venetian Ambassador's Room**—the bed is said to be the one in which King James II awoke at Whitehall on December 18, 1688, the day William of Orange took the crown and forced James into exile. A less imposing but nonetheless notable piece of furniture is the Knole settee in the adjoining ❼ **Museum Room.** This high-armed, high-backed couch may look familiar; the design is still popular and often reproduced. The harpsichord in the ❽ **Spangle Dressing Room** is one of the oldest in England, but your attention will probably be drawn to the 17th-century bed in the adjoining ❾ **Spangle Bedroom,** covered with thousands of silver panels intended to sparkle in the sunlight.

In the next rooms hang Knole's famous paintings. A van Dyck portrait of a teenaged Frances Cranfield, who married a 17th-century owner of Knole, is in the ❿ **Ballroom,** and a collection of paintings by Sir Joshua Reynolds hangs in the appropriately named ⓫ **Reynolds Room.** If you know your Dante, you might recognize the horrible scene of a starving Count Ugolino contemplating eating his dead children. One of the more curious portraits is of Wang-y-Tong, page to the third duke of Dorset, who owned Knole for the last half of the 18th century and was Reynolds's patron.

The last two rooms commemorate royalty—the ⑫ **King's Closet** does so humbly, with what is euphemistically called a "seat of easement" used by Charles II or James II; and the ⑬ **King's Room** shows off a grandiose bed made for Charles, as well as a set of rare silver furniture. Though the remarkable ensemble is lit dimly (to preserve the gilt), the set is one of the Knole's great treasures and, like the house itself, in a somewhat musty manner suggests the grandeur of bygone times.

MORE THINGS TO SEE & DO

From Knole you can visit nearby Ightham Mote and Chartwell. Chartwell is accessible by bus no. 401, which runs from Sevenoaks train station only on Sunday, every 2 hours between 9:53am and 5:53pm; the fare is £1.60 ($2.55). To reach Chartwell at other times, and to reach Ightham Mote, it's necessary to take a taxi; the fare to each is about £6 ($10) one-way.

Ightham Mote One of the oldest residences in England and one of the best-preserved medieval dwellings in the world dates to 1330. Unlike the cold staterooms at Knole, the Great Hall and other rooms of this moated manor exude warmth and familiarity and are filled with textiles, paneling, and furnishings accumulated over the centuries. The gardens are beautiful, and the extensive grounds are laced with footpaths.

Ivy Hatch, 6 miles (9.5km) east of Sevenoaks. ✆ **01732/810-378.** www.nationaltrust.org.uk/places/ighthammote. £6 ($10) adults, £3 ($4.80) children, £15 ($24) families. Mar 23–Nov 7, Mon, Wed–Fri, Sun 10am–5:30pm.

Chartwell For more than 40 years, Sir Winston and Lady Churchill made this handsome brick house their home, entertaining world leaders and engaging in their private pursuits, too. Here England's wartime prime minister wrote his history of the English-speaking peoples and other books and painted his accomplished watercolors. Together the couple transformed the 80-acre (32-hectare) grounds, and their gardens continue to flourish.

2 miles (3.2km) south of Westerham (fork left off B2026 after 1½ miles/2.5km), about 7 miles (11km) southwest of Sevenoaks. ✆ **01732/868-381.** www.nationaltrust.org.uk/places/chartwell. £6.50 ($10) adults, £3.25 ($5) children, £16 ($26) families. Mar 22–June 29 and Sept 3–Nov 9, Wed–Sun 11am–5pm; July 1–Aug 31, Tues–Sun 11am–5pm.

Moments **A Bird's-Eye View**

Ramble through Knole's Deer Park over hills and through woods. Find a high spot and look over the sea of roofs and courtyards—you'll agree with novelist Virginia Woolf that Knole is "a town rather than a house."

---

3 Where to Dine

Greggs LIGHT FARE/TRADITIONAL BRITISH You can eat simply or rather lavishly in this attractive room in the center of town. Soups, pastas, and salads are served on a "light lunch" menu, but calves' liver, steaks, and other hearty British fare are also available. Sunday lunch is very popular with locals.

28–30 High St. ✆ **01732/456-373.** Most items £4–£13 ($6–$21). DC, MC, V. Food served Tues–Sat 12:30–2:30pm and 6:30–9:30pm; Sun noon–2:45pm.

Trip 13

Leeds Castle

"The loveliest castle in the world," as Leeds is billed, is lovely indeed, a vision of turrets, towers, and light gray stone that seems to float in the middle of a swan-filled moat. On the extensive and manicured grounds, streams bubble through copses, exotic flowers bloom in well-tended gardens, and a maze hides a secret grotto. Leeds has a long history, too: It traces its roots to the 9th century and

Leeds Castle

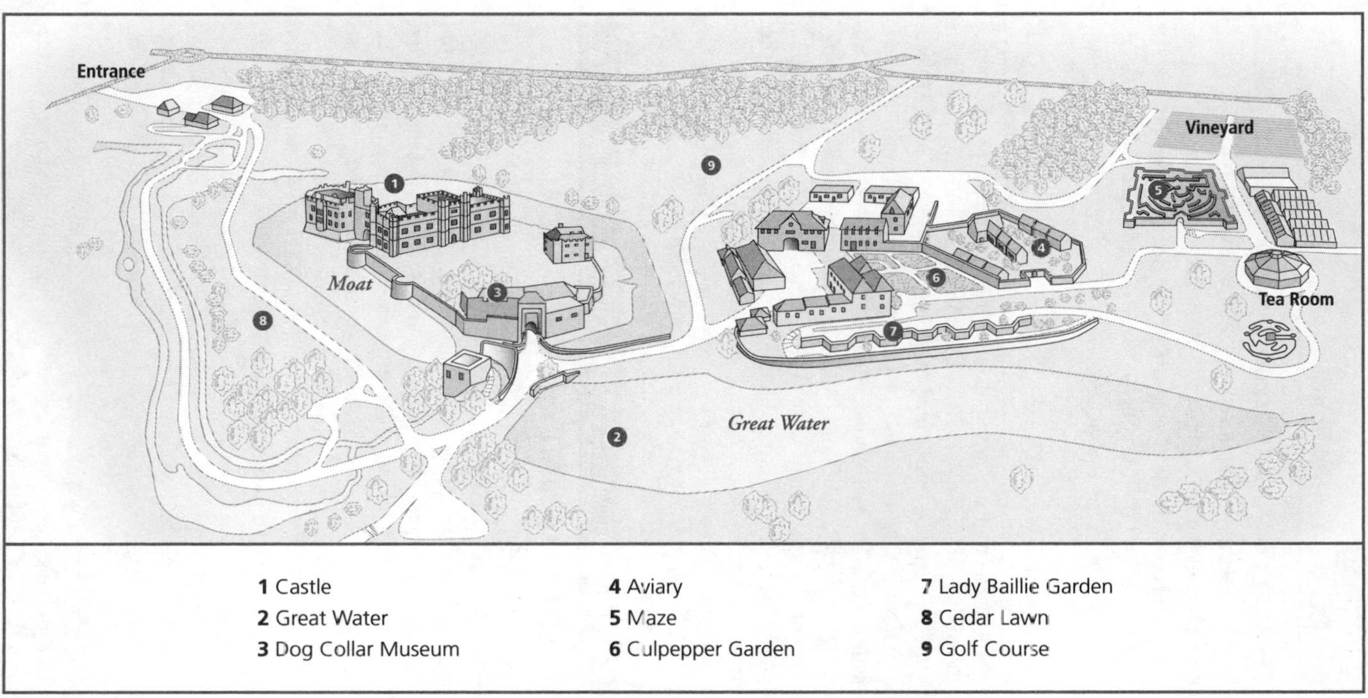

Leeds Castle Highlights

- The sumptuous 20th-century living quarters of the castle.
- The medieval chapel with its paintings and carvings.
- The weird grotto, hidden in the maze.
- Culpepper Garden, a colorful and delightfully informal bower, and the Mediterranean-style Lady Baillie Garden.
- Charming Bearsted village.

was transformed into a royal palace for Edward I in 1278; the castle's vineyard, still producing grapes, is listed in the 11th-century *Domesday Book.* King Henry V imprisoned his stepmother, Queen Joan, at Leeds on charges of witchcraft, and Henry VIII made substantial improvements to Leeds for his first queen, Catherine of Aragon. The castle was later the country seat of Lord Culpeper, colonial governor of Virginia. A wealthy heiress, Olive, Lady Baillie, purchased the castle in 1926, restoring some of Leeds to its medieval splendor and creating in other parts of the castle one of the most sophisticated and tasteful homes of 20th-century Britain. A visit to Leeds provides a dose of English history with a glimpse into the lives of a privileged few.

1 Essentials

VISITOR INFORMATION

Leeds is located 7 miles (11km) east of the town of Maidstone and about 40 miles (64km) southeast of London. Unlike many historic homes in Britain, the castle is open year-round: March to October, from 10am to 6pm (last admission at 5pm); and November to February, from 10am to 4pm (last admission at 3pm). Fees vary with the time of year. From March 1 to October 31, entrance to the castle and grounds costs £11 ($18) for adults, £9.50 ($15) for seniors and students, £7.50 ($12) for children 4 to 16, and £32 ($51) for families of up to two adults and three children. Entrance to the grounds only—but do tour the castle, too—costs £9.50 ($15) for adults, £8 ($13) for seniors and students, £6 ($9.60) for children 4 to 16, and £29 ($46) for families of up to two adults and three children. From November 1 to February 28, entrance to the castle and grounds costs £9.50 ($15) for adults, £8 ($13) for seniors and students, £6 ($9.60) for children 4 to 16, and £27 ($43) for families of up to two adults and three children; lower fees for entrance to the grounds only are not available during this period. For information, call © **0870/600-8880** or visit www.leeds-castle.com.

SCHEDULING CONSIDERATIONS

You may or may not want to arrange your visit to Leeds Castle to coincide with one of the many events the castle hosts. These include a Flower Festival in early April, a food and wine festival in May, open-air concerts on summer evenings, a hot-air balloon and antique car exhibition in September, and an extravagant Guy Fawkes fireworks display on or around November 8.

GETTING THERE

BY TRAIN

The closest train station to Leeds Castle is the one in the village of Bearsted, about 5 miles (8km) away. The trip from London's Victoria Station takes just over an hour, and the cheap day return fare is £8.70 ($14). There are some 20 trains a day from London; the first train to Bearsted is at 6:10am and the last train returns to London at 10:24pm; trains run every half hour during rush hour and every hour throughout the rest of the day and evening. A bus meets trains throughout the day for the trip from the train station to the castle; the return fare is £4 ($6.40). The first bus leaves the train station at 10:35am after meeting the 9:14am train from London. From March to October, the last bus returns to the train station from the castle at 6pm (reaching the station in time for the 6:24pm train to London). From November to February, the last bus returns to the train station at 4pm (in time for the 4:24pm train to London).

An "all in one" ticket from Connex rail service includes train travel to Bearsted, free bus transport between the station and the castle, and admission to the castle and grounds; the fee is £22 ($34) for adults, £11 ($17) for children 4 to 15. You can purchase this ticket from the windows at London's Victoria Station. For more information, call ✆ **0870/603-0405.**

BY BUS

Another way to visit Leeds Castle is on a special National Express coach that departs from London's Victoria Coach Station at 9am each day the castle is open. It arrives at the castle at 10:30am, and departs the castle at 3pm to arrive back at London's Victoria Coach Station at 4:50pm. The fare, including transportation and admission to the castle and grounds, is £15 ($24) for adults and £10 ($16) for children 4 to 15 from Monday to Friday; and £17 ($27) for adults and £12 ($19) for children 4 to 15 on Saturday and Sunday. For more information, call ✆ **08705/808-080** or visit www.nationalexpress.co.uk. If you don't mind the lack of flexibility in travel times, this is an easy and relatively inexpensive way to visit Leeds Castle.

BY CAR

The trip from London takes just under an hour, depending on traffic. Take the M25 to the M20, then take exit 8 and follow the signs to the castle entrance. Parking is free.

GETTING AROUND

A free, open-air bus travels from the main entrance to the castle (a distance of about a quarter mile) and other attractions on the grounds. However, it's much more enjoyable to walk along the paved paths that curve around ponds and cross lawns and woods.

2 A Day at Leeds Castle

To get a good overview of the extent and grandeur of Leeds, and to enjoy views of its moat, turrets, and towers, walk around the grounds before entering the ❶ **castle.** Then, after the castle tour, return to the grounds and take some time to relax in a nice spot—the benches overlooking the lake known as the ❷ **Great Water** are a good choice.

As you tour the grounds, at each turn you seem to come upon another attraction. These can be somewhat surprising, such as the ❸ **Dog Collar Museum,** where canine accessories going back more than 400 years are on display; and the ❹ **aviary,** whose state-of-the-art pavilions house more than 100 feathered species. The most popular attraction at Leeds is the ❺ **maze,** planted with 2,400 yew trees and leading to a fantastically macabre grotto filled with mythical beasts. Two of the most pleasant spots are the ❻ **Culpepper Garden,** a colorful and delightfully informal bower; and the ❼ **Lady Baillie Garden,** where Mediterranean plantings cascade down lakeside terraces.

The prescribed castle tour begins in the dank and dull Norman cellars, then continues into medieval rooms that include the 15th-century bathroom of Catherine of Valois, the wife of Henry V; the room is surprisingly well equipped and luxurious, and invites an interesting comparison with the sumptuous Russian onyx bathroom in another wing that Lady Baillie had installed in the 1920s.

Interiors at Leeds are intimate and appealing—Henry VIII's Banqueting Room is handsome, not overwhelming, and overlooks the grounds through a large bay window. And one of the pleasures of exploring the castle is coming upon treasure after treasure: In the Banqueting Room, the prize is a spring scene by Pieter Brueghel the Younger; in the Chapel are exquisite limewood carved panels and four paintings by the late-14th-century Florentine Niccolò di Pietro Gerini that depict the Passion of Christ—they are some of the earliest known works on canvas. Probably the most charming of the castle's many

Fun Fact Royals & Americans

Leeds Castle traces it origins to the days of William the Conqueror and became a royal home when Edward I, the founder of the British Parliament, acquired the estate around 1290. The castle remained in the hands of the monarchy for the next 3 centuries. Among the royal tenants who left their mark on Leeds is Catherine of Valois, who received the castle upon the death of her husband, Henry V, in 1422; her bedroom and bathroom are on view in the old Keep, known as the Gloriette. (Catherine, then only 21, fell in love with Owen Tudor, clerk of her wardrobe, and they secretly married—their son Edmund was the father of King Henry VII, founder of the Tudor dynasty.) Catherine of Aragon, first wife of Henry VIII, also lived at Leeds, and the fireplace in the Queens Gallery is emblazoned with part of her symbol, the pomegranates of Aragon. A portrait of Edward VI, Henry VIII's only male heir (whom he had with his third queen, Jane Seymour), hangs above the fireplace; notice his misshapen ear. Leeds's connection with America begins in 1663, when Thomas, the second Lord Culpeper, purchased the castle; Lord Culpeper's father had been granted more than 5 million acres (2 million hectares) in Virginia, and Culpeper later became governor of the colony. His daughter, Catherine, married into the Fairfax family, who eventually inherited the Culpeper lands in Virginia and the castle, which they held until the end of the 18th century. One reminder of the castle's American connections is on the grounds—a sundial that's designed to show the time in Virginia.

works of art is Giambattista Tiepolo's *The Punchinello's Kitchen,* which hangs above the mantle in the Yellow Drawing Room and provides an 18th-century view of the Venice Carnival.

In addition to its medieval splendor, Leeds gives visitors a look at a privileged mid-20th-century lifestyle that has all but disappeared. The rooms that Lady Baillie renovated are comfortably luxurious, proving that you don't have to be a king or queen to live like one.

MORE THINGS TO SEE & DO

Before boarding the train back to London, take an hour or so to wander around Bearsted. (The train station is at the edge of the village, only a 5-min. walk from the center.) The village surrounds a large,

Moments Lazing on the Lawn

You won't tire of the vista of Leeds rising from the moat that surrounds it. An especially nice outlook is the one from the ⑧ **Cedar Lawn,** just off the main drive. Stretch out and enjoy the view.

beautifully maintained green, and on the east side you'll see a distinctive Kentish scene: the steep, conical roofs of oast houses, used for drying hops. (The ones here have been converted to residences.)

OUTDOOR ACTIVITIES

On the grounds is a ⑨ **nine-hole golf course** built for Lady Baillie in the 1920s. The course is open daily. Weekday fees are £11 ($18) for adults, £8 ($13) for seniors. On weekends, the fee for all players is £13 ($21). Clubs are available for rent. For more information, call the pro shop at ✆ **01622/767-828.**

3 Where to Dine

The White Horse PUB At this historic village pub, far more appealing than the dining options on the castle grounds, you can find a cozy nook in front of the fire or at a window overlooking the lovely green. Pub fare as well as substantial meals are served.

Bearsted Green. ✆ **01622/738-365.** Most items £3–£10 ($4.80–$16) DC, MC, V. Food served Mon–Sat noon–2:30pm and 6:30–9:30pm; Sun noon–3pm and 6:30–9pm.

Trip 14

Monk's House & Charleston

These two evocative houses are known as "Bloomsbury in Sussex": For the early years of the 20th century they were the country retreats of the artistic, intellectual, and literary set known as the "Bloomsbury Group" for the London neighborhood where many of them lived. The painter Vanessa Bell, her husband Clive Bell, and her friend and sometime lover Duncan

Monk's House & Charleston Highlights

- The village of Rodmell, where Monk's House is located.
- The Sitting Room at Monk's House, where you will have to resist the urge to plop down and read a book.
- The garden and orchard at Monk's House (especially in the autumn, when you may be able to pick fruit in the orchard).
- Vanessa Bell's bedroom at Charleston, the most comfortable room in the house.
- The Dining Room at Charleston, which the residents outdid themselves designing.

Grant moved to Charleston, a rambling and derelict old farmhouse, in 1916. They painted many of the furnishings and surfaces in fanciful patterns and hung works by Picasso and Renoir, creating an artistic setting in which they lived until their deaths many years later. Vanessa's sister, the novelist Virginia Woolf, and her publisher husband Leonard bought modest and "unpretending" Monk's House in the nearby village of Rodmell in 1919. Virginia wrote several of her novels here, and in 1941 she drowned herself in the nearby River Ouse. A visit to one or preferably to both of these beautifully maintained houses is a delightful and enlightening experience. The houses are more than literary and artistic shrines—they evoke a lifestyle, an intellectual climate, and a heady period in English history. Fans of poet Percy Bysshe Shelley may want to make this an overnight trip for a chance to stay in the Shelley family home. (See the last section of this chapter.)

1 Essentials

VISITOR INFORMATION

Monk's House and Charleston are on the Sussex Downs, near the town of Lewes, which is about 50 miles (80km) south of London and 8 miles (13km) northeast of Brighton. Monk's House, in the village of Rodmell, 4 miles (6.5km) southwest of Lewes (© **01372/453-401;** www.nationaltrust.org.uk), is open from April 1 to November 2, Wednesday and Saturday from 2 to 5:30pm. Admission is £2.80 ($4.50) for adults, £1.30 ($2) for children under 16, and £6.50 ($10) for families of up to two adults and two children. Charleston, in open country 7 miles (11km) east of Lewes off A27 (© **01323/811-265;**

Monk's House & Charleston Area

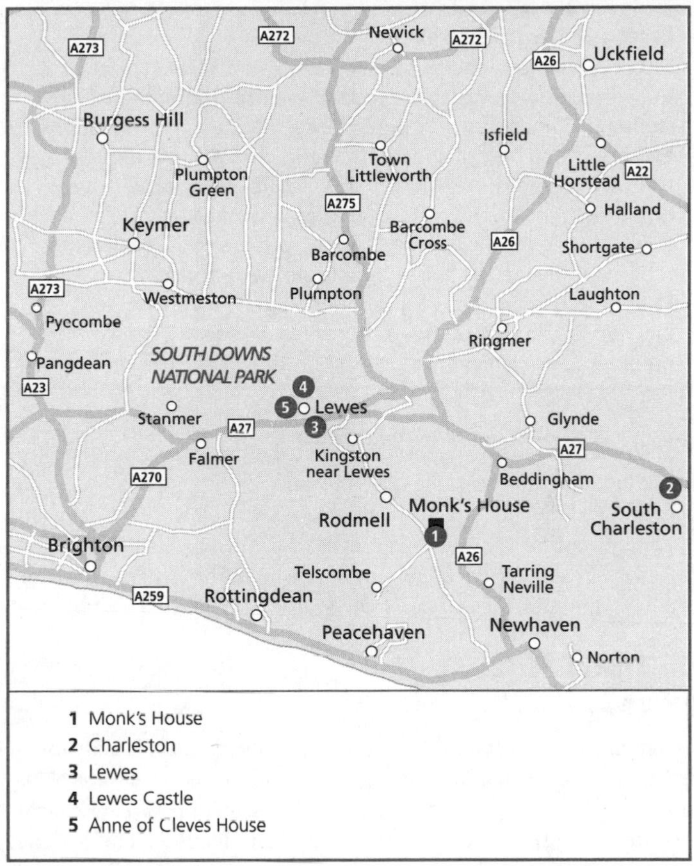

www.charleston.org.uk), is open April 1 through June 30, Wednesday through Sunday from 2 to 6pm; July 1 through August 31, Wednesday through Sunday from 11:30am to 6pm; and September 1 through October 31, Wednesday through Sunday from 2 to 6pm. During these times the house is also open on Bank Holiday Mondays from 2 to 6pm. The last admission is 1 hour before closing. Admission costs £6 ($10) for adults, £4.50 ($7) for seniors and students.

SCHEDULING CONSIDERATIONS

You'll have to plan your trip carefully because, due to limited opening hours, Wednesday and Saturday afternoons are the only times you can pay a combined visit to both houses. Because the houses attract many visitors on weekends, it's best to try to visit on Wednesday. Plus, if you want to explore Lewes, you should do so in the morning before visiting

Living It Up in Lewes

Lewes goes a bit wild (well, with the good taste typical of a British country town) twice a year. May through August, the stunning Glyndebourne opera house mounts six productions and brings the best of the opera world, and many ardent fans, to town. (For information, call ✆ **01273/813-813** or visit www.glyndebourne.com.) On November 5, Lewes stages one of the England's biggest Guy Fawkes Night celebrations, commemorating the events of this evening in 1605—that's when Guy Fawkes and members of the Gunpowder Plot attempted to blow up Parliament but were thwarted. Fireworks, a costumed procession, and an enormous bonfire are part of the show.

the houses, when the shops are still open. (Many close at 5pm.) Keep in mind, too, that the houses are closed November through March. If you plan to spend more than a day in Brighton (see trip 3), you might want to consider visiting the houses as part of that trip. Trains from Brighton to Lewes run about every 20 minutes throughout the day and make the trip in 15 minutes; the ride costs £4 ($6.40).

GETTING THERE

BY TRAIN

The train station closest to the houses is the one in the charming town of Lewes, where you'll want to spend some time before or after your visits. The direct trip from London's Victoria Station to Lewes takes just over an hour, and a day return ticket costs about £16 ($25). The first train to Lewes is at 5:15am and the last train returns to London at 10:42pm; trains run about every half hour. For more information, contact **National Rail Enquiries** (✆ **08457/484-950;** www.nationalrail.co.uk).

BY CAR

It's useful to have a car here, especially if you want to see both houses in a day. The trip from London takes just over an hour, depending on traffic. Take the M25 to the M23, which becomes the A23; follow that to the A27, which leads east to Lewes. If you're driving directly to Monk's House, at the western edge of Lewes turn off A27 at the exit for Kingston, and follow the road to Rodmell; from there, turn left at the pub and follow the lane down to Monk's House. For Charleston, follow A27 east of Lewes; about 7 miles (11km) east of Lewes you'll see a turnoff for Charleston on the right side of the road, between the villages of Firle and Selmeston.

Impressions

I could fancy a very pleasant walk in the orchard under the apple trees, with the grey extinguisher of the church steeple pointing my boundary.

—Virginia Woolf, diary entry for July 3, 1919

GETTING AROUND

From Lewes train station you can continue to Monk's House or Charleston by bus, but service is infrequent and you won't have time to see both houses in one afternoon if you use public transportation. Of the two, Monk's House is the most accessible by bus from Lewes; take bus no. 123, which runs about every hour, get off in the village of Rodmell, and follow the main lane about a quarter of a mile down to the house. For Charleston, take bus no. 125, which runs every 1½ to 2 hours. (Ask the driver to let you off at the foot of the lane leading from A27 to the house; the walk is about 1½ miles/2.4km.) The fare to each house is £1.60 ($2.55). To reach one of the houses from the other, it's necessary to return to Lewes and transfer buses. For additional bus information, call **Traveline** at ✆ **0870/608-2608.**

If you're not traveling by car, the most feasible way to see both houses is by taxi from Lewes. Fares, however, are a bit steep: For example, expect to pay about £8 ($13) for the trip from Lewes to Monk's House, £17 ($27) from Monk's House to Charleston, and £12 ($19) from Charleston back to Lewes. There's a taxi stand outside the Lewes train station, but to ensure that a taxi will be available when you arrive, arrange a pickup in advance by calling **Meridian Taxis** at ✆ **01273/580-099** or **Newhaven/Seaford Taxis** at **01273/611-111.**

2 A Day at Monk's House & Charleston

Your first impression of ❶ **Monk's House** may be just how charming the surrounding village is. Then you might be struck by how small and unassuming the house is. Clearly, the luxury the Woolfs valued most was not a great amount of creature comfort but the leisure to do what they wanted—she to write, and he to run his small, literary Hogarth Press and to garden.

You can wander through the house at your leisure, and since there are only four rooms to see, you should indulge in the luxury of lingering in each room and soaking in the atmosphere. It's quite easy to imagine the couple in the Sitting Room where, Virginia wrote, "we sit, eat, play the gramophone, prop our feet up on the side of the fire and read endless books." The tile-topped, painted table is the work of Duncan Grant and Vanessa Bell, and Vanessa designed the fabric that covers an extraordinarily comfortable-looking reading chair; Duncan and Vanessa also designed the dining room chairs.

"A woman must have money and a room of her own if she is to write fiction," Virginia wrote, and as her novels began earning money she added a rather austere room that didn't suit her as a workroom but became her bedroom. The room's most noticeable attributes are its brightness and the presence of the garden beyond the windows. Virginia wrote in a rustic structure at the far end of the garden known as the Lodge, where apples from the large orchard were stored throughout the winter. The orchard still bears fruit, and if you visit in the autumn, you can get into the spirit of Monk's House by picking some to take away with you.

❷ **Charleston** is a different sort of house altogether—it is much larger than Monk's House, and is as much a design statement as it is a home. Entry is by guided, 1-hour tour Wednesday through Saturday (unguided on Sun), and the knowledgeable docents show remarkable restraint in not resorting to back-fence gossip as they lead tours through the dining room, bedrooms, sitting room, and studio and describe the presences in the house of Vanessa Bell, her husband Clive, her sometime lover Duncan Grant, the children Vanessa had with both men, and visitors who included such luminaries as the economist Maynard Keynes and the biographer Lytton Strachey.

Instead, the focus is on the enormous amount of creativity the house seemed to generate: Vanessa and Duncan were both painters and decorative artists, and they created designs for many of the leading fabric and ceramics producers of the time. Their designs appear on upholstery, draperies, and tilework throughout the house. They also brought a personal style to Charleston by painting their distinctive geometric patterns on walls, window frames, mantelpieces, and just about every other surface. The effect can be a bit gloomy, but it is unique and pays tribute to the fact that in this rather extraordinary house, for more than 60 years, Vanessa and Duncan created a distinctive artistic style.

MORE THINGS TO SEE & DO

❸ **Lewes,** a handsome county seat of brick houses, is far too appealing to be just a jumping-off point for Monk's House and Charleston.

Moments A Garden of Your Own (Almost)

The Woolfs and their visitors enjoyed many happy hours in the garden and orchard of Monk's House, and you can, too. Bring a book, stretch out, and enjoy. The only noise you'll hear will be the hum of bees and the tolling of the church bells just beyond the garden wall.

Impressions

It's most lovely, very solid and simple, with . . . perfectly flat windows and wonderful tiled roofs. The pond is most beautiful, with a willow at one side and a stone or flint wall edging it all round the garden part, and a little lawn sloping down to it, with formal bushes on it.

—Vanessa Bell on Charleston

Take some time to walk along the High Street past shops selling antiques and rare books. Thomas Paine, who argued for American independence in his pamphlet "Common Sense," lived in half-timbered Bull House on High Street and debated politics in the nearby White Hart Hotel. (Step inside to enjoy the excellent selection of British ales in the hotel's atmospheric bar.)

❹ & ❺ Lewes Castle & the Anne of Cleves House Lewes's hilltop castle dates to the days of William the Conqueror. Though largely in ruin, it is still a commanding presence. In the adjoining Barbican House Museum you can learn more about local history than you may want to during the sound-and-light show, "The Story of Lewes Town." From the castle, a steep downhill walk of about 10 minutes brings you to the Anne of Cleves House, which Henry presented to his queen when he divorced her in 1541. The kitchen, bedroom, and Tudor-style garden are touchingly quaint in their simplicity.

Castle, High St.; Anne of Cleves House, Southover High St. ✆ **01273/405-732.** www.sussexpast.com. Admission to castle: £4.40 ($7) adults, £3.70 ($6) students and seniors, £2.10 ($3.35) children 5–15, £11 ($18) families of 2 adults and 2 children. Admission to house: £2.80 ($4.50) adults, £2.50 ($4) students and seniors, £1.40 ($2.25) children 5–15, £7 ($11) families of up to 2 adults and 2 children. Combined admission: £5.80 ($9) adults, £5 ($8) seniors and students, £2.80 ($4.50) children, £14 ($22) families of up to 2 adults and 2 children.

3 Shopping

Charleston has an appealing shop (✆ **01323/811-265**) filled with fabrics, ceramics, prints, and other decorative items based on designs created by Vanessa Bell and Duncan Grant for British design studios, as well as an excellent selection of books. It's open Wednesday to Sunday from 1 to 4pm. As you poke around Lewes, step into the **Church Hill Antiques Centre** at 6 Station St. (✆ **01273/474-842**), where 60 dealers sell such easily portable wares as jewelry, linen, glass, and decorative items.

4 Where to Dine

The Abergavenny Arms PUB This dark, woody pub is the social center of Rodmell and a nice place to enjoy a pint or a meal after visiting Monk's House. The cuisine doesn't get fancier than meat and vegetable pies, ploughman's platters, and other traditional pub fare, but it's quite good.

Rodmell. ✆ **01273/472-416.** Main courses £3.50–£7 ($6–$11). MC, V. Food served Mon–Sat noon–3pm and 6–9:30pm; Sun noon–7pm.

Shelleys CONTINENTAL The dining room of this country-house hotel, once home to the poet's family, is a gracious place to enjoy lunch or dinner. French doors open to a delightful garden, but your attention may well be riveted on the dishes that chef Tim Earley creates from local produce, game, and lamb.

High St., Lewes. ✆ **01273/472-361.** £9.50–£15 ($15–$23) lunch, £16–£17 ($25–$27) dinner. AE, DC, MC, V. Daily 12:15–2:15pm and 7–9:15pm.

5 Extending Your Trip

Lewes, your base for exploring Monk's House and Charleston, is also a pleasant place to spend the night—especially during the Glyndebourne opera season (see "Living It Up in Lewes," above). You might want to visit one of the houses the first afternoon, spend the evening and following morning in Lewes, then visit the other house the following afternoon before returning to London. Or, devote the first afternoon to seeing the two houses, then spend the next morning poking around this pleasant town.

Shelleys The chance to spend the night in this charming house, once the home of the family of the poet Percy Bysshe Shelley, is reason enough to extend your stay in Lewes. Guest rooms are traditionally but not fussily appointed with style and comfort in mind, and many overlook a beautiful garden.

High St., Lewes, E. Sussex BN7 1XS. ✆ **01273/472-361.** www.shelleys-hotel.com. £110–£170 ($176–$272) double. Rates include breakfast. AE, DC, MC, V.

Trip 15

Moreton-in-Marsh & the Cotswolds

The Cotswolds hills, known simply as the Cotswolds, present a gentle landscape of woodland; high, open plateaus known as "wolds"; and lovely villages of soft yellow stone and thatched roofs that date from the Middle Ages, when fortunes were made here in the wool trade. This is rural England as you imagined it—a welcome tonic from busy London, and a chance to

Moreton-in-Marsh & the Cotswolds Highlights

- Moreton-in-Marsh and other charming villages of mellow stone.
- Views over the rolling hills and "wolds" (high plateaus).
- A walk from Chipping Campden to Broadway or elsewhere in the countryside.
- Hidcote Manor Garden, beautiful from spring to fall.

take a peek at British country life. The pretty village of Moreton-in-Marsh is an excellent base, especially if you're not traveling by car—it's centrally located in the region, is the only Cotswolds village on a train line, and is also the hub of a bus network you can use to visit other Cotswolds villages. With travel to and from London and time to poke around a village or two, you should expect to spend a full day visiting the Cotswolds, and you may well be so enchanted with the region that you'll want to stay over at least 1 night. We think it's worth the trip if you can only spend 1 day, but this region, perhaps more than any other in this book, lends itself well to a few days of traveling from village to village to see the sights. For that reason, we've included some good accommodations options at the end of this chapter, and suggested enough activities to last you a few days.

1 Essentials

VISITOR INFORMATION

The **Tourist Information Centre** in Moreton-in-Marsh, Cotswold District Council Offices, High Street (✆ **01608/650881;** www.moreton-in-marsh.co.uk), is well stocked with maps and information on what to see and do and where to stay and dine throughout the Cotswolds. The center is open Monday to Thursday from 8:45am to 5:15pm, Friday from 8:45am to 4:45pm, and Saturday from 10am to 12:30pm.

SCHEDULING CONSIDERATIONS

The bucolic beauty of the Cotswolds attracts hordes of visitors who can put a pall on your rural reveries. In summer it's difficult to find a quiet patch anywhere in the region, and Broadway and Burton-on-Water may be more crowded than Piccadilly Circus. May and October are

Moreton-in-Marsh & the Cotswolds

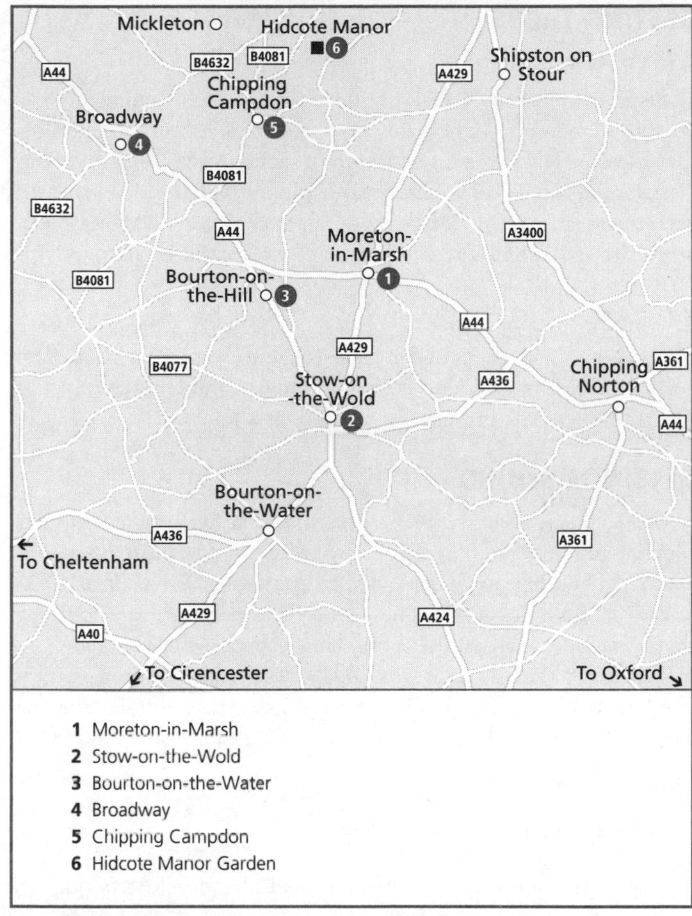

ideal times to visit—the crowds have thinned out, and the landscape is either budding or in majestic fall color. If you are using public transportation, try to visit the Cotswolds on a day other than Sunday, when bus service between the villages is extremely limited. If you only have 1 day in the Cotswolds, and especially if you're relying on public transportation, you'll need to limit your outings from Moreton-in-Marsh to no more than two other villages—this is relatively easy to do if you visit villages that are near each other and on the same bus lines. For example, from Moreton-in-Marsh you might want to travel south to Stow-on-the-Wold and/or Bourton-on-the-Water or south to Chipping Campden and/or Broadway.

GETTING THERE

BY TRAIN

Trains run about every 1 to 1½ hours from London's Paddington Station to Moreton-in-Marsh; the first train departs for Moreton-in-Marsh at 6am and the last train returns to London at 9:38pm. The trip takes about 1½ hours. The cheap day return fare is £21 ($33); standard day return fare is £39 ($62). For information, call **National Rail Enquiries** at ✆ **08457/484-950** or go to www.nationalrail.co.uk.

BY CAR

Moreton-in-Marsh is about 90 miles (145km) west of London. The quickest route from London is the M40 to Oxford, and the A40 and A44 from there; the trip usually takes about 2 hours.

GETTING AROUND

From Moreton-in-Marsh you can reach several other villages by bus Monday through Saturday. For Stow-on-the-Wold and Bourton-on-the-Water, take bus no. 55, operated by **Beaumont Travel** (✆ **01452/309-770**). Buses leave from the Town Hall on High Street and run about every 1 to 1½ hours throughout the day; the first bus is at 6:25am and the last bus is at 5pm. Buses return from Bourton-on-the-Water and Stow-on-the-Wold with similar frequency throughout the day, with the last bus returning from Bourton-on-the-Water at

Wool & Walls

You'll see telltale signs of Cotswolds history just about everywhere you look. The native sheep that graze on the hillsides yield wool of unusually high quality that in the Middle Ages was prized throughout Europe. The wool trade brought enormous wealth into the region, and traders invested their riches in the churches (known as "wool churches") that still rise above every village. The distinctive stone walls you see crisscrossing the fields are known as "drystone walls" and are built without mortar. They were introduced in the 18th and 19th centuries to enclose sheep runs, making it possible to protect fields for farming. While the sheep and stone enclosures were once economic necessities in these parts—and to a degree still are—today they present irresistible photo ops for countless numbers of Cotswolds visitors.

7:05pm. The travel time between Moreton-in-Marsh and Stow-on-the-Wold is 10 minutes, and travel time between Moreton-in-Marsh and Bourton-on-the-Water is 20 minutes.

For Broadway and Chipping Campden, take bus no. 55, operated by **First Midland Red** (© **01905/763-888**). Buses leave from the train station and the Corn Exchange on High Street and operate roughly every hour during peak morning and evening times and every 2 hours throughout the day, with the first departure at 7:02am and the last departure at 6:50pm. Buses return to Moreton-in-Marsh with the same frequency, with the last bus leaving Chipping Campden at 5:59pm. Travel time between Moreton-in-Marsh and Broadway is 20 minutes, and travel time between Moreton-in-Marsh and Chipping Campden is about 35 minutes.

You can also travel between villages, much more expensively, by taxi; the fare from Moreton-in-Marsh to Stow-on-the-Wold is about £8 ($13) each way. Call **Cotswolds Taxis** (© **07710/117-471**) or **Town and Country Taxi** (© **07968/763-379**).

2 A Day (or More) in Moreton-in-Marsh & the Cotswolds

❶ **Moreton-in-Marsh** straddles the Fosse Way, a Roman road that extends from Leicester to Cirencester—in fact, there's not much more to the village than a mile-long string of handsome 17th- and 18th-century buildings along the road, called High Street as it passes through. Among them is White Hart Royal, a manor house in which King Charles I sheltered during the Civil War. Curfew Tower still sports its original clock and bell, dating from 1633, rung to tell the inhabitants to lock themselves in and cover their fires so they couldn't be seen by invaders.

Frequent bus service connects Moreton-in-Marsh with ❷ **Stow-on-the-Wold,** "where the wind blows cold," as the saying goes (a meteorological reality caused by the fact that Stow is the highest of the Cotswolds towns). Stow, just 4 miles (6.5km) south of Moreton-in-Marsh on A429, is still a place where life goes on *somewhat* untouched by the tourist fray. The engaging center of town is the market square, a lovely assemblage of stone buildings housing shops selling antiques as well as everyday essentials.

You may well decide that ❸ **Bourton-on-the-Water** (about 5 miles/8km south of Stow-on-the-Wold on A429 and also served by frequent buses from Moreton-in-Marsh) is a victim of its charm—no small part of the appeal is the River Windrush, which gurgles through the center of town beneath five bridges, each of them presenting another photo op. For visitors not content with rolling hills and sheep, Bourton offers many amusement park–type attractions. **The Model Village,** on High Street behind the Old New Inn (✆ **01451/820-467**), is a ⅑-scale miniature replica of the village built of Cotswold stone in 1937. It's open every day, in summer from 9am to 6pm and in winter from 10am to 4pm; admission is £2.75 ($4.40) for adults, £2.25 ($3.70) for seniors, and £2 ($3.20) for children. **Birdland Park,** on Rissington Road (✆ **01451/820-480**), houses pelicans, penguins, cranes, toucans, and parrots in some 50 different aviaries. The park is open daily, April to October from 10am to 6pm, and November to March from 10am to 4pm; admission is £4.60 ($7) for adults, £3.60 ($6) for seniors, £2.60 ($4) for children, and £13 ($21) for families of up to two adults and two children. **Cotswold Motor Museum** (✆ **01451/821-255**), in the Old Mill, displays vintage cars, motorcycles, and children's pedal cars as well as a small collection of historic toys. It's open February through November, daily from 10am to 6pm; admission is £2.50 ($4) for adults, £1.75 ($2.80) for children.

Artist-craftsman William Morris supposedly "discovered" ❹ **Broadway** (about 8 miles/13km northwest of Moreton-in-Marsh on A44 and also served by frequent buses) in the 19th century, and the village of mellow honey-colored stone has been a hit with sightseers ever since. The width of High Street gave the place its name. This handsome avenue was once lined with inns (some remain) and other establishments that did a brisk business providing travelers and horses with rest, in readiness for the steep climb up the hill towering over the village. The escarpment is crowned with the **Broadway Tower** (✆ **01386/852-390**), an 18th-century folly built by the earl of Coventry. You can climb the tower April through October, daily from 10:30am to 5pm; November through March, Saturday and Sunday from 11am to 3pm. The fee is £4 ($6) for adults, £2.30 ($3.70) for children, and £12 ($18) for families of up to two adults and three children.

❺ **Chipping Campden** (about 4 miles/6.4km west of Broadway and 10 miles/16km northwest of Moreton-in-Marsh via A44 and B4081, and also served by buses) is a beautiful village of 14th- to 17th-century stone buildings. The most photogenic of them are the 17th-century gabled market hall and 14th-century Woolstaplers Hall, both gracing High Street.

MORE THINGS TO SEE & DO

❻ Hidcote Manor Garden This enchanting garden is the creation of Lawrence Waterbury Johnston, son of the wealthy American heiress Gertrude Winthrop. Johnston lived at Hidcote for nearly 40 years, creating a series of rooms (said to have influenced Vita Sackville-West and

Moments **Basking in the Light**

You'll never tire of the mellow, yellow stone of village houses and churches glowing in the sunlight. A good place to appreciate this phenomenon is from one of the bridges in Bourton-on-the-Water, where the sound of the gurgling Windrush River adds another sensation to the scene.

Harold Nicolson in designing Sissinghurst; see trip 21) that incorporate acres of rare plantings, lush borders, pools, lawns, and long vistas. If you're using public transportation, a visit to the garden entails a pleasant country walk: From Moreton-in-Marsh, take bus no. 55 (see "Getting Around," above) one stop past Chipping Campden to the village of Mickleton. Then follow the marked footpath from the village church through fields and parkland to Hidcote Manor; the walk is about 1½ miles (2.4km) each way.

Hidcote Bartrim, outside Chipping Campden. ✆ **01386/438-333.** £5.90 ($9) adults, £2.90 ($4.60) children 5–15, £15 ($23) families of up to 2 adults and 2 children. Open Mar 29–Sept 30, Sat–Wed 10:30am–6pm; Oct 1–Nov 2, Sat–Wed 10:30am–5pm.

OUTDOOR ACTIVITIES

The Cotswolds hills are laced with footpaths, and the country lanes are ideal for cycling. From Moreton-in-Marsh, for example, footpaths lead through the surrounding wolds to the charming hillside village of Bourton-on-the-Hill, and you can return through Batsford Arboretum, founded in the 1880s. The total walk is about 8 miles (13km); for details on this and other easy walks, purchase the pamphlet "The Complete Footpath Guide to Moreton-in-Marsh and Surrounding Areas" for £1.20 ($1.90) at the Tourist Information Centre in Moreton-in-Marsh. If you plan to visit other Cotswolds villages, consider taking the bus to Chipping Campden, walking along the well-marked **Cotswold Way** from there to Broadway, and returning to Moreton-in-Marsh via bus from there; the walk is about 4 miles (6.4km). For cycle rental in Moreton-in-Marsh, contact **Country Lanes Cycle Centre,** at the train station (✆ **01608/650-065**).

3 Shopping

The Moreton-in-Marsh market, held on Tuesday from 8am to 2pm, is the largest in the Cotswolds and attracts some 200 vendors who sell everything from antiques to fresh produce.

4 Where to Dine

Eagle and Child Pub PUB/BRITISH While this cozy beamed room is a popular local gathering spot, the fare is many cuts above what you normally find in a pub—venison, wild mushroom tarts, smoked fish chowder, and an innovative and delicious version of fish and chips are on the menu, and several daily specials are usually available.

Royalist Hotel, Digbeth St., Stow-on-the-Wold. ✆ **01451/830-670.** Main courses £7.75–£14 ($12–$23). AE, MC, V. Food served Mon–Sat noon–2:30pm and 6–10pm; Sun noon–3pm and 6–9pm.

Tillys LIGHT FARE/TEA This bright, airy teashop in the village center serves sandwiches, salads, and pastries throughout the day, and is a handy spot for a quick bite or a cream tea.

18–19 High St. ✆ **01608/650-000.** Most items £4–£7 ($6–$11). MC, V. Mon–Sat 9am–5pm.

5 Extending Your Stay

Cozy inns are about as common as sheep in the Cotswolds, and you may want to settle into and divide your explorations and wanderings over a couple of days. In fact, if you head out into the inviting countryside for a long walk, you'll probably find it a lot more pleasant to come back and relax in front of a roaring fire than to hop on a train for London.

The Cotswolds House Even in London, accommodations don't get much more comfortable and stylish than this elegant manor house with a large garden, centered in one of the most beautiful of the Cotswolds villages. Rooms are equipped with everything you might need, from cushy armchairs to state-of-the-art audio equipment, bathrooms are large and have deep tubs and power showers, meals are excellent, and service is gracious.

The Square, Chipping Campden, Gloucestershire GL55 6AN. ✆ **01386/840-330.** www.cotswoldhouse.com. £110–£120 ($176–$192) double. Rates include full breakfast. AE, MC, V.

The Royalist Hotel Exposed beams and handsome furnishings lend warmth and style to these unusually comfortable accommodations in this centuries-old inn. Two excellent restaurants and a welcoming fireside lounge occupy the ground floor.

Digbeth St., Stow-on-the-Wold, Gloucestershire GL54 1BN. ✆ **01451/830-670.** www.theroyalisthotel.co.uk. £90 ($144) double. AE, MC, V.

Trip 16

Oxford

This "sweet city with her dreaming spires" (to quote the poet Matthew Arnold) is best known as the seat of one of the world's most respected centers of learning. Oxford also happens to be one of the most appealing cities in England. The chapels, quads, and lecture theaters of the 39 Oxford colleges, the oldest of which date to the 13th century, are spread throughout the city and a pleasure to come across, and town and gown converge on lively commercial

Oxford Highlights

- A walk through the water meadows along the Thames and Cherwell rivers.
- The paintings and antiquities at the Ashmolean Museum.
- The beautiful quad at Christ Church College.
- Bustling High and Cornmarket streets and the covered market.

streets. This city is not all about brain power (though there's quite a bit of it in evidence): For every Sir Christopher Wren masterpiece and medieval cobbled lane, there's a snug pub in which to bend an elbow and a lovely riverside walk to enjoy. In fact, there's so much to see and do that you may wish to spend a night in Oxford; see the last section in this chapter for some nightlife and hotel recommendations.

1 Essentials

VISITOR INFORMATION

The **Oxford Tourist Information Centre** (15/16 Broad St.; © **01865/726-871;** www.oxfordcity.co.uk) provides information on what to see and do, where to dine and shop, how to get around, and where to stay. It has a small bookshop where you can purchase photo books on Oxford and other specialized guides. Hours are Monday to Saturday from 9:30am to 5pm, and Sunday (Apr 20–Oct 26) from 10am to 3:30pm. The official website of the University of Oxford (www.ox.ac.uk/visitors) lists opening times of the colleges, as well as concerts, exhibitions, and other events at the university.

SCHEDULING CONSIDERATIONS

It's important to check with the university website or the Tourist Information Centre for hours and admission policies, since colleges are often closed during exams and at other times. If you're visiting Oxford on a Sunday, you might be able to work a concert into your visit: **Oxford Coffee Concerts** is a chamber music series performed on Sunday mornings in the Holywell Music Room on Holywell Street at 11:15am. Tickets cost £8 ($13) and are available from the Oxford Playhouse box office on Beaumont Street (© **01865/305-305**). For schedules and other information, visit www.coffeeconcerts.com.

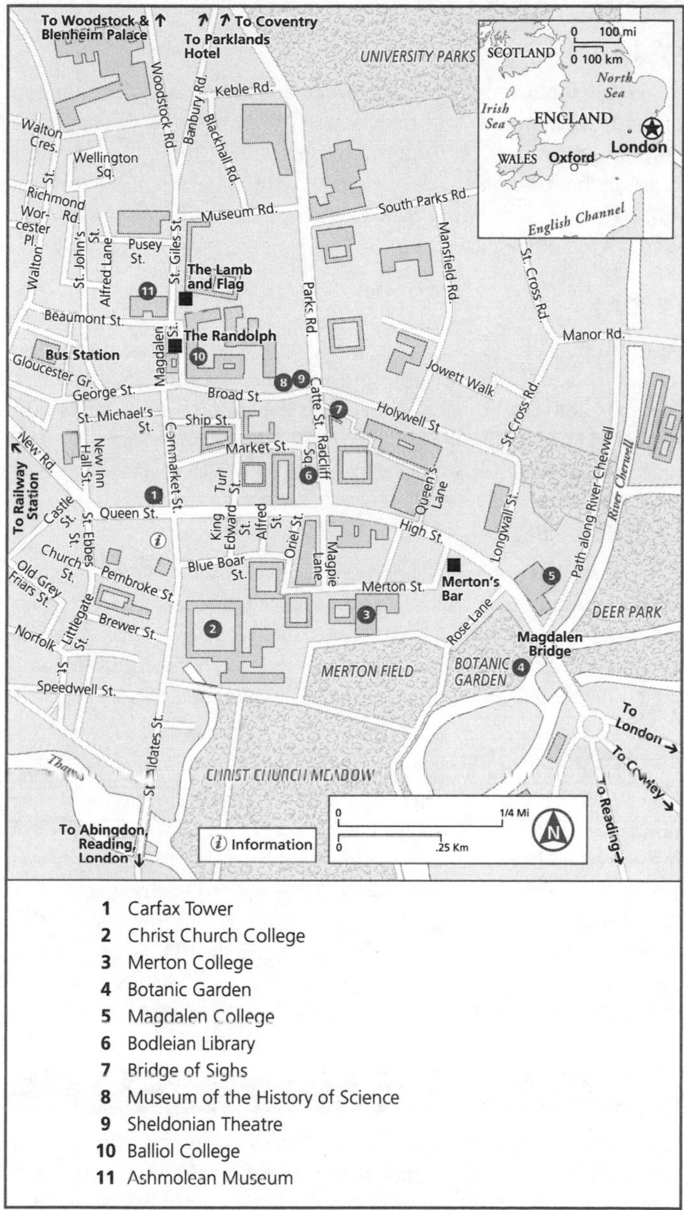

1 Carfax Tower
2 Christ Church College
3 Merton College
4 Botanic Garden
5 Magdalen College
6 Bodleian Library
7 Bridge of Sighs
8 Museum of the History of Science
9 Sheldonian Theatre
10 Balliol College
11 Ashmolean Museum

GETTING THERE

BY TRAIN

Trains run about every 15 to 20 minutes from London's Paddington station to Oxford; the first train departs for Oxford at 6am and the last train returns from Oxford to London at 11:15pm. The trip takes about an hour and the standard day return fare is £30 ($48). For information, call **National Rail Enquiries** at ✆ **08457/484-950** or go to www.nationalrail.co.uk.

BY CAR

Oxford is 60 miles (97km) west of London. The quickest route from London is the M40, and the trip usually takes a little over an hour. The most convenient places to park are the municipal car parks near the city center, off Beaumont Street, Worcester Street, and Norfolk Street; these charge on average about £2 ($3.20) an hour.

BY BUS

National Express buses leave London's Victoria coach station for Oxford about every half hour from about 7am to 9pm, and less frequently outside those times; service is around the clock. The trip takes about an hour and 40 minutes and costs £12 ($19) return. For more information, call ✆ **08705/808-080** or go to www.nationalexpress.co.uk.

GETTING AROUND

You can probably get anywhere you want to go in Oxford on foot. The train station is about a 10-minute walk west of the city center, off Park End Street, and the bus station is on the north side of the city center at Gloucester Green. The two main shopping and business streets are Cornmarket Street, running north–south through the center, and High Street, running east–west through the center. There's a taxi rank outside the train station; if you need one in another part of town, call **001 Taxis** at ✆ **01865/240-000** or **City Taxis** at ✆ **01865/794-000.**

2 A Day in Oxford

An illuminating way to begin a tour of Oxford is with a climb up the spiral staircase of the ❶ **Carfax Tower,** at the crossroads of the town's busiest thoroughfares (Cornmarket, Queen, St. Aldate's, and High sts.). As you look over the surrounding streets and spires, you'll get a good sense of the layout of the university—the colleges sit behind high walls and are built around inner courtyards called "quads." The tower, which once rose above the 14th-century church of St. Martin

Town & Gown

While one of the appeals of modern Oxford is the mix of town and gown, or the way ordinary townsfolk and students mingle (the students wore gowns until fairly recently, and on occasion still do), the relationship has not always been so amicable. On February 10, 1355 (St. Scholastica's Day), widespread rioting broke out when students accused the keeper of an inn near Carfax tower of serving inferior wine—when the hostilities died down several days later, dozens of students had been beaten to death and the colleges ransacked. The moral to be learned from this event, known as the St. Scholastica Day Massacre, is . . . never send back a bottle of wine in Oxford.

(demolished in the late 19th c. to ease traffic flow) is open every day from 10am to 3pm; admission is £1 ($1.60).

Walk south from the tower down Cornmarket Street, which becomes St. Aldate's Street, and step into ❷ **Christ Church College** (✆ **01865/286-573**). As you enter, you'll pass beneath Tom Tower, from which a bell tolls 101 times nightly at 9:05 when the college gates are closed. Cardinal Wolsey, King Henry VIII's powerful associate, founded the college in 1525 and graced it with the largest quad in Oxford. Christ Church also claims a Norman church, St. Frideswide (better known as Oxford Cathedral), and a Picture Gallery graced with works by Sir Joshua Reynolds and William Gainsborough. The college is open Monday to Saturday from 9am to 5:30pm, and Sunday from 1 to 5:30pm; the Picture Gallery is open Monday to Saturday from 10:30am to 1pm and 2 to 5:30pm, and Sunday from 2 to 5:30pm (closes at 4:30pm Oct–Mar). Admission to the college (including the Picture Gallery) is £4 ($6) for adults, £3 ($4.80) for seniors and children.

Now cross Christ Church Meadow and adjoining Merton Field (these two greenswards are on the banks of the River Thames) to ❸ **Merton College** (✆ **01865/276-310**). Rich in medieval ambience and dating to the 13th century, this is one of the earliest centers of learning in Oxford; the 14th-century library houses Geoffrey Chaucer's astrolabe. The college is open Monday to Friday from 2 to 4pm, and Saturday and Sunday from 10am to 4pm; admission is £1 ($1.60).

Across Rose Lane is the ❹ **Botanic Garden** (✆ **01865/276-920**), founded in 1621 for the study of medicinal plants—a rose garden commemorates the Oxford researchers whose work paved the way for the discovery of penicillin. The garden is open from 9am to 5pm daily (last admission is at 4:15pm) and the suggested donation is £2.50 ($4). At dawn on May Day, undergraduates gather in punts beneath nearby Magdalen (pronounced "*maud*-lin") Bridge, as hymns ring out from Magdalen bell tower. The tower rises above ❺ **Magdalen College** (✆ **01865/276-000**), where the grounds encompass a deer park and water meadows (which were once used as a basic irrigation system) along the River Cherwell. Oscar Wilde studied at Magdalen, and Sir Edward Gibbon, who wrote *The Decline and Fall of the Roman Empire,* described his time here as "the most idle and unprofitable of my whole life." The college is open daily, June 25 to September 30 from noon to 6pm, and October 1 to June 24 from 1 to 6pm (or dusk, whichever is earlier). Admission is £3 ($4.80) for adults; £2 ($3.20) for seniors, students, and children.

Follow High Street back toward the town center, and turn right (north) into Radcliff Square to reach the ❻ **Bodleian Library** (✆ **01865/277-224**), established in 1450 and the oldest library in the world. The Bodleian's main reading room is the domed and round **Radcliffe Camera.** Although this and other reading rooms are closed to the public, you can visit the Divinity School; a 15th-century lecture hall; the Exhibition Room, which mounts rotating displays of rare volumes and prints; Duke Humfrey's Library, a collection of early manuscripts; and other parts of the library on guided tours Monday to Friday from 9am to 5pm and Saturday from 9:30am to 12:30pm. The fee is £3.50 ($6).

Just north of Radcliffe Square, turn north onto New College Lane, and follow it a few steps to the enclosed bridge known as the ❼ **Bridge of Sighs** for its resemblance to the Venetian landmark. The bridge connects two parts of Hertford College. Early medical and scientific instruments and such paraphernalia as Albert Einstein's blackboard are on display in the ❽ **Museum of the History of Science,** just north of Radcliffe Square on Broad Street; the 17th-century premises once housed Elias Ashmole's Cabinet of Curiosities, the forerunner of the Ashmolean Museum (see below). The museum is open Tuesday to Saturday from noon to 4pm, and Sunday from 2 to 5pm; admission is free.

Also on this stretch of Broad Street is the ❾ **Sheldonian Theatre** (✆ **01865/277-299**), designed by the famous architect of St. Paul's Cathedral in London, Sir Christopher Wren. (He was a professor of astronomy at Oxford.) The university holds its commencement exercises (in Latin) in the richly paneled hall, and the public can step inside for a look Monday to Saturday from 10am to 12:30pm and from 2 to 4:30pm; the admission fee is £1.50 ($2.40) for adults, and £1 ($1.60) for children under 15.

❿ **Balliol College** (✆ **01865/277-777**), farther west on Broad Street at the intersection of St. Giles Street, was founded in 1263. In the 17th century, bishops Latimer and Ridley and Archbishop Crammer were burned at the college entrance for heresy; the huge gates still bear scorch marks. The college is open daily from 2 to 6pm. Admission is £1 ($1.60).

From St. Giles Street, follow Beaumont Street to two other august Oxford landmarks: the Randolph Hotel, an ornate hostelry that has accommodated visiting parents for more than a century; and the ⓫ **Ashmolean Museum** (✆ **01865/278-000;** www.ashmol.ox.ac.uk), the university's vast and rather musty collections of art and archaeology; it's the oldest public museum in England. Poke around the galleries and you'll come upon many a treasure. Paolo Uccello's *Hunt in the Forest* will alone reward a visit, and the antiquities and Chinese ceramics reflect the bounty of the expeditions the university has sponsored over the years. Admission is free and the museum is open June 1 to August 31, Tuesday to Wednesday and Friday to Saturday from 10am to 5pm; Thursday from 10am to 7:30pm; and Sunday from 2 to 5pm. From September 1 to May 31, it's open Tuesday to Saturday from 10am to 5pm and Sunday from 2 to 5pm.

MORE THINGS TO SEE & DO

Blenheim Palace This 18th-century baroque palace—one of the largest houses in England, home of the dukes of Marlborough, and birthplace of Sir Winston Churchill, Britain's wartime prime minister—is imposing and a bit overwhelming; it's best to take one of the free tours. Your guide will point out such details as the carvings by Grinling Gibbons in the Great Hall and the portraits by Joshua Reynolds and John Singer Sargent. Just as impressive as the house's considerable treasures are the small room where Sir Winston was born in 1874 and, in an exhibition devoted to him, several of his paintings. The grounds, designed in part by the great Capability Brown, are lavish and extensive.

In Woodstock village, 8 miles (13km) north of Oxford on A44. (Buses from Oxford train station run every half hour; fare is £1.60/$2.60.) Admission is £11 ($17) adults, £8 ($13) seniors and students, £5 ($8) children 5–15, and £27 ($43) families. Open Mar 14–Nov 2, 10:30am–4:45pm.

ORGANIZED TOURS

All of the following tours depart from the front of the **Oxford Tourist Information Centre** (✆ **01865/726-871**), where you can purchase tickets. (Buy them from the guide if the center is closed.) For more information, check with the center. You can see a lot of the city and several colleges on Oxford's Guild of Guides 2-hour **walking tours,** every day at 11am and 2pm; try to book early, because each tour is limited to 19 people, and tickets are sold on a first-come, first-served basis. The cost is £6.50 ($10) for adults, £3 ($4.80) for children under 16. Additional tours on Saturday at 11am and 2pm include Christ Church College, not otherwise included; the fee is £7.50 ($12) for adults and £3.50 ($6) for children under 16. **Inspector Morse Tours** show off scenes from the popular PBS series set in Oxford and are led on Saturday only, beginning at 1:30pm; the fee is £7 ($11) for adults and £3.50 ($6) for children. **Ghost Tours** set off for Oxford's spooky medieval lanes at 8pm from July 1 to September 31 and on October 31 (Halloween); the fee is £5 ($8) for adults and £3 ($4.80) for children.

OUTDOOR ACTIVITIES

For a quick escape into bucolic settings, take a riverside walk: From St. Aldate's Street you'll find entrances to Christ Church Meadow and a network of paths that follow the rivers Thames and Cherwell. From Walton Road, northwest of the center, you can enter Port Meadow, where you may be joined by grazing livestock. For a leisurely afternoon, follow the Thames-side path north from Port Meadow to two charming pubs: the **Perch** (✆ **01865/728-891**) and the nearby **Trout** (✆ **01865/302-071**); they are about a 2-mile (3.2km) walk from the center of Oxford and have delightful riverside gardens. You can also enjoy the rivers from a punt, rented by the hour from the **Cherwell Boathouse,** Banbury Road (✆ **01865/515-978**); and from **Old Horse Ford,** off High Street under the Magdalen Bridge (✆ **01865/202-643**). Both are open from mid-March to mid-October and charge £10 ($16) an hour, plus a damage and theft deposit.

3 Shopping

Not too surprisingly, Oxford is well endowed with bookstores. **Blackwell's** (✆ **01865/792-792**), at 48–52 Broad St., is the largest, with more than 200,000 new and rare books and more than 3 miles (4.8km) of shelving in its cavernous underground Norrington Room. **Oxford University Press Bookshop** (✆ **10865/242-913**), at 116–117 High St., sells dictionaries and a complete inventory of other books published by the university's press, founded in the 15th century.

4 Where to Dine

To stock up on provisions for a picnic on the water meadows or simply to grab a quick bite, take a walk through the **covered market** at the intersection of High and Cornmarket streets. Aunt May's is one of many vendors of "fast food"—in this case, authentic Cornish meat or

Moments A Pint in a Pub

Enjoying a pint in a cozy pub is a tradition that goes back centuries in Oxford—the Bear Inn on Alfred Street claims to be the oldest watering hole in town, dating from 1242. At the Head of the River (on the Thames at the end of St. Aldate St.) and at many other pubs there's an added feature—you can arrive by punt, or at least enjoy a river view from a lovely garden.

cheese pasties—deliciously heavy combinations of pastry and a generous filling of meat, cheese, and veggies.

The Lamb and Flag PUB Coziest spot for a pub lunch goes to this charmer, where Thomas Hardy toiled at *Jude the Obscure* and J. R. R. Tolkien and Lewis Carroll took breaks from their writing labors. These literary associations are served up with sandwiches, salads, pizzas, and excellent ales.

12 St. Giles. ✆ **01865/515787.** Main courses £3.50–£6 ($6-$10). MC, V. Food served noon–3pm.

Merton's Bar and Brasserie LIGHT FARE/BRITISH This clubby room, warmed by a fire, is open throughout the day for coffee, tea, and snacks, and serves three squares. Grilled steaks and chops from organic Scottish beef are the specialty at lunch and dinner, but vegetarians will find a few choices, too.

Eastgate Hotel, High St. ✆ **0870/400-8201.** From £4 ($6) breakfast, £5.95–£21 ($10–$34) main courses lunch and dinner. AE, DC, MC, V. Open 8am–10pm (full meals served 8–10am, noon–2:30pm, and 6–10pm).

5 Extending Your Trip

Oxford provides plenty of evening entertainment, and you may wish to overnight to partake of some. Besides, an overnight will allow you to see the town and university in a leisurely day and visit Blenheim the next morning. Check out the offerings of the **Oxford Playhouse,** opposite the Ashmolean Museum on Beaumont Street (✆ **01865/305-305;** www.oxfordplayhouse.com), where Richard Burton, John Gielgud, and Dirk Bogarde have acted. The **Burton-Taylor Theatre** on Gloucester Street was funded by the famous pair and is associated with the Oxford Playhouse. Music venues include the **Apollo Theatre** on George Street (✆ **0870/606-3500**), which often hosts big-name acts and touring companies; and the **Jacqueline du Pré Music Room** at St. Hilda's College (✆ **01865/276-821**), the city's newest concert hall. **Music at Oxford** mounts concerts from January to July, usually on Friday and Saturday evenings, at the Sheldonian Theatre; for more information, call ✆ **01865/242-865** or visit www.musicatoxford.com.

Parklands Hotel This large Victorian home, built for an Oxford don in a leafy residential neighborhood about a mile from the city center, now offers pleasant and quiet accommodations. Newly refurbished bathrooms, some with tubs, adjoin all of the guest rooms.
100 Banbury Rd., Oxford, Oxfordshire OX2 6JU. ✆ **01865/554-374.** www.oxfordcity.co.uk/hotels/parklands. £58–£86 ($92–$138) double. Rates include full breakfast. MC, V.

The Randolph This grand old Victorian hostelry is the best address in town and a favorite with parents checking on their young scholars. The most atmospheric rooms are the high-ceilinged ones in the front of the house. But all guest rooms throughout the hotel—recently refurbished—are smartly and comfortably furnished, and all have large marble bathrooms with large tubs. The Morse Bar and Oyster Bar and Restaurant are justifiably popular gathering spots.
Beaumont St., Oxford, Oxfordshire OX1 2UN. ✆ **0870/400-8200.** www.macdonaldhotels.co.uk. £98–£160 ($157–$256) double. Rate includes buffet breakfast. AE, MC, V.

Trip 17

Rochester

For much of British history, Rochester was on the main route from London to the Continent, and a walk through the town is a heady trip through 2,000 years of history. The Roman legions garrisoned here to protect their crossings over the River Meadway, and the Normans built a mighty castle and cathedral. In the mid–19th century Charles Dickens settled nearby, and the town's Elizabethan and Victorian buildings show up as settings for scenes in

Rochester Highlights

- Attending Evensong at Rochester Cathedral.
- Exploring the remains of Rochester Castle, England's best-preserved example of Norman architecture.
- Eastgate House and other Victorian architecture that inspired Charles Dickens.
- Satis House and Restoration House, architectural gems.

his novels. Not only is there a nice amount to see and do in Rochester, but this compact, easily walkable town is a quick jaunt away from London, making it a good destination for a half-day's outing.

1 Essentials

VISITOR INFORMATION

For maps and information, step into the **Medway Visitor Information Centre** (✆ **01634/843-666**) at 95 High St. The center is open Monday to Saturday from 10am to 5pm and Sunday from 10:30am to 5pm.

SCHEDULING CONSIDERATIONS

If you're visiting in winter, get an early start in London because the Charles Dickens Centre and Rochester Castle close at 4pm. An especially colorful time to visit Rochester is in early December, when the town celebrates a Dickensian Christmas and High Street fills with carolers and characters from the novels.

GETTING THERE

BY TRAIN

Service between London and Rochester is fast and frequent. Trains run to and from both London's Victoria and Charing Cross stations, departing on average about every 15 minutes throughout the day. The first train leaves London for Rochester at 4:55am and the last train returns to London at 11:19pm. The trip takes 45 minutes to an hour and the standard day return fare is £10 ($16).

BY CAR

Rochester is about 40 miles (64km) due west of London on the A2, and the trip takes less than an hour. There are several car parks in the town center, including one on the grounds of the castle and two off Corporation Street, which runs parallel to High Street.

Rochester

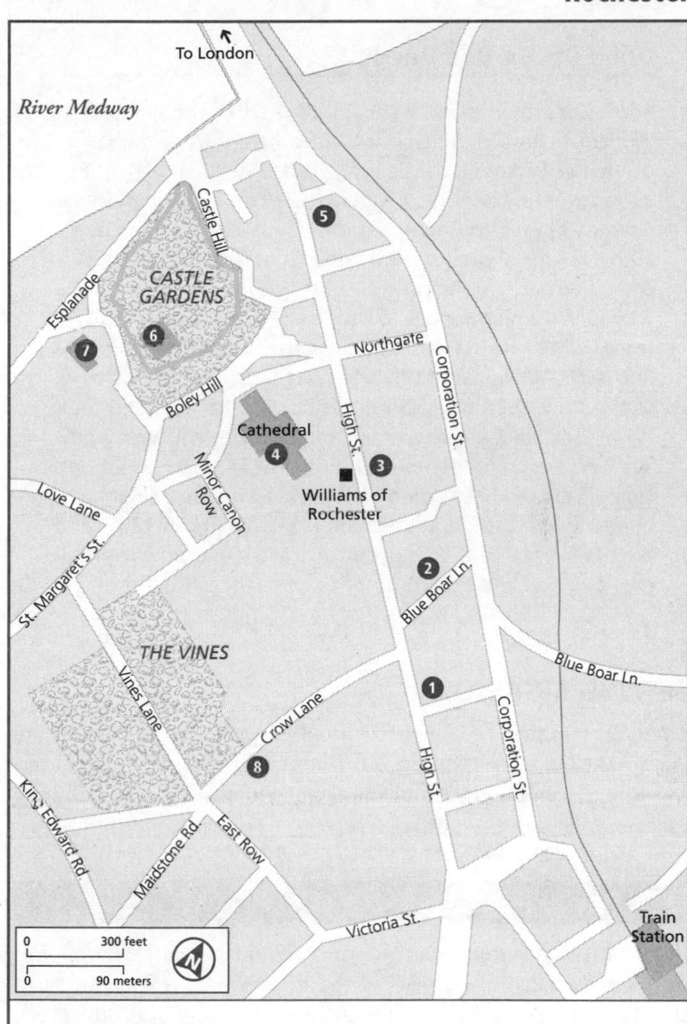

1 Charles Dickens Centre
2 medieval walls
3 Poor Traveler's House
4 Cathedral
5 Guildhall
6 Rochester Castle
7 Satis House
8 Restoration House

Good Deeds, Bad Deeds

Rochester's own saint, William of Perth, also known as William of Rochester, could be a character out of the pages of Charles Dickens. After a wild youth, William settled into a trade as a baker in his native Perth in Scotland and devoted himself to God and good deeds—he set aside every 10th loaf for the poor, and took in a foundling left in a church doorway. Sometime around 1200 William honored a vow to make pilgrimages to the Holy Places, and he took his ward, whom he named David, with him. After a stop in Rochester, William and David set out for Canterbury. David, so the story goes, slew his benefactor on the road and took his money, and a madwoman came upon William's body. She laid a garland of flowers on his head and plaited one for herself, and in so doing became sane again. William was buried in the cathedral and canonized a saint in 1256, and his tomb became a shrine that attracted pilgrims from all over England and the Continent.

GETTING AROUND

Rochester is extremely compact and all of the sights of interest are concentrated in a small area on and around High Street. The train station is at the southern edge of the town center, only a few minutes' walk from the south end of High Street.

2 A Day in Rochester

On a walk through Rochester you won't venture too far off the appealing Victorian High Street, part of the Roman road from London to the Channel coast and these days closed to traffic. Toward the south end of the street is the ❶ **Charles Dickens Centre** (✆ **01634/844-176**), which occupies Eastgate House. This gloomy brick edifice served as a girl's boarding school in Dickens's day, and the author re-created it as Nuns' House, Miss Twinkerton's school for young ladies in *The Mystery of Edwin Drood,* and as Westgate House Seminary for young women in *The Pickwick Papers.* Inside are rather unconvincing exhibits that employ laser disc imagery to re-create scenes from the novel. The most charming bit of Dickens memorabilia is in the garden—a miniature replica of a Swiss chalet that the author used as a workroom at his nearby estate, Gad's Hill. The center is open March 29 to September 30, daily from 10am to 6pm; and October 1 to March 31, daily from 10am to 4pm. Admission is £3.90 ($6) adults; £2.80

($4.50) seniors, students, and children; and £11 ($18) for families of up to two adults and two children or one adult and three children.

As you head up High Street from the Dickens Centre, you'll pass sections of the ❷ **medieval walls,** and if you look carefully you might be able to see some especially weather-worn masonry pieces that are parts of the defenses the Romans built around their settlement here. A little farther along is the ❸ **Poor Traveler's House,** a welcoming structure that from the 16th through mid–20th centuries provided free lodging to indigent travelers; Dickens used this house as a setting for his short story "The Seven Poor Travelers." Just before you come to the Old Corn Exchange, dating from 1706 (its distinctive clock hangs over the street), turn into the ❹ **Cathedral** (✆ **01634/401-301**). The squat, solid-looking edifice, begun in 1080, once welcomed pilgrims who sought the alleged healing powers of the tomb of St. William of Perth, a baker from that Scottish city who was slain outside Rochester in 1201 while traveling to the Holy Land. The cathedral is open daily from 8:30am to 5pm; you can attend Evensong Monday to Friday at 5:30pm and Saturday and Sunday at 3:15pm. If you're feeling peckish, pop into the cathedral tearoom for a snack; it's open daily, 8:30am to 4:30pm.

Farther along High Street, across from the 17th-century ❺ **Guildhall,** is the entrance to the imposing ruins of ❻ **Rochester Castle** (✆ **01634/402-276**), commanding a strategic site above the River Meadway. The Romans built their encampment here to guard the bridge that the legions crossed en route from Dover to London. On orders of William the Conqueror, the Normans reinforced the fortifications with timbers, then built the present stone structure—England's best preserved example of Norman architecture—in 1088; the keep, the tallest in England at 113 feet (34m), dates to 1127. You can explore what remains of the castle on a system of steel stairs and catwalks, and when you're back on terra firma you can enjoy views of the River Meadway from the Esplanade at the edge of the grounds. The castle is open daily from March 29 to September 30, 10am to 6pm; and in October, daily 10am to 4pm. Admission is £3.90 ($6) for adults, £2.80 ($4.50) for seniors and students, and £11 ($17) for families.

As you leave the castle grounds from the west end of the keep, through a gate onto St. Margaret's Street, you'll be in front of ❼ **Satis**

Moments Time Travel

In Rochester, it's easy to forget you're in the 21st century. Walk down High Street and imagine the pavement and shops bustling with Victorian activity, as Charles Dickens experienced it. Or sit on the lawn outside Rochester Castle and feel the presences of Roman legionnaires and Norman soldiers.

House—so-called because Queen Elizabeth I, who stayed here in 1573, expressed her approval of the arrangements with one word, "satis" (Latin for "enough"). Turn onto Boley Hill toward the west front of the cathedral, where the 800-year-old West Portal is graced with elongated figures. Minor Canon Row leads past modest houses built for the clergy in the 18th century and the buildings of King's School, founded by Henry VIII in 1542. The lane ends at a park known as "The Vines," so-called because monks once had their vineyards here. Facing the park on Crow Lane is 8 **Restoration House,** which got its name when Charles II stayed here in 1660 on his return to England to be crowned. Samuel Pepys wrote about the house, which he called a "pretty seat," in his diaries, and also noted an amorous conquest in an adjoining orchard. Dickens used the house as the home of Miss Havisham in *Great Expectations,* but borrowed the name "Satis House" from the property nearby. The house is beautifully furnished with period pieces and is open June to September, Thursday and Friday from 10am to 5pm. In just a few steps, Crow Lane comes to High Street and back where you started, at the Charles Dickens Centre.

MORE THINGS TO SEE & DO

Gad's Hill Place Charles Dickens spent the last years of his life in this large brick house surrounded by pleasant grounds and died here, in 1870, while writing *The Mystery of Edwin Drood.* The story behind his connection with Gad's Hill might have come from one of his own novels. He lived nearby as a child, and his father used to tell him that if he worked hard enough, he could one day live in the house. Gad's Hill is now a school, but several rooms, furnished as the author left them, can be seen on an informative guided tour.

Gad's Hill School Highham, Rochester (off A226; follow signs to Gravesend). ✆ **01474/822-366.** Admission £3.50 ($6) adults, £1.50 ($2.40) children. Easter to May, first Sun of each month 2–5pm; June–Aug daily 11am–4:30pm. Take bus no. 136 from Corporation St. toward Gravesend; buses run every half hour and the fare is £1.60 ($2.55). For bus information, call ✆ 01634/843-666.

3 Where to Dine

Williams of Rochester TEA/BRITISH A bright tearoom in the town center serves breakfast, lunch, and dinner, as well as a satisfying cream tea. Offerings at lunch include sandwiches and salads as well as such sizable entrees (also served at dinner) as pork chops and fish. A rear patio is a pleasant place for tea after a summertime stroll through the town.

86 High St. ✆ **01634/847-776.** Most items £3.50–£15 ($6–$23). MC, V. Daily 7am–midnight.

Trip 18

Rye

"Rye is like an old beautifully jewelled brooch worn at South-England's throat." So wrote Patric Dickinson, one of the many writers who have fallen under the spell of this remarkably beautiful coastal town in East Sussex, 62 miles (100km) southeast of London. Henry James spent the last years of his life here, and E. F. Benson, author of *Mapp and Lucia,* was mayor of Rye in the 1920s. (In his novels, Benson called the town "Tilling.")

Rye Highlights

- Strolling along the winding warren of cobblestone streets lined with ancient stone and half-timbered buildings.
- Climbing the tower of St. Mary's Church for a stunning view over Rye and the Romney Marsh.
- Visiting Lamb House, last residence of Henry James.

Rye's official title, "The Ancient Town of Rye," was bestowed upon it nearly a millennia ago when Rye joined the federation of coastal defense towns known as the Cinque Ports. A powerful seaport, it protected the coast from foreign marauders while carrying on a lively business in smuggling and piracy. That old maritime history still clings to the cobblestone lanes threading through Rye, even though the coastline has receded, leaving Rye in a kind of drydock about 2 miles (3.2km) inland from the English Channel, rising above the flat green expanse of Romney Marsh.

Few English towns are more picturesque or pleasurable to explore. Rye claims to have more historic buildings than any other town in England, and is jam-packed with half-timbered Tudor and Elizabethan houses, handsome Georgian town houses, secret passageways, quaint corners, cobbled lanes, windy viewpoints, enticing shops, and wonderful restaurants. The town is small enough to see in about 3 hours, but it is so charming that you may want to spend the night—see our hotel recommendations at the end of this chapter.

1 Essentials

VISITOR INFORMATION

The Rye Heritage Centre on Strand Quay is also the **Tourist Information Centre** (✆ **01797/226-696;** www.rye-tourism.co.uk). You can obtain a free town map and rent an excellent **audio walking tour** (£2.50/$4) that guides you around the streets. The center can also help you find a room. April through October, the center is open daily from 10am to 5pm; November through March, it's open Monday through Saturday from 10am to 4pm.

SCHEDULING CONSIDERATIONS

Lamb House, home of Henry James, is open April through October on Wednesday and Saturday only from 2 to 6pm. **Ypres Tower,** which houses Rye's local history museum, is closed on Tuesday, Wednesday,

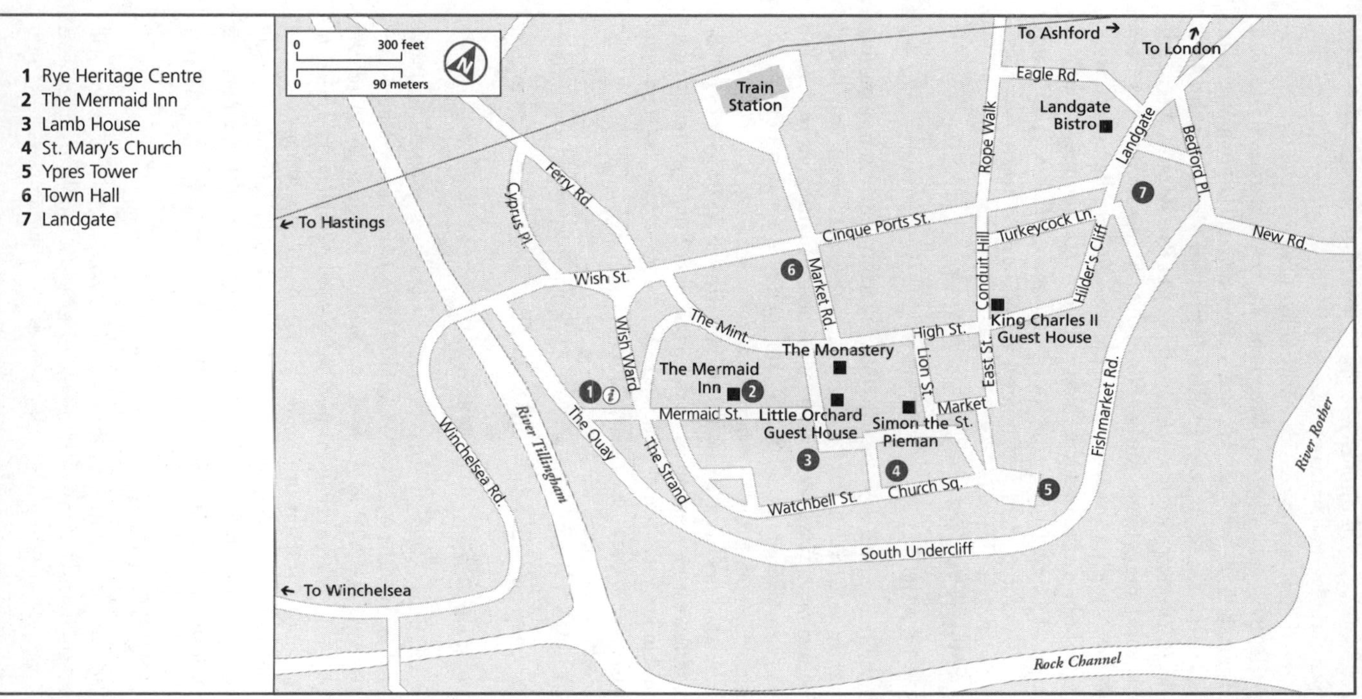
1 Rye Heritage Centre
2 The Mermaid Inn
3 Lamb House
4 St. Mary's Church
5 Ypres Tower
6 Town Hall
7 Landgate
0
300 feet
0
90 meters
To Ashford
To London
Eagle Rd.
Landgate Bistro
Train Station
Rope Walk
Landgate
Bedford Pl.
To Hastings
Ferry Rd.
Cyprus Pl.
Cinque Ports St.
Turkeycock Ln.
New Rd.
Wish St.
Market Rd.
Conduit Hill
Hilder's Cliff
King Charles II Guest House
The Mint.
High St.
The Monastery
Wish Ward
The Mermaid Inn
Lion St.
East St.
Market
Mermaid St.
Little Orchard Guest House
Simon the Pieman
St.
The Quay
The Strand
Winchelsea Rd.
River Tillingham
Fishmarket Rd.
River Rother
Church Sq.
Watchbell St.
South Undercliff
To Winchelsea
Rock Channel

and Saturday April through October; November through March, it's open Saturday and Sunday only.

You might want to consider visiting Rye during one of its town celebrations. During August a **Medieval Weekend** features a parade of costumed locals, a 2-day fair, and a street market on High Street. In September, the town hosts the **Rye Festival of Music and the Arts,** which features concerts and exhibitions. On **Rye Bonfire Weekend,** celebrated around Guy Fawkes Night (Nov 5), bonfire societies from all over Sussex participate in a parade and torchlight procession through the darkened streets before the ceremonial bonfire is lit and fireworks set off. Contact the Tourist Information Centre at the number above for more information on any of these events.

GETTING THERE

BY TRAIN

By train, Rye is an easy day trip. **Connex** trains depart hourly starting as early as 5:25am from London's Charing Cross Station to Ashford International, where you change to the **South Central** line to Rye; the total trip takes about 2 hours. Trains return to London until nearly 8pm. The standard day return fare from London is £19 ($30). For train schedules call **National Rail Enquiries** at **© 08457/484-950,** or visit www.nationalrail.co.uk. The easy walk from Rye train station on Cinque Ports Street to Strand Quay, a good place to start your explorations, takes about 10 minutes.

BY BUS

Currently, no regular daily bus service is available from London to Rye.

BY CAR

By car, Rye is 10 miles (16km) northeast of Hastings on A259. From London, take the M25, M26, and M20 to Maidstone, going southeast along the A20 to Ashford. At Ashford, continue south on the A2070. Cars aren't allowed into the historic center, so you need to park in one of the many lots on the north side of town and near the train station; you can walk from there. If you drive, you can easily combine a trip to Rye with a trip to Battle, scene of the momentous Battle of Hastings in 1066. (See trip 2.)

GETTING AROUND

Cars are not permitted in Rye's historic center, and the town is small enough to make a complete circuit on foot in a couple of hours. This is one place where good walking shoes come in handy. Getting into the center requires a bit of a climb, nothing strenuous, and you'll encounter many uneven cobblestone streets.

2 A Day in Rye

A good place to start your walk is the ❶ **Rye Heritage Centre** on Strand Quay (✆ **01797/226-696**). The center occupies one of Rye's old sail lofts, where ships' sails were repaired. Take 20 minutes to watch "The Story of Rye," which uses an elaborate scale model of the town for a miniature sound-and-light show detailing highlights in Rye's long and sometimes bloody history. The show runs continuously from 10am to 3pm. Admission is £2.50 ($4) for adults, £1.50 ($2.40) for seniors, and £1 ($1.60) for children 5 to 15.

Walk up Mermaid Street, which begins just south of the Heritage Centre. On your left you'll pass ❷ **The Mermaid Inn** (✆ **01787/223-065**), a half-timbered building that houses one of the oldest inns in England. (See "Extending Your Stay," below.)

Continue south on West Street and you'll come to ❸ **Lamb House** (✆ **01892/890-651**), a dignified, redbrick Georgian house that served as the last residence of the American writer Henry James, who became a British citizen and lived here from 1898 to 1916. The writer E. F. Benson acquired the house after James's death. You can see some of the rooms and personal possessions of James and Benson and step into the charming walled garden. Lamb House is open April through October on Wednesday and Saturday from 2 to 6pm. Admission is £2.60 ($4.20) for adults, £1.30 ($2.10) for children 5 to 15.

Turn left on Watchbell Street and follow it to Church Street, site of ❹ **St. Mary's Church** (✆ **01797/222-430**), which has stood on the highest point in Rye for almost 900 years. Step inside for a look at the turret clock, the oldest in the country, dating from 1561 and with an 18-foot (5.4m) long pendulum; it is said to have inspired the nursery rhyme "Hickory Dickory Dock." The beautiful stained-glass window by Sir Edward Burne-Jones dates from 1891. You can climb the church tower for a magnificent view over the rooftops of Rye to Romney Marsh. The church and tower are open daily from 9am to 6pm (to 4pm in winter). Admission to the tower is £1.50 ($2.40).

Just south of the church, on Pump Street, you'll find the 12th-century ❺ **Ypres Tower** (✆ **01797/226-728**), one of Rye's oldest buildings. Originally built as part of the town's defenses, it was later used as a prison and a mortuary. Today it's a small local history museum displaying medieval pottery, ironwork, and items having to do with smuggling. From the terrace, you can view what was once Rye's busy harbor. The tower/museum is open April through October on Monday, Thursday, and Friday from 10am to 1pm and 2 to 5pm, Sunday

Moments **Ghost Walk**

You might see a strange shadow or two as you stroll through Rye's old, winding streets on a dark night with the "Ghost Walks" audio tour (available from the Tourist Information Centre). Spooky fun!

from 10:30am to 1pm; November through March, it's open Saturday and Sunday only from 10:30am to 3:30pm. Admission is £2.90 ($4.60) for adults, £1.50 ($2.40) for children 7 to 16.

From Ypres Tower, take Pump Street north to Market Street and have a look at the arcaded 6 **Town Hall,** dating from 1742 (not open to the public), then continue north on East Street, turning right on East Cliffe. At the end of it you'll see the 7 **Landgate,** a fortified 14th-century stone gate. Backtrack along East Cliffe and follow High Street, full of shops and galleries, to The Mint, which will bring you back to the Heritage Centre.

ORGANIZED TOURS

On Wednesday and the first and third Saturdays of the month, from the last week in May to September, the secretary of the E. F. Benson Society leads a 90-minute **"Mapp and Lucia's Rye" walking tour** past the characters' houses to the Benson memorials in St. Mary's Church, ending at Lamb House. Cost is £4.75 ($8) per person. You do not need to reserve; just show up at The Belvedere, the viewpoint at the eastern end of High Street, at 2pm. For more information, call **© 01797/223-114.**

OUTDOOR ACTIVITIES

Rye Harbor, with its fishing fleet and pleasure boats, runs along the inlet of the River Rother. Its focal point, the **Rye Harbour Nature Preserve,** can easily be reached on foot or bicycle by taking Harbour Road, a small road off the A259 on the Hastings side of the town. (You have to pass some industrial buildings on the road.) The distance is about 2 miles (3km). The road leads to the 209-acre (84-hectare) preserve, a tract of shingle ridges formed over hundreds of years as the sea receded. The varied habitat of grazing marsh, arable fields, and intertidal salt marsh is known for its birdlife, particularly for its 50 or so breeding species of terns, oystercatchers, and plovers. **Rye Hire,** 1 Cyprus Place (**© 01797/223-033**), close to the train station and Tourist Information Centre, rents bicycles for £9 ($14) per day plus deposit.

Winchelsea, the smallest town in England, stands 2 miles (3km) west of Rye on A259 and is also a pleasant bike ride or walk. In 1277, a charter fortified Winchelsea against French invaders and resulted in the town being rebuilt and laid out in grid form, the first such example of town planning in England. At that time, Winchelsea had a harbor and, like Rye, was one of the "Ancient Towns" affiliated with the Cinque Ports defense network. Today Winchelsea is a quiet, unspoiled town with fine old buildings and great views toward the coast. **The Tea Tree,** 12 High St. (✆ **01797/226-102**), serves sandwiches and teas.

3 Shopping

The Rye **Farmers Market,** held on Wednesday from 10am to 1pm on Strand Quay, has stalls selling fish and local organic produce, plus cakes and breads. On Friday, the **Rye Market** is held in the Rye Community Center, Conduit Hill, starting at 10am; here you'll find more local products, including crafts. The **Rye Chocolate Shop,** 5A Market Rd. (✆ **01797/222-522**), sells Charbonnel & Walker chocolates and gifts. **David Sharp Pottery,** 55 The Mint (✆ **01797/222-620**), sells handmade pottery.

4 Where to Dine

Landgate Bistro MODERN BRITISH This highly regarded bistro close to the old town gate is known for the quality of its local produce, fish, and lamb. The cooking is sophisticated but not fussy. For starters, you may have leek and Roquefort tart or wild-mushroom risotto. Main courses may include free-range chicken, wild rabbit, or "very fishy stew," which uses fresh, locally caught fish.

Landgate. ✆ **01797/222-829.** Main courses £9.90–£13 ($16–$20). AE, MC, V. Tues–Sat 7–9:30pm.

The Monastery MODERN BRITISH/ITALIAN The Monastery on busy High Street is one of Rye's top restaurants. A typical menu might include chicken breast stuffed with prawns, poached salmon in white wine and dill, tortellini with tomato and basil sauce, or tagliatelle with porcini mushrooms. In the summer, reserving a table in advance is a good idea.

High St. ✆ **01797/223-272.** Main courses £12–£15 ($19–$24), fixed-price dinner £18 ($26). MC, V. Open Tues–Sat noon–2pm and 7–9:45pm; Sun noon–2pm.

Simon the Pieman LIGHT FARE/AFTERNOON TEA At this charming old tearoom in the shadow of St. Mary's Church, you can get a light lunch, homemade cakes and pastries, or an afternoon cream tea.

Lion St. ✆ **01797/222-207.** Lunch £3.50–£7 ($6–$12). Cream tea £4.40 ($7). No credit cards. Mon–Sat 9:30am–5pm; Sun 1:30–5:30pm.

5 Extending Your Stay

King Charles II Guest House The writer Radclyffe Hall owned and lived in this beautiful half-timbered medieval building that once served as a refuge for King Charles II. The quality of accommodation here is extremely high. The house (completely nonsmoking) and its three guest rooms are beautifully furnished with antiques, tapestries, leaded glass windows, and Persian carpets.

High St., Rye, E. Sussex TN32 7JE. ✆ **01797/22-4954.** www.ryetourism.co.uk/kingcharles. £80–£95 ($132–$157) double. Rates include English breakfast. AE, MC, V. 2-night minimum on weekends.

Little Orchard House This charming, Georgian-era B&B is named for the romantic little orchard garden tucked behind the house. Period antiques and paintings decorate the two guest rooms; both have private bathrooms. The rate includes a generous country breakfast with many local and organic products.

West St., Rye, E. Sussex TN31 7ES. ✆ and fax **01797/223-831.** www.littleorchardhouse.com. £64–£90 ($102–$144) double. Rates include English breakfast. V.

The Mermaid Inn When you enter this famous half-timbered inn, one of the oldest in England, you're instantly wafted back to the "olde England" of your dreams. Full of ancient oak timbers, creaking floors, huge fireplaces with log fires, plus a resident ghost or two, the inn has 31 rooms, every one different, all with modern bathrooms.

Mermaid St., Rye, E. Sussex TN31 7EU. ✆ **01797/223-065.** Fax 01797/225-069. www.mermaidinn.com. £160–£200 ($256–$320) double. Rates include English breakfast. AE, DC, MC, V.

Trip 19

St. Albans

St. Albans, Hertfordshire's oldest town, first appeared as a Celtic Iron Age settlement called Verlamion ("settlement above the marsh"). After the Roman conquest of Britain in A.D. 43, the name changed to Verulamium and the settlement became the third-largest town in Roman Britain. Encircled by gated walls, it was filled with impressive town houses and public buildings, including a large theatre. After the departure of the Roman Army in A.D. 410,

St. Albans Highlights

- Visiting the ancient cathedral with its shrine to St. Alban.
- Strolling through Verulamium Park.
- Exploring the ruins of Britain's largest Roman amphitheatre.

the Roman city fell into decay and its ruined buildings provided building materials for the new Saxon settlement of St. Albans, which grew up around a monastery founded during A.D. 900 to 950 near the site of St. Alban's execution. (Alban was a Roman soldier martyred for his Christian faith.) It developed into a town of significance with a powerful abbot and was one of five venues chosen by the barons and clergy in 1213 for the drafting of the Magna Carta. The town prospered during the Middle Ages, catering to travelers and pilgrims who flocked to St. Alban's shrine in the Abbey Church. In 1877, St. Albans received a Royal Charter giving it city status and the Abbey Church became a Cathedral. Today it's a commuter town with enough character and history to make for a very pleasant day trip.

1 Essentials

VISITOR INFORMATION

The **Tourist & Information Centre,** located in the Town Hall on Market Place (✆ **01727/864-511;** www.stalbans.gov.uk), is open Monday to Saturday from 9:30am to 5:30pm (Nov to Easter until 4pm), and on Sunday mid-June through mid-September from 10:30am to 4:30pm.

GETTING THERE

BY TRAIN

St. Albans is only 40 minutes from London, and the easiest way to reach it is by train. The city is served by two train stations. **Thameslink** trains (www.thameslink.co.uk) run half-hourly throughout the day from London's King's Cross Station and arrive at **City Station** (✆ **08457/484-950**) on Victoria Street; trains depart St. Albans just as frequently, until 11pm. From London's Euston Station you can take a train to Watford Junction and change to a local train, which arrives at **Abbey Station** (✆ **08457/484-950**) on St. Stephens Hill. A day return from either station costs about £7.50 ($12). For train schedules

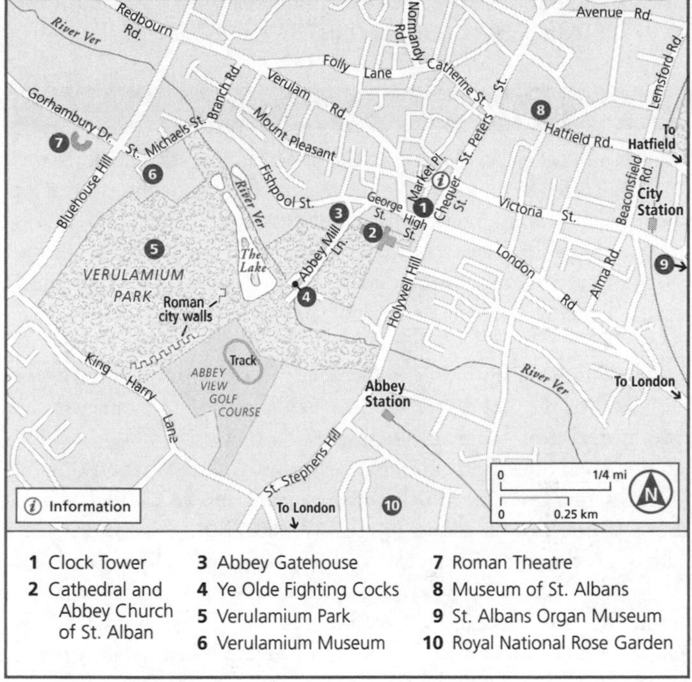

and information, call **National Rail Enquiries** at © **08457/484-950,** or visit www.nationalrail.co.uk.

BY BUS

National Express buses from London go only as far as Luton, where you must change to a local carrier. Take the train; it's easier.

BY CAR

From London, take the M1 or M25 motorways north to the St. Albans turnoff. St. Albans is a historic city with many narrow and residential streets, and street parking is difficult. You'll find parking lots on Victoria Street, London Road, and St. Peter's Street, and at the Verulamium Museum.

GETTING AROUND

The center of town is small enough that you can explore it all on foot. There is a useful bus service (Intalink) from the station to the town center, the Verulamium Museum, and Hatfield House; for more information call **Traveline** (© **0870/608-2608**). Taxis are available outside

City Station, but not Abbey Station. To reserve a cab, call **Gold Line** (© **01727/833-333**) or **Abbey** (© **01727/832-822**).

2 A Day in St. Albans

Begin your day in St. Albans at the city's famous ❶ **Clock Tower** (© **01727/751-826**), located in the marketplace at the intersection of Chequer Street and London Road. Built between 1403 and 1412, it is one of only two medieval belfries in England. Its construction, during a time of growing tension between the church and the townspeople, became a political statement because the tower enabled the town (as opposed to the Abbey) to sound its own hours and curfew. On Saturday and Sunday from Easter to October you can climb the tower for fine views of the Abbey, the Roman Verulamium, and the city; the tower is open from 10:30am to 5pm.

Cross High Street and enter the passageway (called Waxhouse Gate) directly across from the Clock Tower to reach the ❷ **Cathedral and Abbey Church of St. Alban** (© **01727/860-780**). For centuries the church has dominated the city's skyline. A Norman church replaced the original Saxon monastery, and St. Albans, with its attached Benedictine Monastery, became the premier abbey of medieval England. Its architecture is a blend of many different periods, and its great tower includes Roman bricks salvaged from the ruins of the Roman city of Verulamium. It is best known for the ornate shrine of St. Alban, Britain's first Christian martyr, which attracted pilgrims from far and wide and contributed to the growth of the city. Its monastic life ended in 1539 when Henry VIII dissolved England's monasteries, and everything but the Abbey Church and Gatehouse was destroyed. The cathedral is open daily from 8:30am to 5:45pm.

Walk around the church to look at the ❸ **Abbey Gatehouse,** the only other building that remains of the Abbey of St. Albans. Built in 1365, it was used as a prison until 1868 and now forms part of St. Albans school.

From the Gatehouse, follow Abbey Mill Lane, a delightful country-like lane, south. You'll pass ❹ **Ye Olde Fighting Cocks,** one of the oldest pubs in England and an excellent spot for lunch or a drink. (See "Where to Dine," below.) A pathway just beyond the pub brings you into ❺ **Verulamium Park,** set in over 100 acres (40 hectares) of beautiful parkland alongside the River Ver. Named after the Roman city of Verulamium on which it stands, the park contains the remains of the Roman city walls and the main London Gate. From the park you have a wonderful view of the Cathedral and Abbey Church to the east. The park's large ornamental lake is home to a variety of water birds.

Cathedral & Abbey Church of St. Alban

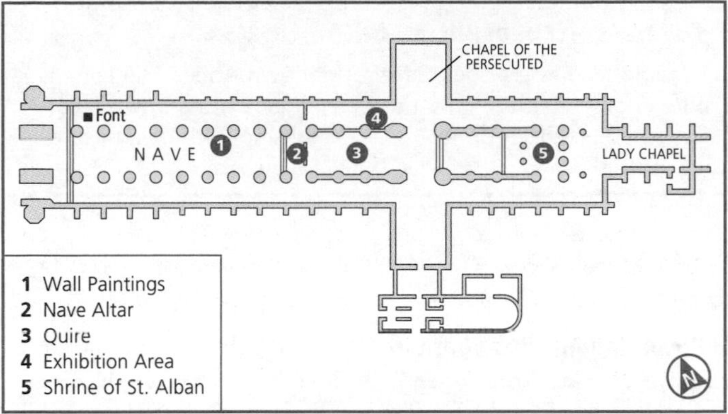

Signposts on the pathway will direct you to the ❻ **Verulamium Museum** (✆ **01727/751-810**). The museum tells the story of everyday life in Roman Britain with displays that include re-created Roman rooms and some of the best Roman mosaics and wall frescoes outside Italy. The museum is open Monday through Saturday from 10am to 5:30pm and on Sunday from 2 to 5pm. Admission is £3.30 ($5).

From the museum, cross Bluehouse Hill Road to the ❼ **Roman Theatre** (✆ **01727/854-051**), the best preserved example of a Roman theatre in Britain. Used originally for bear baiting and cock fighting, its fine acoustics were also perfectly suited to musical and dramatic performances. Within the site are the foundations of a row of Roman shops and the remains of a 3rd-century town house with an underground shrine. The site is open daily year-round from 10am to 5pm (until 4pm Nov–Feb). Admission is £1.50 ($2.50) adults, £1 ($1.60) seniors and students. Free tours are given on Saturday and Sunday in summer at 2:30, 3:15, and 4pm.

If you don't want to walk back into the city center, you can catch bus no. 30 to the train station from the St. Michael's Village stop beside the Verulamium Museum.

MORE THINGS TO SEE & DO

❽ **Museum of St. Albans** The museum tells the story of historic St. Albans, from the departure of the Romans to the present day.
Hatfield Rd. ✆ **01727/819-340.** Free admission. Mon–Sat 10am–5pm; Sun 2–5pm.

❾ **St. Albans Organ Museum** The museum gives live performances of the various mechanical musical instruments in its permanent collection, everything from music boxes to theatre organs, on Sunday from 2 to 4:30pm (the only day it's open). From City Station or the city center, take bus no. S2 or C2.

Moments A Pleasant Stroll

Strolling from the Abbey Gatehouse down Abbey Mill Lane is pure English pleasure. The quiet, leafy lane has a few old cottages and an ancient pub, Ye Olde Fighting Cocks, waiting for you at the end.

320 Camp Rd. (about 2 miles/3.2km east of city center). ✆ **01727/873-896.** Admission £3.50 ($6). Sun 2–4:30pm.

⑩ **Royal National Rose Garden** This is the flagship rose garden of the Royal National Rose Society, with over 30,000 roses on display (as well as clematis, iris, and other flowers). From St. Albans, take a taxi, or take bus no. 727 or no. 320 and ask the driver for the stop nearest the gardens; it's about a 10-minute walk from bus stop to garden entrance.
Chiswell Green Lane (2 miles/3.2km south of city center). ✆ **01727/850-461.** Admission £4 ($6) adults, £3.50 ($6) seniors. June–Sept daily 10am–5pm (Sun until 6pm).

Hatfield House Located 6 miles (9.5km) east of St. Albans, this famous Jacobean house has staterooms loaded with paintings, furniture, and armor. Within the lovely gardens is the Old Palace, childhood home of Queen Elizabeth I and the site of her first Council of State in 1558. From St. Albans, take a taxi or bus no. 30 from City Station; by car, take A414 east.
Hatfield, Hertfordshire. ✆ **01707/262-823.** www.hatfield-house.co.uk. Admission £7 ($11) adults; £3.50 ($6) seniors, students, and children under 16. Easter to Sept, house daily noon–4pm, gardens daily 11am–5:30pm.

ORGANIZED TOURS

Guided city walks start from the Tourist Information Centre, usually at 11:15am and/or 3pm on Saturday and Sunday, and take from 1 to 1½ hours. Tickets (£1/$1.60) can be obtained from the Tourist Information Centre or from the guide. You'll find the current schedule at the tourist center.

Every Sunday at 3pm from April 20 to September, a free, guided **Verulamium Walk** covers the remains of Verulamium, Roman Britain's third largest town. The walk starts from outside the Verulamium Museum.

3 Shopping

With over 170 stalls, **St. Albans market** is one of the most colorful and vibrant street markets in the south of England. Held on Wednesday and Saturday in the city center along the length of St. Peters

Street, it offers everything from fish to fancy goods. The market was granted a special Royal Charter in 1553 but dates as far back as the 9th century.

4 Where to Dine

Ye Olde Fighting Cocks PUB Situated on a quiet, leafy pathway close to the River Ver and Verulamium Park, this is one of the oldest pubs in England. The food is nothing fancy, but the atmosphere is great. You can get a club sandwich, hot soup, sausage, and mash, or a ploughman's lunch of cheese, ham, bread, pickles, apple, and salad. If the weather is nice you can eat at a table outside.

16 Abbey Mill Lane. ✆ **01727/869-152.** Main courses £5.50–£7.50 ($9–$12). MC, V. Open daily 11am–11pm.

Trip 20

Salisbury & Stonehenge

In this beautiful cathedral city dating from the 13th century, half-timbered inns and houses line medieval lanes that surround a still-lively marketplace. The tall spire of a graceful Gothic cathedral pierces the sky, and the Rivers Avon and Nadder sprint through water meadows. Little wonder that John Constable captured Salisbury in his paintings, and that Thomas Hardy and

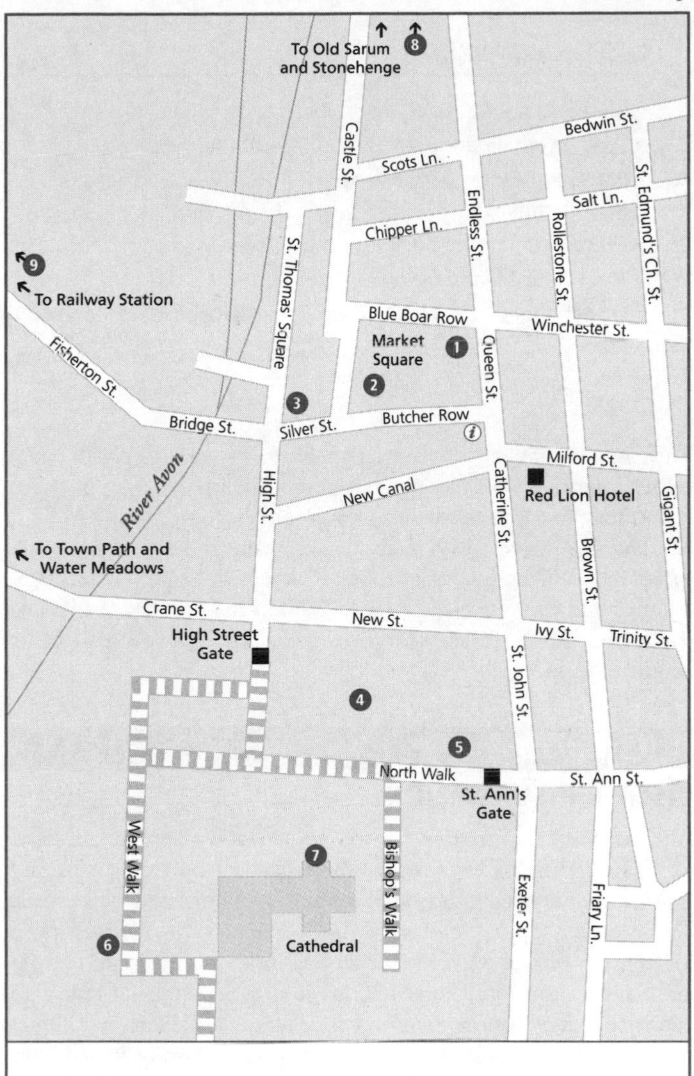

1 marketplace
2 Poultry Cross
3 St. Thomas Church
4 Cathedral Close
5 Mompesson House
6 The Salisbury and South Wiltshire Museum
7 Salisbury Cathedral
8 Stonehenge
9 Wilton House

Salisbury Highlights

- Medieval marketplace, still the scene of a lively market.
- High Street, lined with half-timbered buildings.
- Cathedral Close, with Mompesson House and other elegant landmarks.
- Salisbury Cathedral, a Gothic masterpiece.
- The Water Meadows.
- Stonehenge, the world's most famous prehistoric landmark.

Anthony Trollope set novels here; you'll be inspired simply to enjoy one of England's most pleasant and unspoiled cities.

You may find yourself wishing you didn't have to rush away from Salisbury—you can spend a full day enjoying the city sights, walk through the Water Meadows and Cathedral Close on a warm evening, and visit Stonehenge and/or Wilton the next day. Add a side trip to nearby Winchester (see trip 23) and you may want to stay a couple of days.

1 Essentials

VISITOR INFORMATION

The **Salisbury Information Centre** (in the marketplace on Fish Row; ✆ **01722/334-956;** www.visitsalisburyuk.com) provides maps and information on major attractions, shops, restaurants, and local events. The center is open October to April, Monday to Saturday from 9:30am to 5pm; in May, Monday to Saturday from 9:30am to 5pm and Sunday from 10:30am to 4:30pm; June to September, Monday to Saturday from 9:30am to 6pm and Sunday from 10:30am to 4:30pm; July to August, Monday to Saturday from 9:30am to 6pm and Sunday from 10:30am to 5pm.

SCHEDULING CONSIDERATIONS

This usually sedate city is quite animated for 10 days in late May and early June during the annual Salisbury Festival, when you can enjoy drama, classical music, and jazz at locations around the city, as well as architectural tours and other walks. For information and tickets, call ✆ **01722/332-241** or visit www.salisburyfestival.co.uk.

In late July of alternating years, the choirs of Salisbury, Chichester, and Winchester cathedrals perform in Salisbury Cathedral during the

Southern Cathedrals Festival. For information and tickets, contact the Salisbury Information Centre or visit www.southerncathedralsfestival.org.uk.

GETTING THERE

BY TRAIN

Trains run half-hourly between London's Waterloo Station and Salisbury at morning and evening peak travel times and hourly the rest of the day. The first direct train from London is at 7:10am and the last direct train for the return trip to London is at 9:05pm. (There's an earlier train from London to Salisbury, at 5:35am, and a later train returning to London, at 10:40pm, but these trips require a change at Bassingstoke and take about an hour longer.) The trip takes about 1½ hours, and the standard day return fare is £23 ($37). For information, call **National Rail Enquiries** at ✆ **08457/484-950** or visit www.nationalrail.co.uk. The train station is at the western edge of the city center, off Fisherton Street, and within easy walking distance of Salisbury Cathedral and other sights.

BY CAR

The quickest route from London is the M3, then the A30. The trip takes about 1½ hours. Convenient car parks near the city center are Central Car Park, north of the marketplace on the west side of the River Avon; and Culver Street Car Park, a few blocks northeast of the Cathedral Close. Fees at most car parks near the center are £3 ($4.80) per day.

BY BUS

National Express buses leave London's Victoria Coach Station for Salisbury about every 2 to 3 hours. The bus ride takes at least 3 hours and sometimes requires a change at Southampton or Bristol, making the train a much faster alternative. The trip costs about £20 ($31) return. For more information, call ✆ **08705/808-080** or visit www.nationalexpress.co.uk. The bus station is at the east end of the marketplace.

GETTING AROUND

Salisbury is compact and easy to get around, all the more so because much of the marketplace and surrounding streets, High Street, and the Cathedral Close are closed to traffic. The marketplace is at the north end of the center; from there, High Street leads south to the Cathedral Close. If you need a taxi, call **City Cabs** (✆ **01722/423-000**). The company will take you on excursions to Stonehenge and other nearby sites—the trip to Stonehenge is about £21 ($34).

2 A Day in Salisbury

The best place to begin a walk around Salisbury is the heart of town—the ❶ **marketplace,** where vendors have congregated since 1227 and continue to do so every Tuesday and Saturday. The medieval ❷ **Poultry Cross,** so called because it once marked the poultry section of the market, still rises above the stalls, and the names of the narrow medieval lanes—Fish Street, Silver Street, Butcher Row—represent the trades that once transpired on them.

Just to the west of the marketplace, off Silver Street, is 700-year-old ❸ **St. Thomas Church.** Step inside (the church is open daily 8am–6pm) to see the terrifying painting called "Doom," probably the gift of a medieval pilgrim to the cathedral; it hangs over the chancel arch and depicts ordinary folk rising from their graves and marching toward heaven or hell. High Street leads south toward Salisbury Cathedral, past many half-timbered buildings. The Old George (near the corner of New St.) is a former inn that was already 300 years old when the diarist Samuel Pepys stayed here in 1668. Just across New Street is the Old Bookshop, also dating to the 14th century.

The ❹ **Cathedral Close** is a small city, protected by stone walls and entered through four gates. (Raucous citizens who preyed upon the wealthy clergy once rendered these precautions necessary.) From High Street you'll pass through High Street Gate, with elaborate stonework above its archway. The entrance from Queen Street, to the east, is through St. Anne's Gate, where George Frederick Handel is said to have given his first recital in England in a room over the gatehouse.

Some of Salisbury's finest houses are in the Close, and you can tour the best of them: ❺ **Mompesson House** (✆ **01722/335-659;** www.nationaltrust.org.uk) was built in 1701 and retains its original plasterwork, paneling, and furnishing, including an astonishing collection of 18th-century glassware; the house evokes the Queen Anne period so richly that period dramas are often filmed here. (You might, for instance, recognize the house from director Ang Lee's 1995 *Sense and Sensibility.*) The house is open March 24 to September 28, Saturday to Wednesday from 11am to 5pm, and admission is £3.90 ($6) for adults

---

Moments A Picture-Perfect View

Walk into the water meadow, find a bench, and look back toward the cathedral. Does the scene look familiar? The sight of the tall spire piercing the blue sky has remained unspoiled since John Constable painted the scene 200 years ago. You may have seen his canvases in the National Gallery in London and in other museums.

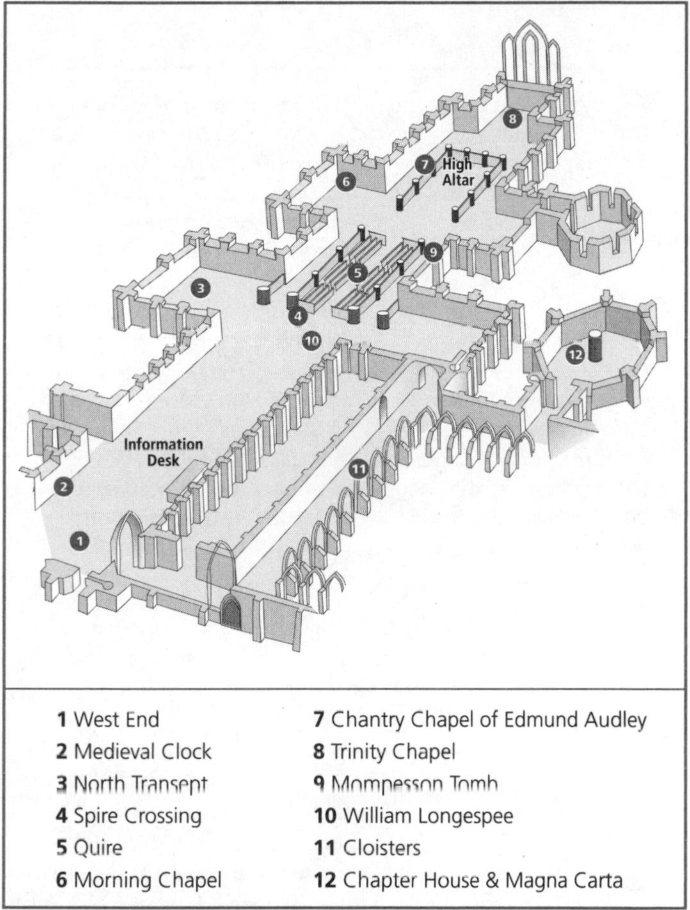

and £1.95 ($3.10) for children; half price if you show a train ticket.

❻ **The Salisbury and South Wiltshire Museum,** 65 The Close (✆ **01722/332-151;** www.salisburymuseum.org.uk), is a good stop if you plan to visit nearby Stonehenge. A few flints and other artifacts from the site are on display, but most interesting are the displays showing how the monument was constructed, as well as Stone Age and Roman finds from around Salisbury. The museum is open Monday to Saturday from 10am to 5pm; in July and August it's also open Sunday from 2 to 5pm. Admission is £3.50 ($6) adults, £2.30 ($3.70) seniors and students, £1 ($1.60) children 5 to 16, and £7.90 ($13) families of up to two adults and three children.

❼ **Salisbury Cathedral** (✆ **01722/555-120;** http://salisbury cathedral.org.uk) was built in just 38 years, from 1220 to 1258, and because the graceful and soaring structure doesn't bear the influence of

The Magna Carta

The light-filled, octagonal Chapter House of Salisbury Cathedral, built in the second half of the 13th century as a meeting hall for the cathedral's governing body, houses one of England's most treasured documents, the Magna Carta. The manuscript here is one of four originals known to exist—one of the others is in Lincoln Cathedral and two are in the British Library in London.

King John granted the charter largely as a concession to meet demands from his barons to ensure their privileges. Drafted and sealed at Runnymede in June 1215, the document protects land rights, guarantees freedoms for the Church, ensures legal reforms, makes the monarchy accountable, and addresses other basic tenets of civil liberties. Portions of the Magna Carta have been incorporated into the U.S. Constitution and many other documents.

other centuries, it is thoroughly Gothic. Join one of the free, highly informative guided tours offered throughout the day. You'll learn that the cloisters are the largest in England; the spire, at 404 feet (123m), is the tallest in the land; and a mechanical clock in the north aisle is one of the oldest pieces of working machinery in the world, telling time since 1386. In the octagonal Chapter House, remarkable stone friezes from the 13th century tell Old Testament stories, and one of four copies of the Magna Carta has been housed here since 1225. The cathedral is open daily from 7:15am to 6:15pm (to 7:15pm Mon–Sat June 9–Aug 30); the Chapter House is open Monday to Saturday from 9:30am to 5:30pm (until 6:45pm June 9–Aug 30) and Sunday from noon to 5:30pm. On Tower Tours, you can climb into the tower via 332 winding steps past medieval scaffolding to enjoy airy views. The tours last 1½ hours and are held January to February and November to December at 2:15pm; in March, Monday to Saturday at 11:15am and 2:15pm; in April, Monday to Saturday at 11:15am, 2:15pm, and 3:15pm; in May and September, Monday to Saturday at 11:15am, 2:15pm, and 3:15pm, and Sunday at 4:30pm; and from June to August, Monday to Saturday at 11:15am, 2:15pm, 3:15pm, and 6:30pm, and Sunday at 4:30pm. Fees are £4 ($6) for adults and £3 ($4.80) for seniors and children.

MORE THINGS TO SEE & DO

Old Sarum (Old Salisbury) The Romans built a settlement on a desolate plain a mile north of the present-day center of Salisbury;

Sarum was a flourishing center by the 13th century, when Salisbury Cathedral was constructed. Sarum was abandoned, but the moody ruins of the Norman castle, cathedral, and Bishop's Palace attest to what an important place this once was. You can reach the site on a well-marked footpath off Husle Road. Bus no. 3 runs from the bus station and elsewhere in the city center every 15 minutes; the fare is 80p ($1.30).

Castle Rd. ✆ **01722/335-398.** www.English-heritage.org.uk. Admission £2.50 ($4) adults, £1.70 ($2.70) seniors and students, £1.10 ($1.80) children 5 to 15. Open daily: Apr–June and Sept, 10am–6pm; July–Aug, 9am–6pm; Oct, 10am–5pm; Nov–Mar, 10am–4pm.

8 Stonehenge The world's most renowned prehistoric site, a stone circle of pillars and lintels, has risen above the Salisbury Plain for almost 4,000 years. Why these stones are here or what they signify is not known. Given the stones' alignment with the summer equinox, the monument may have been intended in part as an astronomical observatory. Stonehenge also seems to have served at times as a burial ground and a ceremonial center. Today's visitors follow an excellent self-guided audio tour and view the stones from a well-designed encircling walkway that does not intrude upon the majesty of the haunting monoliths. **Wiltshire and Dorset** buses (✆ **01722/336-855;** www.wdbus.co.uk) depart from Salisbury bus station for Stonehenge about every 2 hours beginning at 10:25am, and depart from Stonehenge for Salisbury about every 2 hours, with the last return to Salisbury at 3:45pm Monday to Saturday and 6:55pm on Sunday, when there is hourly service. The trip takes 40 minutes and the fare is about £5 ($8) return.

8 miles (13km) north of Salisbury off A360. ✆ **01980/624-715.** www.stonehenge.org.uk. £5 ($8) adults, £3.80 ($6) seniors and students, £2.50 ($4) children 5–15, £13 ($21) families of up to 2 adults and 3 children. Open daily: Mar 16–May 31, 9:30am–6pm; June 1–Aug 31, 9am–7pm; Sept 1–Oct 15, 9:30am–6pm; Oct 16–Mar 15, 9:30am–5pm.

9 Wilton House The 17th-century architect Inigo Jones (whose other works include Covent Garden in London) designed this house. His use of classicism is most in evidence in the Double Cube Room, a harmonious 60 feet long by 30 feet wide and 30 feet high (18m by 9m by 9m). General Dwight D. Eisenhower planned the logistical support for the D-Day Landings in 1944 in this room, when Wilton was a top-secret operations center. Paintings by Anthony van Dyke line the walls, and paintings by Peter Paul Rubens, Pieter Brueghel, Sir Joshua Reynolds, and other masters hang throughout the other staterooms. One of the most striking treasures is not a painting, but the elegant Chippendale bookcase in the Large Smoking Room. The River Avon flows through the lawns and gardens, and is spanned by a Palladian bridge. You can reach Wilton House on bus no. 60 or 61 from the bus station and elsewhere in the city center; the fare is £1.60 ($2.60).

3 miles (5km) northwest of Salisbury on A30, in Wilton village. ✆ **01722/746-720.** www.wiltonhouse.co.uk. Admission £9.25 ($15) adults, £7.50 ($12) seniors and students, £5 ($8) children 5-15, £22 ($35) families. Open Apr 11–Oct 26, daily 10:30am–5:30pm.

ORGANIZED TOURS

The 1½-hour **Salisbury City Walk** (✆ **01725/518-658**) begins at the Tourist Information Centre in Fish Row at 11am, on Saturday and Sunday from November to March, and daily from April to October. The cost is £2.50 ($4) for adults and £1 ($1.60) for children.

OUTDOOR ACTIVITIES

A well-maintained footpath crosses the ❿ **Water Meadows** between Mill Road and the old Harnham Mill, crossing the River Avon and affording wonderful views toward the cathedral. A walk through the meadows and back to the city center covers a little less than 2 miles (3km). For a longer excursion, rent a bike from **Stonehenge Cycles** (86–88 Fisherton St.; ✆ **01722/334-915;** www.stonehengecycles.com) for a spin around town and onto a series of public footpaths that traverse the countryside. For advice on routes, call the **Walking and Cycling Helpline** at ✆ **01980/623-255.**

3 Shopping

Watsons, 8/9 Queen St. (✆ **01722/320-311**), sells a huge selection of British crystal and fine china. The wares are not the only draw, though—the shop occupies two of Salisbury's oldest buildings, from 1306 and 1425. The **National Trust Shop,** 41 High St. (✆ **01722/331-884**), carries needlepoint kits, tea towels, and other handy souvenir-type items.

4 Where to Dine

You can equip yourself with sandwiches, quiches, and delicious pastries at **Reeve the Baker** (2 Butcher Row; ✆ **01722/320-367**) and enjoy a picnic in the Water Meadows. For cheeses, fruit, and other local produce, stroll through the marketplace Tuesday and Saturday mornings.

Harper's Restaurant BRITISH/INTERNATIONAL "Real food is our specialty" is the motto in this pleasant, second-floor room overlooking the marketplace. Excellent meals, including vegetarian dishes, are served a la carte and on reasonably priced prix-fixe menus.

6–7 Ox Row. ✆ **01722/333-118.** Main courses £8.50–£13 ($14–$20). MC, V. Mon–Sat noon–2pm and 6–9:30pm; Sun 6–10pm.

One Minster Street BRITISH Locals may refer to this place as the Haunch of Venison, which is Salisbury's oldest pub, dating from 1320. One Minster occupies a series of small, heavily beamed rooms above the pub and, alas, instead of serving roasted haunch, caters to modern tastes with such fare as burgers and sea bass filets in what is still the town's most atmospheric place to dine.

1 Minster St. ✆ **01722/411-313.** Main courses £6.90–£9.90 ($11–$16). AE, MC, V. Mon–Sun noon–2:30pm and 7–10pm.

5 Extending Your Stay

Red Lion Hotel Atmosphere fills every nook and cranny of this 750-year-old inn, from which the express stagecoach used to depart for London every night at 10pm. The cozy lounge is a popular spot for tea, and drinks are served in the vine-covered courtyard in good weather. Each guest room is uniquely furnished, some with fireplaces and four-poster beds.

Milford St., Salisbury, Wiltshire SP1 2AN. ✆ **01722/323-334.** www.the-redlion.co.uk. £88–£109 ($140–$174) double. AE, DC, MC, V.

Trip 21

Sissinghurst Castle Garden

What has become one of England's favorite gardens is the creation of the poet and novelist Vita Sackville-West (who grew up at Knole; see trip 12) and of her husband, the diplomat and writer Harold Nicolson. The couple bought the nearly ruined remains of a grand Elizabethan house and restored the gatehouse, stables, tower, and other buildings, but most

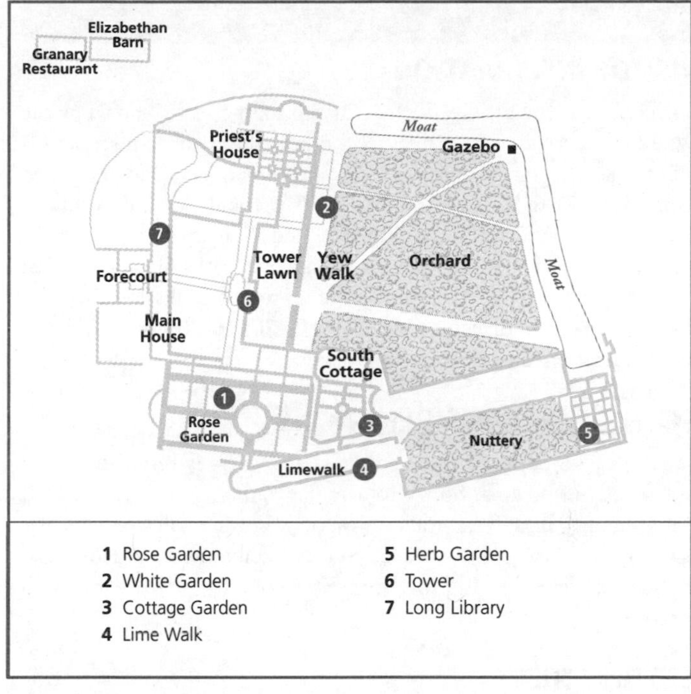

notably turned their attention to the gardens. Here they laid out 10 outdoor rooms, each with a distinct look and feel, separated by hedges and walls. Walking through the gardens, you make a discovery around every corner and through every archway. The experience is delightful, and it's little wonder that Sissinghurst has become the model of gardens around the world. None, however, can be quite as enticing as the original.

Sissinghurst Highlights

- Vita Sackville-West's study in the Tower.
- The Rose Garden, especially when it is in bloom in June.
- The White Garden, at its best in early July when the central rose blooms form a huge canopy.
- The Cottage Garden, at any time of the year.
- The Lime Walk, just after the limes have come into leaf and the spring flowers are in bloom.

1 Essentials

VISITOR INFORMATION

Sissinghurst is beautifully situated in the rolling lands known as the Weald of Kent, about 50 miles (80km) southwest of London and 7 miles (11km) south of the town of Staplehurst. The garden is open from March 22 to November 2 on Monday, Tuesday, and Friday from 11am to 6:30pm, and on Saturday and Sunday from 10am to 6:30pm. Admission is £6.50 ($10) for adults, £3 ($4.80) for children under 16, and £16 ($26) for families of up to two adults and two children. For more information, call ✆ **01580/710-700** or visit www.nationaltrust.org.uk/places/sissinghurst.

SCHEDULING CONSIDERATIONS

You'll want to linger in these gardens, and there is very little to do indoors at Sissinghurst. So try to arrange your visit on a day when it is not raining. Since the garden is especially crowded on weekends, it's best to visit during the week if you can. Like most gardens, Sissinghurst is at its prime in June, but it is colorful from early spring well into the fall.

GETTING THERE

BY TRAIN

The train station closest to Sissinghurst is the one in the village of Staplehurst, about 7 miles (11km) away. The direct trip from London's Charing Cross Station to Staplehurst takes just over an hour and costs about £12 ($19) return. There are some 35 trains a day from London. The first train to Staplehurst is at 5:30am and the last train returns to London at 10:50pm; trains run about every half hour. For more information, call **National Rail Enquiries** at ✆ **08457/484-950** or go to www.nationalrail.co.uk.

From the Staplehurst train station, you can continue to Sissinghurst by bus no. 4/5. Buses run roughly every half hour throughout the day (less frequently before 9:30am and after 7pm), and the fare is £1.60 ($2.55). Tell the driver you want to get off at the gates to Sissinghurst. (You'll have to walk a quarter mile or so up the drive.) Or get off in Sissinghurst village and follow the well-marked footpath through surrounding woods and hops fields to the garden; the walk is delightful and less than a mile. (As you near the grounds of Sissinghurst, the path passes beneath a magnificent spreading beech.) For additional bus information, call **Traveline** at ✆ **0870/608-2608.**

Alternatively, you can take a taxi from Staplehurst. The advantage is a ride right to the garden entrance; the disadvantage is the steep fare, about £8 ($13). If you wish to return via taxi, arrange to have the driver pick you up at a set time, because public phones are scarce at the garden. There's a taxi stand outside the Staplehurst train station, but to ensure that a taxi will be available when you arrive, arrange a pickup in advance by calling the **Maidstone Taxi Company** at © **01580/890-003.**

BY CAR

The trip from London takes just over an hour, depending on traffic. Take the M25 to Maidstone, where you will get on A229 and travel south through Staplehurst to A262; Sissinghurst is about 3 miles (4.8km) west of the junction. Parking is free.

GETTING AROUND

Travelers with disabilities will want to consider the fact that a visit to the garden involves quite a bit of walking when using public transportation—you will have to walk about a quarter of a mile up the drive from the bus stop on the main road. A taxi from Staplehurst (see "By Train," above) may be a better option.

2 A Day at Sissinghurst Castle Garden

If you are a royalist at heart, you will pleased to know that you will enter the gardens—through an arch in the stable and servants' block into the courtyard and past the base of a tall tower of pale pink brick—the same way that Queen Elizabeth I did when she paid a visit to then-owner Sir Richard Baker in 1573. The two rooms of the house you can visit, the Long Library and Vita's study in the Tower, are reached off the courtyard, but save them for later; instead, focus on the gardens that lie just on the other side of the Tower.

There's no best route through the garden; in fact, it's best just to wander across these 6 acres (2.4 hectares) wherever your curiosity takes you. The garden is designed so that you rarely see one section from another, so each time you come through a gap in a hedge or wall, you're in for a surprise.

As you move from outdoor room to outdoor room, take note of the way the garden incorporates classical symmetry and romantic abandon—in this way, the garden is said to capture the personalities of the couple who created it. In the ❶ **Rose Garden,** to your right as you pass through the arch through the base of the tower, Harold designed the disk of mown lawn surrounded by yew hedges, and Vita, whose preference was for colorful beds and flowers straying over paths, planted the luxuriant, old-fashioned varieties that bloom in June. In the ❷ **White Garden,** Vita planted white flowers that bloom throughout the season among the paths and hedges laid out by Harold. The ❸ **Cottage Garden** also combines formality and a sense of abundance, and in it grows the white rose the couple planted the day they bought Sissinghurst. The classically oriented Harold planted the formal, Italian-style ❹ **Lime Walk,** and Vita lavished care on the ❺ **Herb Garden;** supposedly she could identify every herb in it with her eyes closed, by smell alone.

Once you've seen the gardens, return to the ❻ **Tower,** where you can look into Vita's study (an extremely romantic room). Just across the courtyard is the ❼ **Long Library,** a handsome room dating from 1490 and filled with centuries-old family furniture. Don't turn your back on the gardens yet, though—you might want to return for another walk around and to find a spot in which to sit and do what Harold and Vita did for many years—simply enjoy this splendid creation.

Portrait of a Marriage

Vita Sackville-West and her husband, the diplomat Harold Nicolson, are famous for the gardens they cultivated at Sissinghurst and for their literary achievements—Vita's poem "The Land" is one of many works in which she pays homage to her beloved Kent, and Harold's books include biographies of Tennyson and Byron and studies of politics and diplomacy. The couple is also notable for a long, harmonious, and unconventional marriage that began in 1913 and came to an end with Vita's death from cancer in 1962. Both were homosexual, and Vita's extramarital affairs included a rather scandalous and much publicized liaison with Violet Keppel Trefusis in 1920 (Violet was the daughter of Alice Keppel, mistress of King Edward VII) and a close friendship with the novelist Virginia Woolf. Vita often visited Monk's House, the country home that Virginia and Leonard Woolf bought near Lewes in 1920. (See trip 14.) She was the model for the gender-changing hero/heroine of *Orlando,* Woolf's brilliant novel set in part at Knole, Vita's family estate in nearby Sevenoaks and one of the greatest houses in England. (See trip 12.) The couple had two children, the art critic Benedict Nicolson, and the writer and publisher Nigel Nicolson. Nigel wrote about his parents' enduring union in *Portrait of a Marriage,* published in 1973.

Moments A Bird's-Eye View

After you've toured the garden, climb to top of the Tower for one more look. From this vantage point, you can clearly see the separate outdoor rooms and appreciate just what an accomplishment the garden is. You'll also see why Vita Sackville-West enjoyed spending her days here in the Tower.

3 Where to Dine

Granary Restaurant CAFETERIA/LIGHT FARE An airy outbuilding on the estate near the garden entrance is an unusually pleasant setting for a cafeteria-style restaurant that overlooks fields through a wall of glass. Sandwiches, salads, and a few hot dish specials are on offer, as are tea and other beverages, including wine and beer.

✆ **01580/710-704.** Most items £3–£7 ($4.80–$11). DC, MC, V. Mar 22–Nov 2, Mon–Tues and Thurs–Sun 11am–5:30pm; Nov 5–Dec 21, Wed–Sun 11am–4pm.

Trip 22

Stratford-upon-Avon

This market town on the River Avon, 91 miles (146km) northwest of London, is a shrine to the world's greatest playwright, William Shakespeare, who was born, lived much of his life, and is buried here. Stratford boasts many fine Tudor, Elizabethan, and Jacobean buildings, but it's not really a quaint village anymore. If you arrive by train, your first glimpse will be of a vast

Stratford-upon-Avon

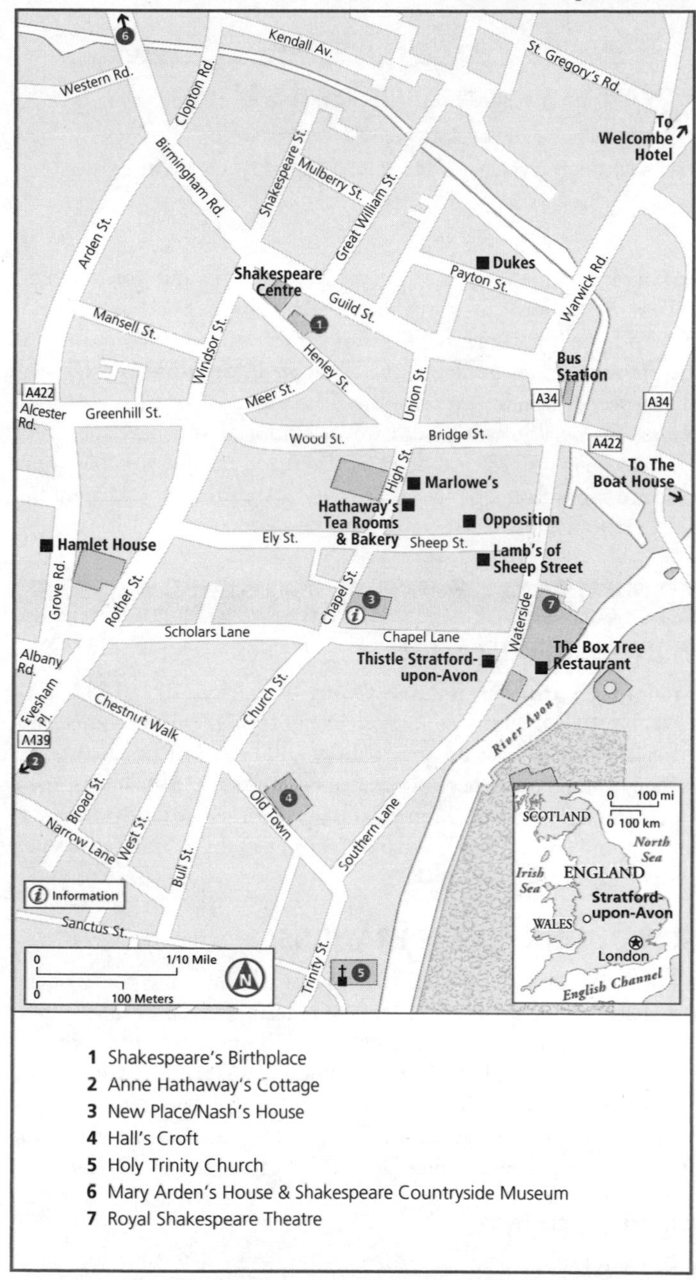

Stratford-upon-Avon Highlights

- Visiting the Bard's birthplace and grave.
- Strolling over to Anne Hathaway's Cottage.
- Attending a play at the Royal Shakespeare Theatre.

parking lot across from the station. Don't let this put you off. The charms of Stratford's formerly bucolic setting haven't been completely lost, and you'll find plenty of quaint corners as you explore. Besides the literary pilgrimage sights, the top draw in Stratford is the Royal Shakespeare Theatre, where Britain's foremost actors perform. Nearby Warwick Castle is also worth visiting if you have the time. With all there is to see and do in Stratford and nearby, you may want to spend more than 1 day here. See the last section in this chapter for hotel recommendations.

1 Essentials

VISITOR INFORMATION

Stratford's **Tourist Information Centre,** Bridgefoot (✆ **01789/293-127;** www.shakespeare-country.co.uk), provides information and maps of the town and its principal sights. The center has a currency exchange and a room-booking service (✆ **01789/415-061**). It's open Easter through October, Monday through Saturday from 9am to 6pm (until 5pm Nov to Easter), and Sunday from 11am to 5pm (until 4pm Nov to Easter).

SCHEDULING CONSIDERATIONS

All of the Shakespeare properties keep basically the same hours, opening daily between 10 and 11am and closing at 5pm. They open slightly earlier in the summer and close an hour earlier in the winter. All of them are closed December 24 through 26; some are also closed January 1 and Good Friday. If you want to see a play at the Royal Shakespeare Theatre (see "More Things to See & Do," below), book ahead and don't come during October, when the theatre is closed.

GETTING THERE

BY TRAIN

Direct trains leave frequently from London's Paddington Station; the journey takes about 2 hours and costs £23 ($37) for a day return ticket. From London there are three morning trains (two on Sun); trains depart Stratford throughout the afternoon and evening until 8pm. Contact **National Rail Enquiries** (✆ **08457/484950;** www.nationalrail.co.uk) for information and schedules.

BY BUS

National Express (✆ **0990/808-080;** www.nationalexpress.co.uk) offers daily bus service from London's Victoria Coach Station; the trip takes just over 3 hours and costs £17 ($27) return.

BY CAR

By car from London, take the M40 toward Oxford and continue to Stratford-upon-Avon on A34.

GETTING AROUND

Stratford is compact, and you can walk everywhere. The train and bus stations are less than a 15-minute walk from the town center. **Guide Friday** (see under "Organized Tours," below) runs a convenient hop-on/hop-off bus service to all the Shakespeare properties, including Anne Hathaway's Cottage (about 1 mile/1.6km from Stratford town center) and Mary Arden's House (about 2 miles/3km from the center).

2 A Day in Stratford-upon-Avon

One money-saving ticket gets you into the five sites administered by the **Shakespeare Birthplace Trust** (✆ **01789/201-807;** www.shakespeare.org.uk): Shakespeare's Birthplace, Anne Hathaway's Cottage, New Place/Nash's House, Hall's Croft, and Mary Arden's House, all of which are described below. You can pick up the ticket at your first stop; it costs £13 ($21) for adults, £12 ($19) for seniors and students.

Start your walking tour of Stratford at ❶ **Shakespeare's Birthplace** on Henley Street (✆ **01789/204-016**), where the Bard, son of a glover and wool merchant, first saw the light of day on April 23, 1564. You enter through the modern **Shakespeare Centre,** where exhibits illustrate his life and times. The house, filled with Shakespeare memorabilia, is actually two 16th-century half-timbered houses joined together: The house and gardens are open daily from 10am to 5pm (from 10:30am on Sun; June–Aug from 9am weekdays and from 9:30am Sun; Nov–Mar until 4pm). Admission is £6.50 ($10) adults, £5.50 ($9) seniors and students.

Make ❷ **Anne Hathaway's Cottage** (✆ **01789/204-016**) your next stop. It's located on Cottage Lane in Shottery, about 1 mile (1.6km) south of Stratford. To get there, walk along the well-marked country path from Evesham Place or hop on a bus from Bridge Street. Anne Hathaway, who came from a family of yeomen farmers, lived in this thatched cottage until 1582, the year she married 18-year-old Shakespeare. (Anne was 7 years older.) Many original 16th-century furnishings are preserved inside the house, which was occupied by Anne's family until 1892. Before leaving, be sure to stroll through the beautiful garden and orchard. The hours are the same as for Shakespeare's Birthplace. Admission is £5 ($8) adults, £4 ($6) seniors and students.

From Anne Hathaway's Cottage, retrace your steps to Shakespeare's Birthplace and then walk east on Henley Street and south on High Street, which becomes Chapel Street. Here you'll find the gardens of ❸ **New Place** (**✆ 01789/204-016**), all that remains of the Stratford house where a relatively prosperous Shakespeare retired in 1610 and died in 1616. You enter the garden through **Nash's House,** which belonged to Thomas Nash, husband of Shakespeare's granddaughter. The house contains 16th-century period rooms and an exhibit illustrating the history of Stratford. New Place/Nash's House is open daily from 11am to 5pm (June–Aug from 9:30am weekdays and from 10am Sun; Nov–Mar until 4pm; opens at 1:30pm Jan 1 and Good Friday). Admission is £3.50 ($6) adults, £3 ($4.80) seniors and students.

From New Place, walk south on Chapel and Church streets and turn east on Old Town to reach ❹ **Hall's Croft** (**✆ 01789/204-016**), a magnificent Tudor house once lived in by Shakespeare's daughter Susanna and her husband, Dr. John Hall. The house is furnished in the style of a middle-class 17th-century home and also has exhibits illustrating the theory and practice of medicine in Dr. Hall's time. It has the same opening hours and admission as New Place/Nash's House.

From Hall's Croft, walk south to Southern Lane, which runs beside the River Avon, and follow it south to Trinity Street and the path to ❺ **Holy Trinity Church** (**✆ 01789/266-316**), where Shakespeare is buried. (He died on his birthday, Apr 23, 1616, at age 52.) A bust of the immortal Bard looks down on his gravesite in front of the altar. Holy Trinity is open Monday through Saturday from 8:30am to 6pm (Nov–Feb until 4pm), and Sunday year-round from 2 to 5pm.

The last Shakespeare site, ❻ **Mary Arden's House & Shakespeare Countryside Museum** (**✆ 01789/204-016**), is located in Wilmcote, about 3½ miles (5.5km) north of Stratford on A34. To reach it, you'll probably want to drive or take the Guide Friday bus. (See "Organized Tours," below.) Mary Arden, Shakespeare's mother, lived in this house dating from 1514. Inside are country furniture and domestic utensils; the extensive collection of farm implements in the barns and outbuildings illustrate life and work in the local countryside from Shakespeare's time to the present. The house and museum are open daily from 10am to 5pm (Nov–Mar and Sept–Oct until 4pm; Sun from 10:30am). Admission is £5.50 ($9) adults, £5 ($8) seniors and students.

The ❼ **Royal Shakespeare Theatre,** Waterside (✆ **01789/403-403;** www.rsc.org.uk), is the home of the **Royal Shakespeare Company,** which stages Shakespeare plays from November to September. It's a good idea to order your tickets 2 to 3 weeks in advance. (A few tickets are always held for sale on the day of a performance.) The box office is open Monday through Saturday from 9am to 8pm, but closes at 6pm on days when there are no performances. Ticket prices are £8 to £42 ($13–$67).

MORE THINGS TO SEE & DO

Warwick Castle Mighty Warwick Castle, one of the most popular tourist attractions in England, is located 8 miles (13km) northeast of Stratford in the town of Warwick. Dramatically sited above the Avon River, the castle is a splendid example of a medieval fortress that's been adapted over the centuries to reflect the tastes and ambitions of its inhabitants. If you're going to visit the castle and the lovely gardens and parkland around it, you need at least 2 hours. **Chiltern Railways** (✆ **08705/165-165**) runs direct trains to Warwick from Stratford-upon-Avon; the trip takes about 15 minutes. **National Express** (✆ **0990/808-080;** www.nationalexpress.co.uk) runs buses to Warwick from Riverside bus station in Stratford-upon-Avon; the 15-minute journey costs £2 ($3.20) return. By car from Stratford, take Junction 15 of the M40 and continue on for 2 miles (3km). Bus tours of Warwick Castle from Stratford-upon-Avon are available through **Guide Friday** (see below).

Warwick Castle. ✆ **0870/442-2000.** www.warwick-castle.co.uk. Admission varies depending on day and season: £11–£14 ($18–$22) adults, £8–£9.75 ($13–$16) seniors, £8.50–£10 ($14–$16) students, £6.95–£8 ($11–$13) children ages 4 to 16, £32–£36 ($51–$58) family tickets (2 adults and 2 children). Daily 10am–6pm (Oct–Mar until 5pm, Aug until 7pm).

ORGANIZED TOURS

The **Stratford Town Walk** (✆ **01789/292-478**) departs Monday through Thursday at 11am and Friday through Sunday at 2pm from the Swan Fountain near the Royal Shakespeare Theatre, year-round except for the last few days in December. This is a 90-minute "insider's tour" of Shakespeare's Stratford. All the Shakespeare sights are visited, and you're given a lively commentary on the Bard's life. No need to reserve, just show up. The tour costs £4 ($6).

Guide Friday, 14 Rother St. (✆ **01789/294-466;** www.guidefriday.com), offers guided tours of Stratford in open-top, double-decker buses that leave from outside the Tourist Information Centre every 15 minutes daily between 9:30am and 5:30pm in summer. You can take the 1-hour ride without stops or get off and on at any or all of the town's five Shakespeare properties, including Mary Arden's

Moments Shakespeare's Grave

He wrote some of the world's most immortal lines, but the epitaph you see scratched on Shakespeare's grave in Holy Trinity Church is little more than doggerel: GOOD FREND FOR JESUS SAKE FORBEARE/TO DIGG THE DUST ENCLOASED HEARE/BLESTE BE YE MAN YT [THAT] SPARES THES STONES/AND CURST BE HE YT MOVES MY BONES.

House in Wilmcote. The tour ticket is valid all day but does not include admission into any of the houses. The bus tour costs £7.50 ($12) for adults, £6 ($10) for seniors and students. You can buy your ticket on the bus.

OUTDOOR ACTIVITIES

Avon Boating (✆ **01789/267-073**) offers half-hour cruises on the Avon River with regular departures Easter through October (10am to dusk) from Bancroft Gardens adjacent to the Royal Shakespeare Theatre. The cost is £3 ($4.80) for adults, £2 ($3.60) for children. Rowboats, punts, and canoes can be rented for £2.50 ($4) per hour.

3 Shopping

Stratford's weekly **Market,** held on Friday, dates back over 800 years. The **Shakespeare Bookshop,** in the Shakespeare Centre, Henley Street (✆ **01789/201-819**), is the region's best bookshop for Shakespeare-related material.

The nearby **Pickwick Gallery,** 32 Henley St. (✆ **01789/294-861**), carries a wide variety of old and new engravings. **Elaine Rippon Craft Gallery,** Shakespeare Craft Yard off Henley Street (✆ **01789/415-481**), designs, creates, and sells sumptuous silk and velvet accessories and carries fine British contemporary crafts.

4 Where to Dine

The Boat House MODERN BRITISH/INTERNATIONAL This chic bistro above a boathouse on the River Avon is a fun and flavorful place to dine. The inventive menu is truly international in scope and the food never loses out in the translation. You may find spicy Thai spring rolls, Szechuan-style tuna, roast halibut with tomato risotto, or spinach lasagne. The nautical decor features wooden tables, bare floorboards, and rope.

Swan's Nest Lane (on the river between Clopton Bridge and footbridge). ✆ **01789/297-733.** Reservations recommended for dinner. Main courses: £9–£15 ($14–$24), fixed-price lunch £11 ($18). MC, V. Wed–Sat noon–2pm; Mon–Sat 6–11pm.

The Box Tree Restaurant BRITISH/CONTINENTAL This lovely restaurant in the Royal Shakespeare Theatre looks out on the River Avon's gliding white swans. The menu offers a bit of everything—French, Italian, and English dishes. You can dine by candlelight after a performance. Use a special phone in the theater's lobby to make a reservation here.

In the Royal Shakespeare Theatre. ✆ **01789/293-226.** Reservations required. Fixed-price matinee lunch £16 ($26); 3-course fixed-price dinner £26–£27 ($42–$43). AE, MC, V. Noon–2:30pm on matinee days (call for schedule) and Mon–Sat 5:45pm–midnight.

Hathaway's Tea Rooms & Bakery TEAROOM For afternoon tea in atmospheric surroundings, try this tearoom on the second floor of a building that dates from 1610. Cream tea comes with homemade fruit scones, clotted cream, and jam, and high tea includes a variety of sandwiches. You can also get an English breakfast and light meals throughout the day.

19 High St. ✆ **01789/292-404.** Cream tea £4 ($6), high tea £6 ($10). No credit cards. Open daily 9am–5:30pm;.

Lamb's of Sheep Street MODERN BRITISH Housed in one of Stratford's oldest buildings, with low ceilings and timber framing, Lamb's serves up modern British cooking with flair. Typical menu offerings include pan-fried pork with sage prosciutto, chargrilled ribeye steak, breast of chicken roasted in mango with lime butter, and vegetarian dishes such as tomato risotto with grilled vegetables and pesto.

12 Sheep St. ✆ **01789/292-554.** Reservations recommended. Main courses £12–£14 ($19–$22); fixed-price lunch and dinner £12–£14 ($18–$22). AE, MC, V. Open Mon–Sat noon–2pm and 5–10pm; Sun noon–2pm and 6–9:30pm.

Marlowe's Restaurant & Georgie's Bistro BRITISH/MODERN BRITISH An Elizabethan town house is the setting for these two adjoining eateries. Marlowe's is the classier "silver service" restaurant. The bar, where a fire blazes in winter, leads to an oak-paneled dining room where you can dine on specialties such as Drunken Duck (duck marinated in gin, red wine, cracked pepper, and juniper berries). In summer, you can eat on the patio. Georgie's, the bistro area, is great for a relaxed, informal meal. Try the fish and chips or the pork and leek sausages.

18 High St. ✆ **01789/204-999.** Reservations required for Marlowe's. Main courses: Marlowe's £9–£15 ($14–$24), Georgie's £6–£8 ($10–$13). Fixed-price lunch and dinner at Marlowe's £20–£23 ($32–$36). AE, MC, V. Daily noon–2pm and 5:45–11pm.

Opposition BRITISH/INTERNATIONAL Good bistro fare is served up in this cozy, oak-beamed restaurant housed in a 16th-century building in the heart of Stratford. Lunch and dinner choices are a mix of traditional and Modern British cuisine with some pasta dishes and Cajun breast of chicken. For dessert, you may want to try Eton Mess, a concoction of strawberries, meringue, and cream.

13 Sheep St. ✆ **01789/269-980.** Reservations recommended. Main courses: £7–£16 ($11–$26). MC, V. Daily noon–2pm and 5–11pm.

5 Extending Your Stay

Dukes In the center of Stratford, close to Shakespeare's Birthplace, Dukes was formed from two Georgian town houses. The nicely restored public areas and 22 guest rooms are attractive, and the hotel's restaurant serves good English and Continental cuisine.

Payton St., Stratford-upon-Avon, Warwickshire CV37 6UA. ✆ **01789/269-300.** Fax 01789/414-700. £65–£100 ($104–$160) double. Rates include English breakfast. AE, MC, V.

Glebe Farm House This lovely house, set within 30 acres (12 hectares) of gardens and lawns, is 3 miles (4km) from Stratford, 7 miles (11km) from Warwick, and 5 miles (8km) from the Cotswolds. From the three guest rooms, there are panoramic views of the countryside. The pretty units have en-suite bathrooms, oak furniture, and four-poster beds. Excellent meals are prepared using organic produce. From Stratford, cross River Avon on Clopton Bridge, make an immediate left on Tiddington Road, and make an immediate right on Loxley Road. Continue on Loxley to the last house on the left (white gates).

Stratford Rd., Loxley, Stratford-upon-Avon, Warwickshire CV35 9JW. ✆ **01789/842-501.** Fax 01789/841-194. scorpiolimited@msn.com. £110–£140 ($176–$224) double. 3-course dinner £29 ($46). MC, V.

Hamlet House This unpretentious, well-maintained B&B in a Victorian town house is a convenient 3-minute walk from the train station and close to everything else in Stratford. Two of its five guest rooms have private bathrooms; the others share a toilet and shower. Yvonne and Paul, the owners, are helpful and hospitable, and welcome children. The breakfast is hearty.

52 Grove Rd., Stratford-upon-Avon, Warwickshire CV37 6PB. ✆ **01789/204-386.** www.hamlethouse.com. £40–£56 ($64–$90) double. Rates include English breakfast. No credit cards.

Thistle Stratford-upon-Avon If this hotel were any closer to the Royal Shakespeare Festival theatres, the guests would be onstage. Thistle is a British chain of upscale full-service hotels, offering well-decorated rooms (63 of them in this hotel) with an abundance of amenities. The building dates back to 1791 and has been decorated to look like a traditional Georgian town house. Bards Restaurant serves fine English and Continental cuisine.

Waterside, Stratford-upon-Avon, Warwickshire CV37 6BA. ✆ **800/847-4358** in U.S. and Canada, or 01789/294-949. Fax: 01789/415-874. www.thistlehotels.com. £128–£185 ($204–$296) double. AE, DC, MC, V.

Welcombe Hotel This is the place to stay if you're feeling to the manor born. Located 1½ miles (2.5km) northeast of the town center, Welcombe Hotel is housed in one of the county's great Victorian (Jacobean-style) houses. An 18-hole golf course and 157 acres (63 hectares) of grounds surround this luxurious, full-service hotel.

Warwick Rd., Stratford-upon-Avon, Warwickshire CV37 0NR. ✆ **01789/295-252.** Fax 01789/414-666. www.welcombe.co.uk. £175–£205 ($280–$328) double. Rates include English breakfast. AE, DC, MC, V.

Trip 23

Winchester

One of the best-kept and prettiest small cities in England, Winchester evokes its ancient heritage with pride. An important Roman military headquarters, it became capital of the ancient kingdom of Wessex after the Romans withdrew from Britain, and remained the most important city in England up until the time of the Norman Conquest. Winchester Cathedral, the town's chief glory, was founded by William the Conqueror, who came to Winchester

Winchester

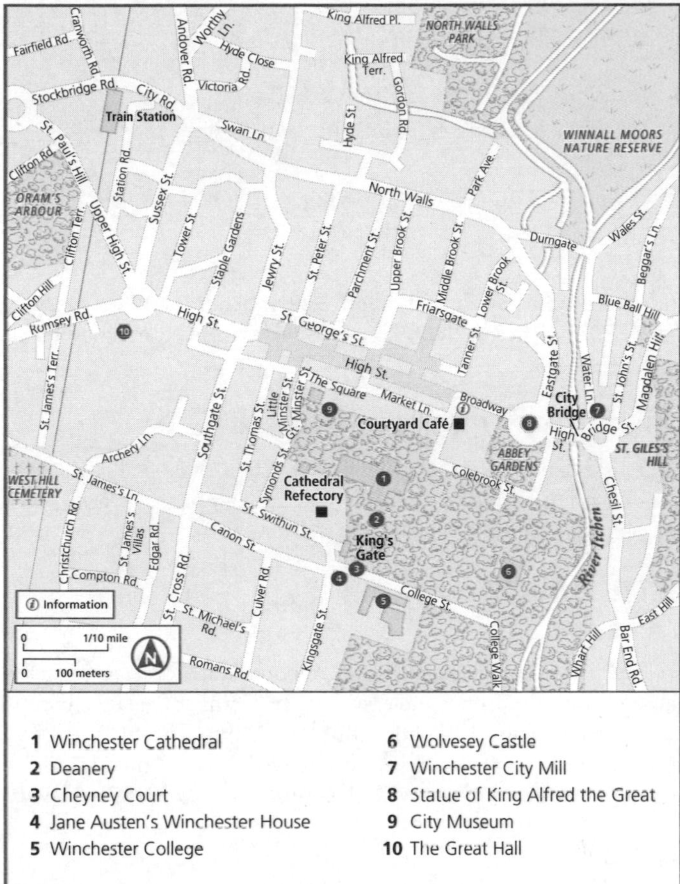

to claim his throne after the Battle of Hastings in 1066. It was in Winchester that William compiled his inventory of England, the famous *Domesday Book.* The ancient cathedral alone is worth a trip, but there are many other charms to be discovered in Winchester. Jane Austen fans can visit the great novelist's home in the nearby village of Chawton and her grave in Winchester Cathedral.

1 Essentials

VISITOR INFORMATION

The **Tourist Information Centre,** in the Guildhall on Broadway (✆ **01962/840-500;** www.visitwinchester.co.uk), is open year-round Monday through Saturday from 11am to 6pm (until 5pm Oct–May),

Winchester Highlights

- Visiting ancient Winchester Cathedral.
- Jane Austen associations in Winchester and nearby Chawton.
- Exploring the charming streets and byways of Winchester.

and also on Sunday June through September from 11am to 2pm. They distribute free maps of the town and provide information on all local attractions.

SCHEDULING CONSIDERATIONS

The world-famous Winchester Cathedral Choir sings at all main services, including Evensong, held Monday though Saturday at 5:30pm and Sunday at 3:30pm. Visitors are welcome to attend.

GETTING THERE

BY TRAIN

Frequent, direct train service from London's Waterloo Station makes getting to Winchester fast and easy. Service begins at 6:42am and runs hourly; trains return to London until 10:13pm. The trip takes just over 1 hour; a day return ticket costs £19 ($31). For train schedules and information, call **National Rail Enquiries** at ✆ **08457/484-950.**

BY BUS

National Express (✆ **0990/808-080**) runs several buses a day from London's Victoria Coach Station. The fastest trip takes 2 hours (the longest, over 4 hr.); a ticket costs £12 ($19) return. The bus lets you off on Broadway, in the center of town.

BY CAR

If you're driving from London, take the M3 to Junction 9. You can't drive in the town center, but there are 29 car parks, including two on the east side of the cathedral. Convenient long-term car parks are located on Friarsgate, Chesil Street, Cattle Market, Durngate, Gladstone Street, St. Peters, and Worthy Lane.

GETTING AROUND

The center of town is about a half-mile from the station. To get there, you can easily walk (10 min.), hop on a white Park and Ride bus

(20p/30¢), or take a taxi (about £3.50/$6) from the rank outside the station. If you want to reserve a taxi, call **Wessex** (© **01962/877-749**) or **Wintax** (© **01962/878-727**). Anyone can use Park and Ride buses around town for the 20p (30¢) rate along the circuit of stops: Broadway, Brooks, Jewry Street, Castle, Station, City Road, North Walls, and Broadway.

2 A Day in Winchester

Winchester is a walking city par excellence, with all sorts of fascinating corners. The following tour hits the main sights and takes about 2 hours, longer if you linger:

Begin your tour at ❶ **Winchester Cathedral** (© **01962/853-224**), in the center of town. One of Europe's greatest cathedrals, the 900-year-old structure is the repository of many historic treasures. The cathedral you see today was begun in 1079 and has the longest nave in Europe. Jane Austen's grave is a simple, stone-floor marker in the north aisle, near a 12th-century font made of Tournai marble carved with stories of St. Nicholas, the patron saint of pawnbrokers long before he became known as Old Saint Nick. Mortuary chests containing the remains of Saxon kings and bishops sit atop the 15th-century Great Screen. In all, 12 English kings lie here, indicative of Winchester's long reign as capital of Wessex and England after the Norman Conquest. The beautiful choir stalls were carved in about 1308. The Winchester Bible, an extraordinary illuminated manuscript, is displayed in the library. Suggested donation for admission is £3.50 ($6). The cathedral is open daily from 7:15am to 6pm; free 50-minute tours are given at 11am and 3pm Monday through Saturday.

Adjacent to the cathedral is the ❷ **Deanery,** formed from 13th-century buildings that belonged to the Priory of St. Swithin (which stood here before Henry VIII dissolved all the monasteries in 1539). ❸ **Cheyney Court,** the picturesque half-timbered porter's lodge beside the ancient priory gate (King's Gate) was formerly the bishop of Winchester's courthouse. The Deanery and Cheyney Court buildings are not open to the public.

Walk through King's Gate and turn left onto College Street. Almost immediately you come to ❹ **Jane Austen's House,** with a plaque on it. (The house is not open to the public.) This is where Jane Austen

---

Moments **Evensong**

Sitting in the choir of Winchester Cathedral and listening to Evensong (5:30pm Mon–Sat, 3:30pm Sun) is nothing less than sublime.

---

died on July 18, 1817, at the age of 42. The ailing writer came to Winchester from the nearby village of Chawton (see "More Things to See & Do," below) so she could be close to her doctor. She is buried in Winchester Cathedral. Further down Queen Street are the buildings of ❺ **Winchester College,** the oldest public school in England, founded in 1382. There's no public access to the college.

Follow College Street to the end, turn left, and take the short, lovely walk along the narrow River Itchen, which served as part of the Roman defense system. To your left are the remains of ❻ **Wolvesey Castle,** a 12th-century bishop's palace destroyed during the Civil War of 1642 to 1649. At the end of Bridge Street, you come to the City Bridge, an 1813 reconstruction of a Saxon span built 1,000 years earlier. On the opposite side of the bridge is the ❼ **Winchester City Mill** (✆ **01962/870-057**). You can stop in to have a look at the mill's restored machinery, an exhibition on the history and surroundings, and a pretty island garden that's home to kingfishers, otters, and water voles. The mill is open Saturday and Sunday in March, and Wednesday through Sunday from April to the end of June and from September to October; in July and August it's open daily. Admission is £2 ($3.30).

Turn left on Bridge Street and you come to the famous bronze ❽ **statue of King Alfred the Great** holding his sword aloft. What made Alfred so "great"? Probably that he was an enlightened man in the Dark Ages, and drove off the marauding Danes. A soldier, statesman, and scholar, he made Winchester capital of his southern England kingdom, called Wessex. Winchester remained as powerful and prosperous as London up to and beyond the Norman Conquest of 1066.

Walk down Broadway to The Square, where you find the small, attractive ❾ **City Museum** (✆ **01962/863-064**). A room devoted to Roman Winchester contains a fine Roman mosaic centerpiece. Admission is free. Hours are Monday through Saturday from 10am to 5pm, Sunday from noon to 5pm (Nov–Mar until 4pm and closed Mon).

Continue down High Street and turn left (south) through the Westgate, a fortified medieval gateway. All that remains of once-mighty Winchester Castle is the ❿ **Great Hall** (✆ **01962/846-476**) on Castle Avenue. The stone hall is famous for displaying what has for centuries been called the "Round Table" of King Arthur and his knights. Looking like a giant Wheel of Fortune, the painted wooden table has hung here for some 600 years. The hall is open daily 10am to 5pm (until 4pm on winter weekends) and admission is free.

MORE THINGS TO SEE & DO

If you're a Jane Austen fan, you might enjoy a visit to **Jane Austen's House** (✆ **01420/83262**) in Chawton, about 17 miles (28km)

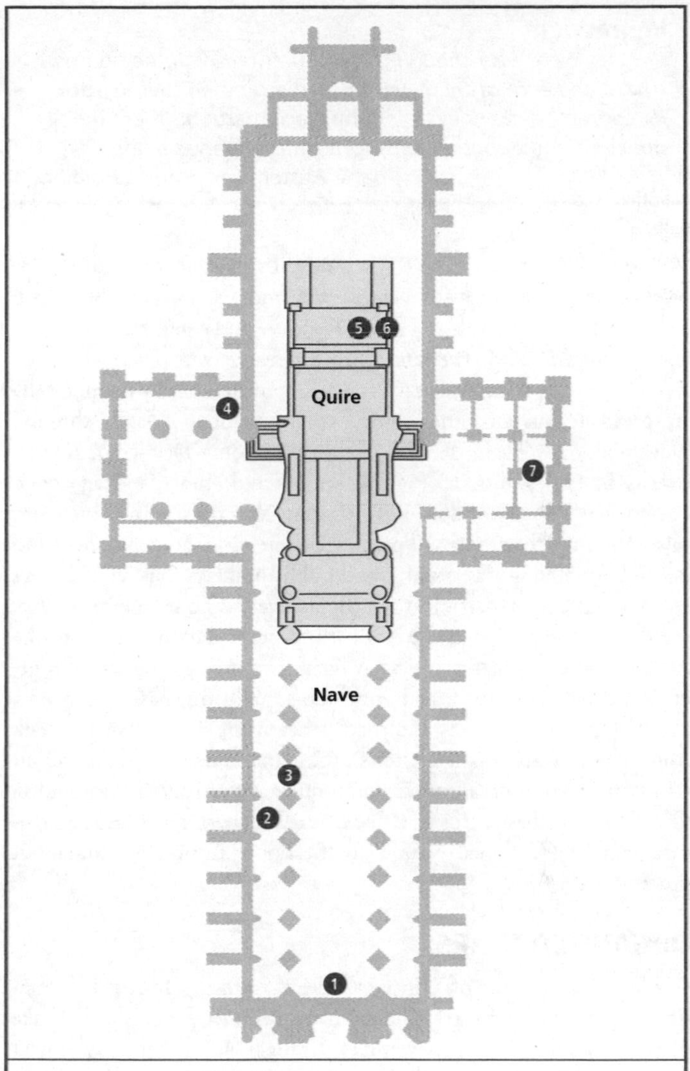

1 West Door & stairs to Treasury
2 Jane Austen's grave
3 Font
4 Entrance to Crypt
5 High Altar and Great Screen
6 Ancient kings' and bishops' mortuary chests
7 Stairs to Cathedral Library & Triforium Gallery

Impressions

. . . they were wise enough to be contented with the house as it was, and each of them was busy in arranging their particular concerns and endeavoring, by placing around them their books and other possessions, to form themselves a home.

—Jane Austen, *Sense and Sensibility*

northeast of Winchester. The witty novelist lived in this sturdy red-brick Georgian house with her mother and sister from 1809 until 1817, revising her novels *Pride and Prejudice* and *Sense and Sensibility,* and writing *Mansfield Park* and *Emma.* Creatively, this was where she spent the most productive years of her life. Austen family memorabilia is spread throughout the house, which is open March through November daily 11am to 4pm (Sat and Sun only Dec–Feb). Admission is £4 ($6) adults, £3 ($4.80) seniors and students. **Stagecoach Hampshire Bus** (**© 01256/464-501**) no. X64 runs from Winchester bus station to Chawton at 10 past each hour Monday to Saturday and takes about 30 minutes; Sunday and public holidays, bus no. 64 leaves at 20 past the hour starting at 10:20 and every 2 hours thereafter. Ask the driver to drop you at the Alton Butts stop, the one closest to the Austen house. From the bus stop, walk towards the railway bridge, cross the very busy road, and continue straight on, passing a brown tourist sign and following the road beneath the underpass; the walk from the bus stop to Jane Austen's House in Chawton will take about 15 minutes. For more information, inquire at the Tourist Information Centre in Winchester. If you drive from Winchester, take A31 northeast; you'll see a signed turnoff to the house from the roundabout junction with A32.

ORGANIZED TOURS

Guided walking tours of Winchester leave from the Tourist Information Centre and make a 1½-hour circuit around the city. Tours take place at the following times: January through March, Saturday only at 11am and 2:30pm; April, Monday through Friday at 11am and Saturday at 11am and 2:30pm; May and June, Monday through Friday at 11am, Saturday at 11am and 2:30pm, and Sunday at 2:30pm; July and August, Monday through Saturday at 11am and 2:30pm, and Sunday at 2:30pm; October, Monday through Saturday at 11am and 2:30pm; and November and December, Saturday at 11am. Tour price is £3 ($4.80).

3 Shopping

Carol Darby Jewellery, 23 Little Minster St. (© **01962/867-671**), is owned by designer Carol Spring, who designed and made the engagement and wedding rings for Princess Anne and Commander Laurence. She can design specialty pieces and make them to your specifications. **Cadogan & James,** 30–31 The Square (© **01962/877-399**), sells clothes from around the British Isles, including colorful cashmeres and waistcoats. **The Clock-Work Shop,** 6a Parchment St. (© **01962/842-331**), stocks a large selection of restored antique clocks and barometers. Food, flowers, and crafts are found at **Winchester Street Market** (© **01962/848-325**), held Wednesday through Saturday on Middle Brook Street.

4 Where to Dine

Courtyard Café LIGHT MEALS This pleasant cafe right behind the Tourist Information Centre is a great, informal spot for a morning cappuccino; homemade soups, salads, and sandwiches at lunchtime; or an afternoon tea.

Winchester Guildhall, Broadway. © **01962/622-177.** Lunch £5–£7 ($8–$11). MC, V. Open daily 9:30am–5pm.

Cathedral Refectory LIGHT MEALS Located behind a medieval wall next to the cathedral, this appealing spot specializes in desserts and meals made from fresh local ingredients.

Inner Close, Cathedral. © **01962/853-224.** Lunch £6–£10 ($10–$16). No credit cards. Mon–Sat 9:30am–5pm; Sun 10am–5pm.

Trip 24

Windsor & Eton

Located in Windsor, Berkshire, 20 miles (32km) from the center of London, **Windsor Castle** is one of the queen's official residences. Constructed some 900 years ago by William the Conqueror, the imposing castle with its skyline of towers and battlements rises from the center of the 4,800-acre (1,920-hectare) Great Park. Eton, a town right across the Thames from Windsor, is the site of Eton College, one of the most exclusive boys' schools in the world.

Windsor & Eton

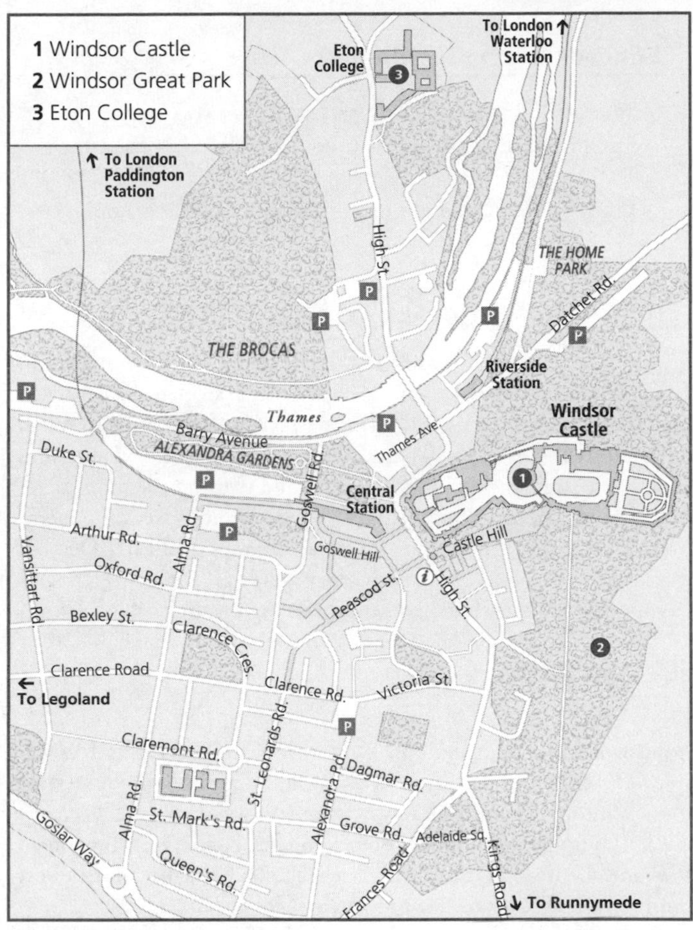

If you're traveling with children, you may want to combine your trip to the castle with a visit to nearby Legoland.

1 Essentials

VISITOR INFORMATION

The **Royal Windsor Information Centre,** 24 High St. (© **01753/743-900;** www.windsor.gov.uk), can provide detailed information about Windsor, Eton, and nearby attractions such as Legoland and Runnymede. The center is open daily year-round from 10am to 5pm (to 4pm Oct–Mar and most Sun; to 5:30pm July and Aug).

Windsor & Eton Highlights

- Touring 900-year-old Windsor Castle.
- Strolling through Windsor Great Park and alongside the Thames.
- Visiting Eton, England's most prestigious public school.

SCHEDULING CONSIDERATIONS

Windsor Castle is open year-round, but visiting hours are subject to change at short notice; be sure to verify that it's open, especially in June when there are many official engagements. If you want to watch the 11am Changing of the Guard from outside the castle, you need to be on High Street by 10:50am; keep in mind that the ceremony takes place on alternate days August through March and never on Sunday. Eton College is open to visitors from late March until early October (closed May 28–June 17), with daily guided tours at 2:15 and 3:15pm. Legoland is closed November through March.

GETTING THERE

BY TRAIN

Windsor has two train stations, Windsor Central Station and Windsor and Eton Riverside Station, both of them about a 10-minute walk from Windsor Castle. **Thames Trains** (www.thamestrains.co.uk) operate hourly or more often from London's Paddington Station to **Windsor Central Station** with a change at Slough. **South West Trains** (www.swtrains.co.uk) operates a direct 55-minute service from London's Waterloo Station to **Windsor & Eton Riverside Station.** Service begins at 7:42am on weekdays from Waterloo, with trains departing Windsor for London until 8:43pm. The day return fare is £6.50 ($10). For train information and schedules, call **National Rail Enquiries** (✆ **08457/484-950**).

BY BUS

Greenline (✆ **0870/6087261;** www.greenline.co.uk) has frequent direct bus service starting at 7:45am from London's Victoria Coach Station to Windsor (and Legoland). Buses depart as often as every 15 minutes for the journey, which takes from 55 minutes to 1 hour and 15 minutes. A "Days Out" return ticket costs £8 ($13) for adults, £4 ($6) for children.

BY CAR

If you're driving from London, take M4 west. Windsor is a historic town, and parking is carefully managed. You'll find outdoor and indoor car parks as you approach the town center. Follow the LONG STAY signs for cheaper all-day parking. Windsor's Park and Ride, based at Legoland, provides daily bus service into the town center every 30 minutes or more frequently during the Park and Ride's open season.

GETTING AROUND

Walking is the best way to see Windsor and the town of Eton. A hop-on/hop-off bus service makes a circuit of all the main sights in town. (See "Organized Tours," below.) There are taxi ranks outside both train stations. If you want to reserve a cab, call **Windsor Radio** (© **01753/677-677**) or **5 Star** (© **01753/858-888**).

2 A Day in Windsor & Eton

Start your day in Windsor at the town's main attraction, ❶ **Windsor Castle** (© **01753/868-286**), one of three official residences of the queen and home to the sovereign for over 900 years. The castle (visible and signposted from both train stations) is the largest inhabited castle in the world and the oldest in continuous occupation. No other royal residence has played such an important role in the nation's history. When the queen is in residence, the Royal Standard flies from the Round Tower. At all other times you will see the Union Flag.

On a self-guided tour you can visit the **State Apartments,** from the intimate chambers of Charles II to the enormous Waterloo Chamber, built to commemorate the victory over Napoléon in 1815. All are furnished with important works of art from the Royal Collection and are open year-round. Open from October until late March, the **semi-state**

Royal Remains at Windsor

St. George's Chapel in Windsor Castle is one of the finest ecclesiastical buildings in England and the final resting place of 10 English monarchs, including Edward IV; Henry VIII and his third wife, Jane Seymour (who died in childbirth in 1537); Charles I; George V and his wife, Queen Mary; and George VI. Construction of the chapel began in 1475 and took 50 years to complete. St. George's is the Chapel of the Most Noble Order of the Garter, Britain's highest order of chivalry, founded by Edward III in 1348. The Albert Memorial Chapel, just beyond St. George's Chapel, was converted by Queen Victoria into a memorial to her husband, Prince Albert, who died in 1861.

---

rooms were created by George IV in the 1820s as part of a new series of Royal Apartments for his personal occupation, and they continue to be used by the queen for official entertaining. Damaged in a 1992 fire, they have been restored to their original appearance and contain furniture and works of art chosen by George IV. The semi-state rooms include the Green Drawing Room, Crimson Drawing Room, State Dining Room, and Octagon Dining Room. In a separate area of the castle, you'll find **Queen Mary's Dollhouse,** a marvelous miniature palace designed by the architect Sir Edwin Lutyens as a present for Queen Mary (wife of King George V) in 1921. Windsor Castle opens daily at 9:45am; November through February, it closes at 4:15pm (last entry 3pm); March through October, it closes at 5:30pm (last entry 4pm). It's closed March 28, June 16, and December 25 and 26. Admission is £12 ($19) for adults, £9.50 ($15) for seniors and students, and £6 ($10) for children under 17.

The **Changing of the Guard** is one of the highlights of a visit to Windsor. The guards are usually accompanied by a band, although this is subject to weather conditions. April through July, the ceremony takes place at 11pm Monday through Saturday (on alternate days the rest of the year). The guards can be watched as they march up High Street and into the castle, but to see the actual ceremony, you need to be inside the castle (ticket required).

From the castle, walk down Castle Hill and follow High Street south to Park Street, which takes you to Long Walk, a pedestrian walkway through 4,800-acre (1,920-hectare) ❷ **Windsor Great Park** (✆ **01753/743-900**), open year-round from dawn to dusk. The current contours of the park, once a favored hunting spot for Saxon kings, were established in the 1360s. The park today is a perfect place for picnics, walking, and cycling. A footpath map of the park is available from the Royal Windsor Information Centre.

To explore the town of **Eton** and its famous school, stroll north on Windsor High Street and follow it as it becomes Thames Street, crosses the river, and becomes Eton High Street. Eton High Street leads you to the entrance of ❸ **Eton College** (✆ **01753 671177;** www.etoncollege.co.uk), founded in 1440 by King Henry VI to provide free education for poor scholars who would go on to study at King's College, Cambridge. Over the centuries, the school has expanded to about 1,280 boys ages 13 to 18 who are admitted by competitive examination, and has become one of the most exclusive schools in the world. Some 18 former British prime ministers have been educated here. The cloisters, the chapel, the oldest classroom in the college, and the Museum of Eton Life are all open to visitors daily: March 27 to April 22 and June 28 to September 2, from10:30am to 4:30pm; April 23 to June 27 and September 3 to October 5, from 2 to

Fun Fact **Dress Code**

Strolling down Eton High Street, you may see some boys wearing black tailcoats and waistcoats and pinstriped trousers. They're Eton boys, and they're wearing the School Dress, started in the 1850s and still in effect today.

4:30pm. Admission is £3.70 ($6) for adults, £2.50 ($4) for children. With a 1-hour guided tour (at 2:15 and 3:15pm), the cost is £4.70 ($8) for adults and £3.50 ($6) for children.

MORE THINGS TO SEE & DO

Legoland Windsor *Kids* Few theme parks are as impressive as Legoland Windsor, or as expensive. It took 20 million of the famous Danish toy company's little plastic building bricks just to create Miniland, one of seven different zones offering over 50 attractions and rides (wet ones, high ones, fast ones, scaled-down ones for little kids). It's a good idea to buy your ticket in advance, because the lines can be extremely long, especially during school holidays. You can buy tickets by phone, online, and at all train stations from Waterloo to Windsor. Winkfield Rd. © **08705/040-404.** www.legoland.co.uk. 1-day admission £23 ($37) adults, £20 ($32) kids under 16 (kids under 3 free), and £17 ($27) seniors. These are peak, at-the-gate prices; you can save several pounds by going off-peak (weekdays, no school holidays). Open daily, Apr–Oct, 10am–6pm (to 5pm Tues–Thurs). A shuttle bus from either Windsor train station is free with a pre-booked Legoland ticket. If you're driving from Windsor, follow Legoland signs from M4 (Junction 6), M3 (Junction 3), and M25 (Junction 13).

Runnymede Located 3 miles (4km) southeast of Windsor on the banks of the Thames, Runnymede is the famous meadow where King John sealed the Magna Carta in 1215, establishing the principle of the constitutional monarchy and affirming the individual's right to justice and liberty. In 1957 the American Bar Association erected a memorial to commemorate the fact that the American Constitution is based on the Magna Carta. Nearby, on an acre of ground given to the U.S. by Queen Elizabeth, is a memorial erected in 1965 to the memory of former U.S. president John F. Kennedy. High on the hill is a memorial to the men and women of the Air Forces of the British Commonwealth who lost their lives in World War II. Runnymede is a peaceful place with magnificent views across the Thames Valley. A boat trip to Runnymede makes a fun excursion: **French Brothers** (© **01735/851-900;** www.boat-trips.co.uk) provides service from Windsor to Runnymede on Wednesday and Friday through Sunday at 4pm, from the last week in April to the third week in September. The fare is £7.70 ($12) return.

On the A308, 3 miles (4km) southeast of Windsor. Free admission. Open daily, dawn–dusk. By car, take the A308 from Windsor towards Staines.

ORGANIZED TOURS

City Sightseeing Open Top Tour (© **01708/865-656;** www.city-sightseeing.com) offers guided bus tours through Windsor, Old Windsor, and Eton. Buses depart year-round (every 15–60 min., depending on the season) from outside Windsor Castle beside the statue of Queen Victoria. The complete loop tour lasts an hour but tickets are valid all day, and you can hop on and off along the route as often as you wish. The tickets, available at the Information Centre or on the bus, cost £6 ($10) for adults, £5 ($8) for seniors and students.

Orchard Poyle Carriage Rides (© **01784/435-983**) are a fun and elegant way to tour Windsor in a horse-drawn carriage. You're taken along High Street, into Park Street, then down the Long Walk into Windsor Great Park. Carriage rides are available year-round from 12:30 to 5:30pm (later in summer), subject to weather conditions. The cost is £19 ($30) per carriage for a 30-minute ride, £39 ($62) per carriage for a 1-hour ride. The carriage collects visitors from High Street, opposite the Harte and Garter Hotel in front of the castle wall, to the left of the statue of Queen Victoria. In high season, it's a good idea to book in advance.

French Brothers Boats Ltd (© **01735/851-900;** www.boat-trips.co.uk) offer 35-minute and 2-hour boat rides from the promenade, next to the bridge over to Eton. River trips are subject to weather conditions, but they generally operate daily from the third week in February through October and into November. The 35-minute trips (£4.40/$7) run every half hour between 11am and 5pm from Easter onwards; 2-hour trips (£6.80/$11) are also available at 1:30pm and 2:30pm.

OUTDOOR ACTIVITIES

The splendid 180-mile (288km) **Thames Path National Trail,** which begins at Thames Head near Kemble in the Cotswolds and runs all the way to the Thames Barrier, east of London, passes through Windsor. You'll find lovely paths on both sides of the river.

With its Great Park and paved riverside paths, Windsor is a great place for biking. You can rent bicycles for a half or full day at **Windsor Roller Rink & Cycle Hire,** Alexander Gardens (© **01753/830-220**).

3 Shopping

Windsor Royal Station is a compact shopping area with designer-name shops. **High Street/Thames Street** in Windsor has many small shops. **Peascod Street** has larger stores, and boutiques line **St. Leonard's Road.** Eton's historic half-mile **High Street** has a diverse range of small family businesses, including clothing boutiques, jewelers, bookshops, art galleries, and gift shops.

4 Where to Dine

Gilbey's Bar & Restaurant WINE BAR This specialist importer sells its French wines at shop prices alongside bottles from its own English vineyard. The bar menu is delicious and reasonable. Try a starter of soup with crusty bread, followed by smoked haddock fishcakes. In the summer, you can eat out in the garden.

82–83 High St., Eton. ✆ **01753/854-921.** Bar main courses £7.95 ($13); 2-course set menu £10 ($16). AE, DC, MC, V. Mon–Fri noon–2:30pm; Sat–Sun noon–3pm; daily 6–11pm.

Trip 25

York

York, 195 miles (314km) north of London, is close enough for a day trip by fast train but worlds apart in character. One of the most historic cities in England, it began life as a Roman fort and settlement known as Eboracum. After the Romans left, York became a thriving Viking settlement called Jorvik. And finally, after the Norman Conquest, it became York, Queen of the North. Enormous York Minster, the largest Gothic

York

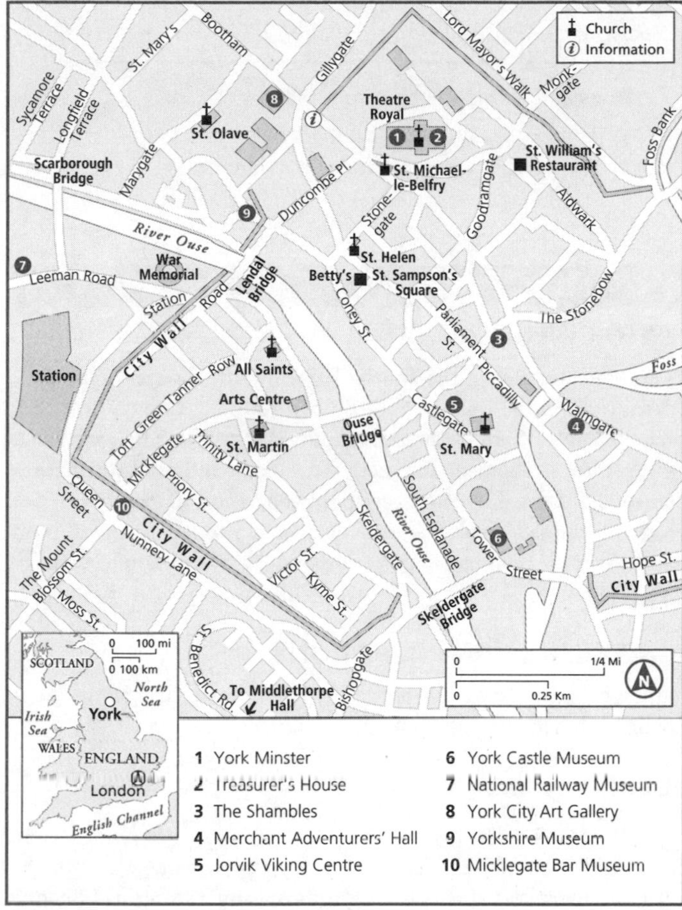

structure north of the Alps, dominates the city. And, amazingly, 800-year-old walls and fortified gateways still girdle the old town center, making York the best-preserved medieval walled city in England. You can soak up the city's history while exploring its maze of ancient streets and hidden alleyways, known as *snickelways.* Most of York's attractions can be visited in a day, but there's plenty here to induce an overnight stay. (See our hotel recommendations at the end of this chapter.) You may want to combine your trip to York with a visit to Castle Howard, one of Yorkshire's stateliest of stately homes, located just a few miles east.

York Highlights

- Marveling at magnificent York Minster.
- Walking along the circuit of medieval walls.
- Exploring York's ancient streets and lanes.

1 Essentials

VISITOR INFORMATION

A convenient branch of the **Tourist Information Centre** (no phone), located right in the train station, is open Monday through Saturday from 9:30am to 5pm (to 6pm in summer), and Sunday from 10am and 4pm (to 4:30pm in summer). The main **Tourist Information Centre,** De Grey Rooms, Exhibition Square (✆ **01904/621-756;** www.york-tourism.co.uk), is open Monday through Saturday from 9am to 5pm (to 6pm in summer), and Sunday from 10am to 4pm (to 5pm in summer). This branch is near York Minster.

SCHEDULING CONSIDERATIONS

You might want to attend Evensong in York Minster at 5:30pm Monday through Saturday and 3:30pm on Sunday.

GETTING THERE

BY TRAIN

The only way to make York a viable day trip is to take one of the super-fast intercity trains that leave hourly from 7am from London's King's Cross Station for the 2-hour trip to York's Rougier Street Station; returning trains depart York hourly until 8pm. The cheapest super-saver fare is £64 ($102) return. For train schedules and information, call **National Rail Enquiries** (✆ **08457/484-950**). The train station is a 5-minute walk from York's historic center.

BY BUS

National Express buses (✆ **0990/808-080**) are considerably cheaper than trains at £28 ($45) return, but the trip to York takes a minimum of 5 hours.

BY CAR

If you're driving from London, take the M1 expressway north to Junction 45, east of Leeds, and from there continue northeast on A64 to York.

GETTING AROUND

The historic city center, where you will want to spend your time, is mostly pedestrianized and easily walkable. If you need a taxi, contact **Station Taxis** (✆ **01904/623-332**).

2 A Day in York

Begin your explorations at awesome ❶ **York Minster,** Minster Yard (✆ **01904/557-216**). The largest Gothic cathedral in northern Europe, it was built between 1220 and 1472 and contains half of all the medieval stained glass in England. A 15th-century choir screen decorated with statues of 15 kings of England, from William I (the Conqueror) to Henry VI, separates the nave from the choir. In the south transept, you can descend into the undercroft, where excavations have revealed the Roman basilica that stood here nearly 2,000 years ago. From the nave, a separate entrance leads to the 13th-century octagonal chapter house, filled with fine stone carvings and medieval glass. Admission to the church and chapter house is by donation; admission to the crypt, undercroft, and treasury is £3.80 ($6) for adults, £1.80 ($2.90) for children 5 to 15. The minster and chapter house are open daily from 7am to 6pm (to 6:30pm in Apr, 7:30pm in May, 8:30pm June–Aug, 8pm in Sept, and 7pm in Oct). The crypt, undercroft, treasury, and tower are open Monday to Saturday from 10am to 4pm, later in summer.

Next to the cathedral, in Minster Yard, stands an elegant town house known as ❷ **Treasurer's House** (✆ **01904/624-247**). Built in 1620 to house the treasurers of York Minster, the house was extensively remodeled during the Victorian era. Inside are beautiful period rooms with collections of 17th- and 18th-century furniture, glass, and china. The house is open April through October, Saturday through Thursday from 10:30am to 5pm. Admission is £3.50 ($6) for adults, £1.75 ($2.80) for children 5 to 15.

From the cathedral, walk southeast on High Petergate and Low Petergate, and you'll come to one of England's most famous medieval streets, ❸ **The Shambles.** Up until 150 years ago, The Shambles was a street where butchers displayed their finest cuts in open windows on wide shelves called *shammels.* Today, this narrow winding lane with buildings so close they shut out the light is filled with gift shops.

Follow the Shambles to Pavement, turn south, and then turn east on Piccadilly to reach the ❹ **Merchant Adventurers' Hall** (✆ **01904/654-818**), one of England's largest and best-preserved guildhalls. This 14th-century stone and half-timbered structure, with a great hall, a hospital, and a chapel, belonged to York's most powerful guild, the Merchant Adventurers. (They controlled trade into and out of the

Fun Fact Guy Fawkes: York's Infamous Son

Who, you may ask, was Guy Fawkes (1570–1606), and what does he have to do with the fireworks set off throughout England on November 5? Guy, born in York, was the most famous guy behind the Gunpowder Plot, a conspiracy of Catholic extremists to blow up Protestant King James and the Houses of Parliament. On November 4, 1605, poor Guy was caught red-handed in the Palace of Westminster. The treasonous plot, and Guy Fawkes's subsequent execution, gave rise to a popular rhyme:

> Please to remember / The 5th November:
> Gunpowder, Treason and Plot.
> We know of no reason / Why Gunpowder Treason
> Should ever be forgot.

Every year since 1605, on November 5, towns, villages, and cities throughout England light bonfires, toss firecrackers, and parade or burn an effigy of Guy Fawkes to celebrate his failure to blow up the king and the parliament. Guy Fawkes Night is perhaps the longest-running tradition in England, even though the religious and royalist sentiments that inspired it have long vanished.

city.) It's open Monday through Thursday 9am to 5pm, Friday and Saturday 9am to 3pm, and Sunday noon to 4pm. (Oct–Mar, it's open Mon–Sat 9am–3pm.) Admission is £2 ($3.20) for adults, £1.70 ($2.75) for seniors/students.

Backtrack on Piccadilly to Coppergate, where you turn south and then turn east on Castlegate to the ❺ **Jorvik Viking Centre** (✆ **01904/643-211**). There you can hop into one of the time cars and be transported back to A.D. 948, when Eric Bloodaxe was king and York was Jorvik, a thriving Viking port and trading town. The scenes you see—of village life, market stalls, crowded houses, and the wharf—are meticulous re-creations based on archaeological finds in this area; even the heads and faces of the animatronic characters were modeled on Viking skulls. Jorvik is open daily from 9am to 5:30pm (Nov–Mar until 4:30pm). Admission is £6.95 ($11) for adults, £6.10 ($10) for seniors and students, and £5.10 ($8) for children 5 to 15.

Continue on Castlegate to ❻ **York Castle Museum** (✆ **01904/653-611**), the most popular folk museum in the country. Using a treasure trove of now-vanished everyday objects, the exhibitions re-create slices of life from 400 years of past epochs. The museum is open daily 9:30am to 5pm. Admission is £6 ($10) for adults, £3.50 ($6) for children 5 to 15.

MORE THINGS TO SEE & DO

7 **National Railway Museum** *Kids* This museum devoted to Britain's railroads is a bit of a hike from the city center, but well worth the effort. The earliest train cars on display date from the 1840s and look like stagecoaches on tracks. You can peek into the windows of private royal coaches, from Queen Victoria's of 1869 to Queen Elizabeth's streamlined carriage, used until 1977.

Leeman Rd. ✆ **01904/621-261.** Free admission. Daily 10am–6pm.

8 **York City Art Gallery** Seven centuries of western European painting and an outstanding collection of 20th-century studio pottery are displayed.

Exhibition Sq. ✆ **01904/551-861.** Free admission. Daily 10am–5pm.

9 **Yorkshire Museum** Set in 10 acres (4 hectares) of landscaped gardens amid the ruins of St. Mary's Abbey, this museum gives a solid presentation of Yorkshire's history from 2 millennia ago up through the 16th century, with displays of elegant Roman jewelry, mosaics, Viking swords and battleaxes, and Anglo-Saxon silver.

Museum Gardens in the center of York. ✆ **01904/551-800.** Admission £4 ($6) adults, £2.50 ($4) children 5–15. Daily 10am–5pm.

10 **Micklegate Bar Museum** Housed in an 800-year-old fortified tower, this tiny museum looks at the social history of the gate in a quirky, humorous light.

Micklegate Bar. ✆ **01904/634-436.** Admission £1.50 ($2.40) adults, £1 ($1.65) seniors and students. Feb–Oct, daily 9am–5pm; Nov–Dec, Sat–Sun 9am–dusk; closed Jan.

ORGANIZED TOURS

The **York Association of Voluntary Guides** (✆ **01904/640-780**) offers free, 2-hour guided tours of the city. The tours depart daily, year-round, at 10:15am from the Tourist Information Centre in Exhibition Square in the city center. Additional tours are offered at 2:15

Moments **How the Other Half Rides**

Take a peek through the windows of Queen Victoria's ornate private railway carriage, on display in the National Railway Museum. When the queen wished to move from one car to the next, the driver had to stop the train. What a hoot!

---

and 6:45pm in summer. You don't need to make a reservation; just show up.

Guide Friday (✆ **01904/625-618;** www.guidefriday.com) runs open-top, double-decker tour buses on a circuit of all the main sights in York (1 hr. total). The ticket, valid all day so you can hop on and off as you wish, costs £7.50 ($12) for adults, £5 ($8) for students, £3 ($4.80) for children 5 to 15. The buses run year-round from about 9:30am to 5pm; you can board at the train station and buy your ticket from the driver.

Departing from the pier below Lendal Bridge, **York Boat** (✆ **01904/647-204;** www.yorkboat.co.uk) provides a 45-minute tour with live commentary that nicely complements a walking tour. February 9 through November 24, at least four boats depart each day; you can buy your ticket on board. The cost is £6 ($10) for adults, £5.50 ($9) for seniors.

OUTDOOR ACTIVITIES

Fortified gateways (or "bars") that still serve as entrances into the old part of town are found along the almost 3 miles (4km) of medieval walls enclosing the center of York. A path (open daily 8am to dusk) runs along the top of the walls, with plenty of great views along the way. You find stairways up to the top of the walls at the four gates. A good place to start a wall walk is Micklegate, the southern entry used by royalty.

3 Shopping

High-end shops, including designer clothes boutiques and fine jewelry, are found on **Swinegate,** a street that was once a hog market. The **Quarter** area around Swinegate is known for its independent, one-of-a-kind shops. **Newgate Market,** between Parliament Street and The Shambles (✆ **01904/551-355**), is York's biggest open-air market, open daily with over 100 stalls selling crafts, clothes, candles, you name it. If you're looking for antiques, head over to **The Red House Antiques Centre,** 1 Duncombe Place (the street runs south from York Minster; ✆ **01904/637-000**), where over 60 dealers sell quality merchandise in a beautiful Georgian building.

4 Where to Dine

Betty's TRADITIONAL ENGLISH/SWISS/TEAS Founded in 1919, Betty's is a wonderfully old-fashioned Art Nouveau tearoom-patisserie-restaurant. A dozen or so hot dishes, both fish and meat, are available. The pastries, all made according to secret recipes, are superb. At the shop in front, you can buy specialties such as Yorkshire fat rascals: warm scones with citrus peel, almonds, and cherries.

6–8 St. Helen's Sq. ✆ **01904/659-142.** Main courses £6–£8 ($10–$13); cream tea £5.50 ($9). AE, MC, V. Daily 9am–9pm.

St. William's Restaurant TRADITIONAL/MODERN BRITISH For an affordable lunch, dinner, or tea, check out this small, attractive restaurant in front of St. William's College at the east end of York Minster. The menu changes daily but always has some delicious choices, such as wild mushroom and leek risotto, pork loin wrapped in Cumbrian ham, or roast loin of venison. This is a good spot for a simple cappuccino or an afternoon cream tea with scones and cakes.

3 College St. ✆ **01904/634-830.** Lunch buffet £7.95 ($13), fixed-price dinner £15–£18 ($24–$29). AE, DC, MC, V. Daily 10am–5pm and 6:30–9:30pm.

5 Extending Your Stay

Middlethorpe Hall One of the country's finest hotels, Middlethorpe Hall is set in a 26-acre (10-hectare) park, 1½ miles (2.4km) south of York. Built in 1699, it was the residence of Lady Mary Wortley Montagu, a famous diarist of the early 18th century. The hotel offers a high standard of personal service and comfort and features beautifully restored rooms, lovely gardens, a health spa, and a fine restaurant.

Bishopthorpe Rd., York YO23 2GB. ✆ **800/260-8338** in the U.S., or 01904/641-241. Fax 01904/620-176. www.middlethorpe.com. £160–£210 ($256–$336) double. AE, MC, V.

Appendix A: England in Depth

by Darwin Porter & Danforth Prince

The history of England is an inexhaustible subject. Huge tomes have been written on individual monarchs, colorful personalities, architectural styles, and historical epochs. This overview of England covers the bare essentials and should help put into context some of the historical landmarks you'll be visiting.

1 History 101

FROM MURKY BEGINNINGS TO ROMAN OCCUPATION Britain was probably split off from the continent of Europe some 8 millennia ago by continental drift and other natural forces. The early inhabitants, the Iberians, were later to be identified with stories of fairies, brownies, and "little people." These are the people whose

Dateline

- **54 B.C.** Julius Caesar invades England.
- **A.D. 43** Romans conquer England.
- **410** Jutes, Angles, and Saxons form small kingdoms in England.
- **500–1066** Anglo-Saxon kingdoms fight off Viking warriors.
- **1066** William, duke of Normandy, invades England, defeats Harold II at the Battle of Hastings.

ingenuity and enterprise are believed to have created Stonehenge, but despite that great and mysterious monument, little is known about them.

The Iberians were replaced by the iron-wielding Celts, whose massive invasions around 500 B.C. drove the Iberians back to the Scottish Highlands and Welsh mountains, where some of their descendants still live today.

In 54 B.C., Julius Caesar invaded England, but the Romans did not become established there until A.D. 43. They went as far as Caledonia (now Scotland), where they gave up, leaving that land to "the painted ones," or the warring Picts. The wall built by Emperor Hadrian across the north of England marked the northernmost reaches of the Roman Empire. During almost 4 centuries of occupation, the Romans built roads, villas, towns, walls, and fortresses; they farmed the land and introduced first their pagan religions, then Christianity. Agriculture and trade flourished.

FROM ANGLO-SAXON RULE TO THE NORMAN CONQUEST When the Roman legions withdrew, around A.D. 410, they left the country open to waves of invasions by Jutes, Angles, and Saxons, who established themselves in small kingdoms throughout the former Roman colony. From the 8th to the 11th centuries, the Anglo-Saxons contended with Danish raiders for control of the land.

- **1154** Henry II, first of the Plantagenets, launches their rule (which lasts until 1399).
- **1215** King John signs the Magna Carta at Runnymede.
- **1337** Hundred Years' War between France and England begins.
- **1485** Battle of Bosworth Field ends the War of the Roses between the Houses of York and Lancaster; Henry VII launches the Tudor dynasty.
- **1534** Henry VIII brings the Reformation to England and dissolves the monasteries.
- **1558** The accession of Elizabeth I ushers in an era of exploration and a renaissance in science and learning.
- **1588** Spanish Armada defeated.
- **1603** James VI of Scotland becomes James I of England, thus uniting the crowns of England and Scotland.
- **1620** Pilgrims sail from Plymouth on the *Mayflower* to found a colony in the New World.
- **1629** Charles I dissolves Parliament, ruling alone.
- **1642–49** Civil War between Royalists and Parliamentarians; the Parliamentarians win.
- **1649** Charles I beheaded, and England is a republic.
- **1653** Oliver Cromwell becomes Lord Protector.
- **1660** Charles II restored to the throne with limited power.
- **1665–66** Great Plague and Great Fire decimate London.
- **1688** James II, a Catholic, is deposed, and William and Mary come to the throne, signing a bill of rights.
- **1727** George I, the first of the Hanoverians, assumes the throne.
- **1756–63** In the Seven Years' War, Britain wins Canada from France.

continues

By the time of the Norman Conquest, the Saxon kingdoms were united under an elected king, Edward the Confessor. His successor was to rule less than a year before the Norman invasion.

The date 1066 is familiar to every English schoolchild. It marked an epic event, the only successful military invasion of Britain in history, and one of England's great turning points: King Harold, the last Anglo-Saxon king, was defeated at the Battle of Hastings; and William of Normandy was crowned William I.

One of William's first acts was to order a survey of the land he had conquered, assessing all property in the nation for tax purposes. This survey was called the *Domesday Book,* or "Book of Doom," as some pegged it. The resulting document was completed around 1086 and has been a fertile sourcebook for British historians ever since.

Norman rule had an enormous impact on English society. All high offices were held by Normans, and the Norman barons were given great grants of lands; they built Norman-style castles and strongholds throughout the country. French was the language of the court for centuries—few people realize that heroes such as Richard the Lionheart probably spoke little or no English.

FROM THE RULE OF HENRY II TO THE MAGNA CARTA In 1154, Henry II, the

- **1775–83** Britain loses its American colonies.
- **1795–1815** The Napoleonic Wars lead, finally, to the Battle of Waterloo and the defeat of Napoleon.
- **1837** Queen Victoria begins her reign as Britain reaches the zenith of its empire.
- **1901** Victoria dies, and Edward VII becomes king.
- **1914–18** England enters World War I and emerges victorious on the Allied side.
- **1936** Edward VIII abdicates to marry an American divorcée.
- **1939–45** In World War II, Britain stands alone against Hitler from the fall of France in 1940 until America enters the war in 1941. Dunkirk is evacuated in 1940; bombs rattle London during the blitz.
- **1945** Germany surrenders. Churchill is defeated; the Labour government introduces the welfare state and begins to dismantle the empire.
- **1952** Queen Elizabeth II ascends the throne.
- **1973** Britain joins the European Union.
- **1979** Margaret Thatcher becomes prime minister.
- **1982** Britain defeats Argentina in the Falklands War.
- **1990** Thatcher is ousted; John Major becomes prime minister.
- **1991** Britain fights with Allies to defeat Iraq.
- **1992** Royals jolted by fire at Windsor Castle and by marital troubles of two of their sons. Britain joins the European Single Market. Deep recession signals the end of the booming 1980s.
- **1994** England is linked to the Continent by rail via the Channel Tunnel, or Chunnel. Tony Blair elected Labour party leader.

first of the Plantagenets, was crowned (reigned 1154–89). This remarkable character in English history ruled a vast empire—not only most of Britain but Normandy, Anjou, Brittany, and Aquitaine in France.

Henry was a man of powerful physique, both charming and terrifying. He reformed the courts and introduced the system of common law, which still operates in moderated form in England today and also influenced the American legal system. But Henry is best remembered for ordering the infamous murder of Thomas Becket, archbishop of Canterbury. Henry, at odds with his archbishop, exclaimed, "Who will rid me of this turbulent priest?" His knights, overhearing and taking him at his word, murdered Thomas in front of the high altar in Canterbury Cathedral.

Henry's wife, Eleanor of Aquitaine, the most famous woman of her time, was no less of a colorful character. She accompanied her first husband, Louis VII of France, on the Second Crusade, and it was rumored that she had a romantic affair at that time with the Saracen leader, Saladin. Domestic and political life did not run smoothly, however, and Henry and Eleanor and their sons were often at odds. The pair has been the subject of many plays and films, including *The Lion in Winter, Becket,* and T. S. Eliot's *Murder in the Cathedral.*

Two of their sons were crowned kings of England. Richard the Lionheart actually spent most of his life outside England, on crusades, or in France. John was forced by his nobles to sign the Magna Carta at Runnymede, in 1215—another date well known to English schoolchildren.

The Magna Carta guaranteed that the king was subject to the rule of law and gave certain rights to the king's subjects, beginning a process that eventually led to the development of parliamentary democracy as it is known in Britain today. This process would have enormous influence on the American colonies many years later. The

- **1996** The IRA breaks a 17-month cease-fire with a truck bomb at the Docklands that claims two lives. Charles and Di divorce. The government concedes a possible link between mad cow disease and a fatal brain ailment afflicting humans; British beef imports face banishment globally.
- **1997** London swings again. The Labour party ends 18 years of Conservative rule with a landslide election victory. The tragic death of Diana, princess of Wales, prompts worldwide outpouring of grief.
- **1998** Prime Minister Tony Blair launches "New Britain"—young, stylish, and informal.
- **1999** England rushes toward the 21st century with the Millennium Dome at Greenwich.
- **2000** London presides over millennium celebration. Gays allowed to serve openly in the military.
- **2001** Foot-and-mouth disease epidemic affects cattle, pigs, and sheep, and brings hard times to the British economy.
- **2002** Queen Elizabeth, the Queen Mother, dies at age 101.
- **2003** Britain backs the U.S. and sends troops to help fight the war in Iraq.

Magna Carta became known as the cornerstone of English liberties, though it only granted liberties to the barons. It took the rebellion of Simon de Montfort half a century later to introduce the notion that the boroughs and burghers should also have a voice and representation.

THE BLACK DEATH & THE WARS OF THE ROSES In 1348, half the population died as the Black Death ravaged England. By the end of the century, the population of Britain had fallen from four million to two million.

England also suffered in the Hundred Years' War, which went on intermittently for more than a century. By 1371, England had lost much of its land on French soil. Henry V, immortalized by Shakespeare, revived England's claims to France, and his victory at Agincourt was notable for making obsolete the forms of medieval chivalry and warfare.

After Henry's death in 1422, disputes arose among successors to the crown that resulted in a long period of civil strife, the Wars of the Roses, between the Yorkists, who used a white rose as their symbol, and the Lancastrians with their red rose. The last Yorkist king was Richard III, who got bad press from Shakespeare, but who is defended to this day as a hero by the people of the city of York. Richard was defeated at Bosworth Field, and the victory introduced England to the first Tudor, the shrewd and wily Henry VII.

THE TUDORS TAKE THE THRONE The Tudors were unlike the kings who had ruled before them. They introduced into England a strong central monarchy with far-reaching powers. The system worked well under the first three strong and capable Tudor monarchs, but it began to break down later when the Stuarts came to the throne.

Henry VIII is surely the most notorious Tudor. Imperious and flamboyant, a colossus among English royalty, he slammed shut the door on the Middle Ages and introduced the Renaissance to England. He is best known, of course, for his treatment of his six wives and the unfortunate fates that befell five of them.

When his first wife, Catherine of Aragon, failed to produce an heir, and his ambitious mistress, Anne Boleyn, became pregnant, he tried to annul his marriage but the pope refused, and Catherine contested the action. Defying the power of Rome, Henry had his marriage with Catherine declared invalid and secretly married Anne Boleyn in 1533.

The events that followed had profound consequences and introduced the religious controversy that was to dominate English politics for the next 4 centuries. Henry's break with the Roman Catholic Church and the formation of the Church of England, with himself as supreme head, was a turning point in English history. It led eventually to the Dissolution of the Monasteries, civil unrest, and much social dislocation. The confiscation of the church's land and possessions brought untold wealth into the king's coffers, wealth that was distributed to a new aristocracy that supported the monarch. In one sweeping gesture, Henry destroyed the ecclesiastical culture of the Middle Ages. Among those executed for refusing to cooperate with Henry's changes was Sir Thomas More, humanist, international man of letters, and author of *Utopia.*

Anne Boleyn bore Henry a daughter, the future Elizabeth I, but failed to produce a male heir. She was brought to trial on a trumped-up charge of adultery and beheaded; in 1536, Henry married Jane Seymour, who died giving birth to Edward VI. For his next wife, Henry looked farther afield and chose Anne of Cleves from a flattering portrait, but she proved disappointing—he called her "The Great Flanders Mare." He divorced her the same year and next picked a pretty young woman from his court, Katherine Howard. She was also beheaded on a charge of adultery but, unlike Anne Boleyn, was probably guilty. Finally, he married an older woman, Catherine Parr, in 1543. She survived him.

Henry's heir, sickly Edward VI (reigned 1547–53), did not live long. He died of consumption—or, as rumor has it, overmedication. He was succeeded by his sister, Mary I (reigned 1553–58), and the trouble Henry had stirred up with the break with Rome came home to roost for the first time. Mary restored the Roman Catholic faith, and her persecution of the adherents of the Church of England earned her the name "Bloody Mary." Some 300 Protestants were executed, many burned alive at the stake. She made an unpopular and unhappy marriage to Philip of Spain; despite her bloody reputation, her life was a sad one.

Elizabeth I (reigned 1558–1603) came next to the throne, ushering in an era of peace and prosperity, exploration, and a renaissance in science and learning. An entire age was named after her: the Elizabethan age. She was the last great and grand monarch to rule England, and her passion and magnetism were said to match her father's. Through her era marched Drake, Raleigh, Frobisher, Grenville, Shakespeare, Spenser, Byrd, and Hilliard. During her reign, she had to face the appalling precedent of ordering the execution of a fellow sovereign, Mary, Queen of Scots. Her diplomatic skills kept war at bay until 1588, when at the apogee of her reign, the Spanish Armada was defeated. She will be forever remembered as "Good Queen Bess."

FROM THE RESTORATION TO THE NAPOLEONIC WARS

The reign of Charles II was the beginning of a dreadful decade that saw London decimated by the Great Plague and destroyed by the Great Fire.

Charles's successor, James II, attempted to return the country to Catholicism, an effort that so frightened the powers-that-be that Catholics were for a long time deprived of their civil rights. James was deposed in the "Glorious Revolution" of 1688 and succeeded by his daughter Mary (1662–94) and William of Orange (1650–1702). (William of Orange was the grandson of Charles I, the tyrannical king whom Cromwell helped depose.) This secured a Protestant succession that has continued to this day. These tolerant and levelheaded monarchs signed a bill of rights, establishing the principle that the monarch reigns not by divine right but by the will of Parliament. William outlived his wife, reigning until 1702.

Queen Anne then came to the throne, ruling from 1702 until her own death in 1714. She was the sister of Mary of Orange and was another daughter of James II. The last of the Stuarts, Anne marked her reign with the most significant event, the 1707 Act of Union with Scotland. She outlived all her children, leaving her throne without an heir.

Upon the death of Anne, England looked for a Protestant prince to succeed her and chose George of Hanover, who reigned from 1714 to 1727. Though he spoke only German and spent as little time in England as possible, he was chosen because he was the great-grandson of James I. Beginning with this "distant cousin" to the throne, the reign of George I marked the beginning of the 174-year rule of the Hanoverians who preceded Victoria.

George I left the running of the government to the English politicians and created the office of prime minister. Under the Hanoverians, the powers of Parliament were extended, and the constitutional monarchy developed into what it is today.

The American colonies were lost under the Hanoverian George III, but other British possessions were expanded: Canada was won from the French in the Seven Years' War (1756–63), British control over India was affirmed, and Captain Cook claimed Australia and New Zealand for England. The British became embroiled in the Napoleonic Wars (1795–1815), achieving two of their greatest victories and acquiring two of their greatest heroes: Nelson at Trafalgar and Wellington at Waterloo.

THE INDUSTRIAL REVOLUTION & THE REIGN OF VICTORIA The mid– to late 18th century saw the beginnings of the Industrial Revolution. This event changed the lives of the laboring class, created a wealthy middle class, and transformed England from a rural, agricultural society into an urban, industrial economy. England was now a world-class financial and military power. Male suffrage was extended, though women were to continue under a series of civil disadvantages for the rest of the century.

Queen Victoria's reign (1837–1901) coincided with the height of the Industrial Revolution. When she ascended the throne, the monarchy as an institution was in considerable doubt, but her 64-year reign, the longest tenure in English history, was an incomparable success.

The Victorian era was shaped by the growing power of the bourgeoisie, the queen and her consort's personal moral stance, and the perceived moral responsibilities of managing a vast empire. During this time, the first trade unions were formed, a public (state) school system was developed, and railroads were built.

Victoria never recovered from the death of her German husband, Albert. He died of typhoid fever in 1861, and the queen never remarried. Though she had many children, she found them tiresome; nonetheless, she was a pillar of family values. One historian said her greatest asset was her relative ordinariness.

Middle-class values ruled Victorian England and were embodied by the queen. The racy England of the past went underground. Our present-day view of England is still influenced by the attitudes of the Victorian era, and we tend to forget that English society in earlier centuries was famous for its rowdiness, sexual license, and spicy scandal.

Victoria's son Edward VII (reigned 1901–10) was a playboy who had waited too long in the wings. He is famous for mistresses, especially Lillie Langtry, and his love of elaborate dinners. During his brief reign, he, too, had an era named after him: the Edwardian age. Under Edward, the country entered the 20th century at the height of its imperial power. At home, the advent of the motorcar and the telephone radically changed social life, and the women's suffrage movement began.

World War I marked the end of an era. It had been assumed that peace, progress, prosperity, empire, and even social improvement would continue indefinitely. World War I and the troubled decades of social unrest, political uncertainty, and the rise of Nazism and fascism put an end to these expectations.

THE WINDS OF WAR World War II began in 1939, and soon thereafter Britain found a new and inspiring leader, Winston Churchill. Churchill led the nation during its "finest hour." From the time the Germans took France, Britain stood alone against Hitler. The evacuation of Dunkirk in 1940, the blitz of London, and the Battle of Britain were dark hours for the British people, and Churchill is remembered for urging them to hold onto their courage. Once the British forces were joined by their American allies, the tide finally turned, culminating in the D-day invasion of German-occupied Normandy. These bloody events are still remembered by many with pride, and with nostalgia for the era when Britain was still a great world power.

The years following World War II brought many changes to England. Britain began to lose its grip on an empire (India became independent in 1947), and the Labour government, which came into power in 1945, established the welfare state and brought profound social change to Britain.

QUEEN ELIZABETH RULES TO THE PRESENT DAY Upon the death of the "wartime king," George VI, Elizabeth II ascended the throne in 1953. Her reign has seen the erosion of Britain's once-mighty industrial power and, in recent years, a severe recession.

Political power has seesawed back and forth between the Conservative and Labour parties. Margaret Thatcher, who became prime minister in 1979, seriously eroded the welfare state and was ambivalent toward the European Union. Her popularity soared during the successful Falklands War, when Britain seemed to recover some of its military glory for a brief time.

Though the queen has remained steadfast and punctiliously has performed her ceremonial duties, rumors about the royal family abounded, and in the year 1992, which Queen Elizabeth labeled an *annus horribilis,* a devastating fire swept through Windsor Castle, the marriages of several of her children crumbled, and the queen agreed to pay taxes for the first time. Prince Charles and Princess Diana agreed to a separation, and there were ominous rumblings about the future of the House of Windsor. By 1994 and 1995, Britain's economy was improving after several glum years, but Conservative prime minister John Major, heir to Margaret Thatcher's legacy, was coming under increasing criticism.

The IRA, reputedly enraged at the slow pace of peace talks, relaunched its reign of terror across London in February 1996, planting a massive bomb that ripped through a building in London's Docklands, injuring more than 100 people and killing two. Shattered, too, was the 17-month cease-fire by the IRA, which brought hope that peace was at least possible. Another bomb went off in Manchester in June.

Headlines about the IRA bombing gave way to another big bomb: the end of the marriage of Princess Diana and Prince Charles. The Wedding of the Century had become the Divorce of the Century. The lurid tabloids had been right all along about this unhappy pair. But details of the $26 million divorce settlement didn't satisfy the curious: Scrutiny of Prince Charles's relationship with Camilla Parker-Bowles, as well as gossip about Princess Diana's love life, continued in the press.

In 1997, the political limelight came to rest on the young Labour leader Tony Blair. From his rock-star acquaintances to his "New Labour" rhetoric, which is chock-full of pop-culture buzzwords, he is a stark contrast to the more staid Major. His media-savvy personality obviously registered with the British electorate. On May 1, 1997, the Labour Party ended 18 years of Conservative rule with a landslide election victory. At age 44, Blair became Britain's youngest prime minister in 185 years, following in the wake of the largest Labour triumph since Winston Churchill was swept out of office at the end of World War II.

Blair's election—which came just at the moment when London was being touted by the international press for its renaissance in art, music, fashion, and dining—had many British entrepreneurs poised and ready to take advantage of what they perceived as enthusiasm for new ideas and ventures. Comparisons to Harold Macmillan and his reign over the Swinging Sixties were inevitable, and insiders agreed that something was in the air.

However, events took a shocking turn in August 1997 when Princess Diana was killed—along with her companion, Harrods heir Dodi al-Fayed—in a high-speed car crash in Paris.

"The People's Princess" continued to dominate many headlines with bizarre conspiracy theories about her death. But the royal family isn't the real force in Britain today. The spotlight remains on Tony Blair, who is moving ahead in streamlining the government.

Blair continues to lead Britain on a program of constitutional reform without parallel in the last century. Critics fear that Blair will one day preside over a "dis-united" Britain, with Scotland breaking away and Northern Ireland forming a self-government.

Of course, the future of the monarchy still remains a hot topic of discussion in Britain. There is little support for doing away with the monarchy in Britain today in spite of wide criticism of the royal family's behavior in the wake of Diana's death. Apparently, if polls are to be believed, some three-quarters of the British populace want the monarchy to continue. Prince Charles is even making a comeback with the British public and has appeared in public—to the delight of the paparazzi—with his longtime mistress, Camilla Parker-Bowles. At the very least, the monarchy is good for the tourist trade, on which Britain is increasingly dependent. And what would the tabloids do without it?

The big news among royal watchers in Britain early in 2002 was the death of Princess Margaret at age 71, followed 7 weeks later by the death of Queen Mother Elizabeth at the age of 101. The most popular royal, the Queen "Mum" was a symbol of courage and dignity, especially during the tumultuous World War II years when London was under bombardment by Nazi Germany. The remains of the Queen Mother were laid to rest alongside her husband's in the George VI Memorial Chapel at St. George's at Windsor Castle. The ashes of Princess Margaret were interred with those of her parents in the same chapel.

At the dawn of the millennium, major social changes occurred in Britain. No sooner had the year 2000 begun than Britain announced a change of its code of conduct for the military, allowing openly gay men and women to serve in the armed forces. The action followed a European court ruling in the fall of 1999 that forbade Britain to discriminate against homosexuals. This change brings Britain in line with almost all other NATO countries, including France, Canada, and Germany. The United States remains at variance with the trend.

After promising beginnings, the 21st century got off to a bad start in Britain. In the wake of mad cow disease flare-ups, the country was swept by a foot-and-mouth disease epidemic that disrupted the country's agriculture and threatened one of the major sources of British livelihoods, its burgeoning tourist industry. After billions of pounds in tourism were lost, the panic has now subsided. The government has intervened to take whatever preventive measures it can.

Following the September 11, 2001, terrorist attacks on New York City and Washington, D.C., Tony Blair and his government joined in a show of support for the U.S. by condemning the aerial bombardments and loss of lives. Not only that, the British joined the war in Afghanistan against the dreaded Taliban. However, by 2003 Blair's backing of George Bush's stance against President Saddam Hussein of Iraq had brought his popularity to an all-time low.

2 Pies, Pudding & Pints: The Lowdown on British Cuisine

The late British humorist George Mikes wrote that "the Continentals have good food; the English have good table manners." But the British no longer deserve their reputation for soggy cabbage and tasteless dishes. Contemporary London—and the country as a whole—boasts many fine restaurants and sophisticated cuisine.

If you want to see what Britain is eating today, just drop in at Harvey Nichol's Fifth Floor in London's Knightsbridge for its dazzling display of produce from all over the globe.

The new buzzword for British cuisine is *magpie,* meaning borrowing ideas from global travels, taking them home, and improving on the original.

WHAT YOU'LL FIND ON THE MENU On any pub menu, you're likely to encounter such dishes as the **Cornish pasty** and **shepherd's pie.** The first, traditionally made from Sunday-meal leftovers and taken by West Country fishers for Monday lunch, consists of chopped potatoes, carrots, and onions mixed together with seasoning and put into a pastry envelope. The second is a deep dish of chopped cooked beef mixed with onions and seasoning, covered with a layer of mashed potatoes, and served hot. Another version is **cottage pie,** which is minced beef covered with potatoes and also served hot. Of course, these beef dishes are subject to availability. In addition to a pasty, Cornwall also gives us **Stargazy Pie**—a deep-dish fish pie with a crisp crust covering a creamy concoction of freshly caught herring and vegetables.

The most common pub meal, though, is the **ploughman's lunch,** traditional farmworker's fare, consisting of a good chunk of local cheese, a hunk of homemade crusty white or brown bread, some butter, and a pickled onion or two, washed down with ale. You'll now find such variations as pâté and chutney occasionally replacing the onions and cheese. Or you might find **Lancashire hot pot,** a stew of mutton, potatoes, kidneys, and onions (sometimes carrots). This concoction was originally put into a deep dish and set on the edge of the stove to cook slowly while the workers spent the day at the local mill.

Among appetizers, called **starters** in England, the most typical are potted shrimp (small buttered shrimp preserved in a jar), prawn cocktail, and smoked salmon. You might also be served pâté or fish pie, which is very light fish pâté. Most menus will feature a variety of soups, including cock-a-leekie (chicken soup flavored with leeks), and perhaps a game soup that has been doused with sherry.

Among the best-known traditional English meals is **roast beef and Yorkshire pudding.** (The pudding is made with a flour base and cooked under the roast, allowing the fat from the meat to drop onto it.) The beef could easily be a large sirloin (rolled loin), which, so the story goes, was named by James I when he was a guest at Houghton Tower, Lancashire. "Arise, Sir Loin," he cried, as he knighted the leg of beef before him with his dagger. Another dish that makes use of a flour base is toad-in-the-hole, in which sausages are cooked in batter. Game, especially pheasant and grouse, is also a staple on British tables.

On any menu, you'll find **fresh seafood:** cod, haddock, herring, plaice, and Dover sole, the aristocrat of flatfish. Cod and haddock are used in making British **fish and chips** (chips are fried potatoes or thick french fries), which the true Briton covers with salt and vinegar. If you like **oysters,** try some of the famous Colchester variety.

The British call desserts **sweets,** though some people still refer to any dessert as **pudding. Trifle** is the most famous English dessert, consisting of sponge cake soaked in brandy or sherry, coated with fruit or jam, and topped with cream custard. A **fool,** such as gooseberry fool, is a light cream dessert whipped up from seasonal fruits. Regional sweets include **northern flitting dumpling** (dates, walnuts, and syrup mixed with other ingredients and made into a pudding that is easily sliced and carried along when you're "flitting" from place to place). Similarly, **hasty pudding,** a Newcastle dish, is supposed to have been invented by people in a hurry to avoid the bailiff. It consists of stale bread, to which dried fruit and milk are added before it is put into the oven.

Cheese is traditionally served after dessert as a savory. There are many regional cheeses, the best known being cheddar, a good, solid, mature cheese. Others are the semi-smooth Caerphilly, from a beautiful part of Wales, and Stilton, a blue-veined, crumbly cheese that's often enjoyed with a glass of port.

ENGLISH BREAKFASTS & AFTERNOON TEA Britain is famous for its enormous breakfast of bacon, eggs, grilled tomato, and fried bread. Some places have replaced this cholesterol festival with a continental breakfast, but you'll still find the traditional morning meal available.

Kipper, or smoked herring, is also a popular breakfast dish. The finest come from the Isle of Man, Whitby, or Loch Fyne, in Scotland. The herrings are split open, placed over oak chips, and slowly cooked to produce a nice pale-brown smoked fish.

Many people still enjoy afternoon tea, which may consist of a simple cup of tea. A formal tea starts with tiny crustless sandwiches filled with cucumber or watercress and proceeds through scones, crumpets with jam or clotted cream, and cakes and tarts—all accompanied by a proper pot of tea.

WHAT TO WASH IT ALL DOWN WITH English pubs serve a variety of cocktails, but their stock-in-trade is beer: brown beer, or bitter; blond beer, or lager; and very dark beer, or stout. The standard English draft beer is much stronger than American beer and is served "with the chill off," because it doesn't taste good cold. Lager is always chilled, whereas stout can be served either way. Beer is always served straight from the tap, in two sizes: half pint (8 oz.) and pint (16 oz.).

One of the most significant changes in English drinking habits has been the popularity of wine bars, and you will find many to try, including some that turn into discos late at night. Britain isn't known for its wine, though it does produce some medium-sweet fruity whites. Its cider, though, is famous—and mighty potent in contrast to the American variety.

Whisky (spelled without the *e*) refers to scotch. Canadian and Irish whiskey (spelled with the *e*) are also available, but only the very best stocked bars have American bourbon and rye.

While you're in England, you may want to try the very English drink called **Pimm's,** a mixture developed by James Pimm, owner of a popular London oyster house in the 1840s. Though it can be consumed on the rocks, it's usually served as a Pimm's Cup—a drink that will have any number and variety of ingredients, depending on which part of the world (or empire) you're in. Here, just for fun, is a typical recipe: Take a very tall glass and fill it with ice. Add a thin slice of lemon (or orange), a cucumber spike (or a curl of cucumber rind), and 2 ounces of Pimm's liquor. Then finish with a splash of either lemon or club soda, 7-Up, or Tom Collins mix.

The English tend to drink everything at a warmer temperature than Americans are used to. So if you like ice in your soda, be sure to ask for lots of it, or you're likely to end up with a measly, quickly melting cube or two.

Appendix B: England's Art & Architecture

by Reid Bramblett

No one artist, period, or museum defines England's art and architecture. You can see the country's art in medieval illuminated manuscripts, Thomas Gainsborough portraits, and Damien Hirst's pickled cows. Its architecture ranges from Roman walls and Norman castles to baroque St. Paul's Cathedral and towering postmodern skyscrapers. This chapter will help you make sense of it all.

1 Art 101

CELTIC & MEDIEVAL (CA. 800 B.C.–16TH CENTURY)

The Celts, mixed with plenty of Scandinavian and Dutch tribes of varying origins, ruled England until the Romans established rule there in A.D. 43. **Celtic art** survived the Roman conquest and medieval Christianity mainly as carved swirls and decorations on the "Celtic Crosses" peppering cemeteries. During the medieval period, colorful

Celtic images and illustrations decorated the margins of Bibles and Gospels, giving the books their moniker **"illuminated manuscripts."**

Important examples and artists of this period include:

- **Wilton Diptych, National Gallery, London.** The first truly important, truly British painting, this diptych (a painting on two hinged panels) was crafted in the late 1390s for Richard II by an unknown artist who combined Italian and northern European influences.
- **Lindisfarne Gospels, British Library, London.** One of Europe's greatest illuminated manuscripts from the 7th century, this work is particularly well crafted and well preserved.
- **Matthew Paris (d. 1259).** A Benedictine monk who illuminated his own writings, Paris put his significant artistic gifts to good use as the official St. Albans Abbey chronicler. Examples of his work are now in London's **British Library** and Cambridge's **Corpus Christi College.**

RENAISSANCE & BAROQUE (16TH–18TH CENTURIES)

The **Renaissance** hit England late, but its museums contain many important Old Master paintings from Italy and Germany. Renaissance means "rebirth"; in this case, it means the renewed use of classical styles and forms originating in ancient Greece and Rome. Artists strove for greater naturalism, using newly developed techniques such as linear perspective. A few foreign Renaissance masters did come to work at the English courts and had an influence on some local artists, but significant Brits didn't emerge until the baroque period.

The **baroque,** a more decorative version of the Renaissance approach, mixes compositional complexity and explosions of dynamic fury, movement, color, and figures with an exaggeration of light and dark, called *chiaroscuro,* and a kind of super-realism based on using peasants as models. The **rococo** period is baroque art gone awry, frothy, and chaotic.

Significant artists of this period include:

- **Pietro Torrigiano (1472–1528).** An Italian Renaissance sculptor, Torrigiano had to flee Florence after breaking the nose of classmate Michelangelo. He ended up in London crafting elaborate tombs for the Tudors in **Westminster Abbey,** including Lady Margaret Beaufort, and Henry VII and Elizabeth of York. London's **Victoria and Albert Museum** preserves Torrigiano's terracotta bust of Henry VII.

- **Hans Holbein the Younger (1497–1543).** A German Renaissance master of penetrating portraits, Holbein the Younger cataloged many significant figures in 16th-century Europe: Sir Thomas More's family (**Nostel Priory** outside Wakefield in West Yorkshire; this may be a copy); Henry VIII and the duke of Norfolk (**Castle Howard** outside York); and Erasmus (whom Holbein knew; **Longford Castle,** Wiltshire). More portraits are in London's **National Gallery** and **National Portrait Gallery** and in **Windsor Castle.**

- **Anton van Dyck (1599–1641).** This Belgian artist painted passels of portraits in the baroque style for the Stuart court, setting the tone for British portraiture for the next few centuries. You'll find his works in London's **National Portrait Gallery, National Gallery, Wallace Collection,** and **Wilton House,** with more in Oxford's **Ashmolean Museum** and Liverpool's **Walker Art Gallery.**

- **Joshua Reynolds (1723–92).** A fussy baroque painter and first president of the Royal Academy of Arts, Reynolds was a firm believer in a painter's duty to celebrate history. Reynolds spent much of his career casting his noble patrons as ancient gods in portrait compositions cribbed from Old Masters. Many of his works are in London's **National Gallery, Tate Britain, Wallace Collection,** and **Dulwich Picture Gallery;** Oxford's **Cathedral Hall;** Liverpool's **Walker Art Gallery;** and Birmingham's **Museum and Art Gallery** and **Barber Institute of Fine Arts.**

- **Thomas Gainsborough (1727–88).** Although he was a classical/baroque portraitist like his rival Reynolds, at least Gainsborough could be original. Too bad his tastes ran to rococo pastels, frothy feathered brushwork, and busy compositions. When not immortalizing noble patrons such as Jonathan Buttell (better known as "Blue Boy"), he painted a collection of landscapes just for himself. His works grace the **Victoria Art Gallery** in Bath (where he first came to fame), London's **National Gallery** and **National Portrait Gallery,** Cambridge's **Fitzwilliam Museum,** Oxford's **Cathedral Hall** and **Ashmolean Museum,** Liverpool's **Walker Art Gallery,** and Birmingham's **Museum and Art Gallery** and **Barber Institute of Fine Arts.**

THE ROMANTICS (LATE 18TH–19TH CENTURIES)

The romantics felt that the classically minded Renaissance and baroque artists had gotten it wrong; the Gothic Middle Ages was the place to be. They idealized the romantic tales of chivalry; had a deep respect for nature, human rights, and the nobility of peasantry; and were suspicious of progress. Their paintings tended to be heroic, historic, dramatic, and beautiful. They were inspired by critic and art theorist **John Ruskin** (1819–1900), who traveled throughout northern Italy and was among the first to sing the praises of pre-Renaissance painting and Gothic architecture.

Significant artists of this period include:

- **William Blake (1757–1827).** Romantic archetype, Blake snubbed the stuffy Royal Academy of Arts to do his own engraving, prints, illustrations, poetry, and painting. His works were filled with melodrama, muscular figures, and sweeping lines; modern, angst-ridden, "Goth" teens really dig his stuff. Judge for yourself at London's **Tate Britain** and Manchester's **Whitworth Art Gallery.**

- **John Constable (1776–1837).** Constable was a great British landscapist, whose scenes (especially those of happy, agricultural peasants) became more idealized with each passing year—while his compositions and brushwork became freer. You'll find his best works in London's **National Gallery** and **Victoria and Albert Museum,** and in Liverpool's **Walker Art Gallery.**

- **J. M. W. Turner (1775–1851).** Turner, called by some "The First Impressionist," was a prolific and multitalented artist whose mood-laden, freely brushed, watercolor landscapes influenced Monet. The River Thames and London, where he lived and died, were frequent subjects. He bequeathed his collection of some 19,000 watercolors and 300 paintings to the people of Britain with the request that they be kept in one place. London's **Tate Britain** displays the largest number of Turner's works, while others grace London's **National Gallery,** Cambridge's **Fitzwilliam Museum,** Liverpool's **Walker Art Gallery,** Birmingham's **Museum and Art Gallery** and **Barber Institute of Fine Arts,** and Manchester's **Whitworth Art Gallery.**

- **Pre-Raphaelites (1848–1870s).** This "brotherhood" of painters declared that art had gone all wrong with Italian Renaissance painter Raphael (1483–1520) and set about to emulate the Italian painters who preceded him—though they were not actually looking at specific examples. Their symbolically imbued, sweetly idealized, hyperrealistic work depicts scenes from romantic poetry and Shakespeare as much as from the Bible. There were seven founders and many followers, but the most important were Dante Rossetti, William Hunt, and John Millais; you can see work by all three at London's **Tate Britain,** Oxford's **Ashmolean Museum,** Liverpool's **Walker Art Gallery,** and Manchester's **City Art Gallery.**

THE 20TH CENTURY

The only artistic movement or era in which the Brits can claim a major stake is contemporary art, with many young British artists bursting onto the international gallery scene just before and after World War II. Art of the last century often followed international schools or styles—no major ones truly originated in Britain—and artists tended to move in and out of styles over their careers. If anything, the greatest artists of this period strove for unique and individual expression rather than adherence to a particular school.

In the examples below, a city name refers to the major modern art gallery in that location; "London" stands for the **Tate Modern,** "Birmingham" for the **Museum and Art Gallery,** and "Liverpool" for the **Walker Art Gallery.** Important British artists of the 20th century include:

- **Henry Moore (1898–1986).** A sculptor, Moore saw himself as a sort of reincarnation of Michelangelo. He mined his marbles from the same quarries as the Renaissance master and let the stone itself dictate the flowing, abstract, surrealistic figures carved from it. The **Henry Moore Institute** in Leeds, where he studied, preserves his drawings and sculpture. You'll also find his work in London, Liverpool, Birmingham, and Cambridge's **Fitzwilliam Museum** and **Clare College.**

- **Francis Bacon (1909–92).** A dark and brooding expressionist (a style that expresses an artist's inner thoughts and feelings), Bacon presented man's foibles in formats usually reserved for religious subjects(such as the triptych, a set of three panels, often hinged and used as an altarpiece). His works may be found in London, Birmingham, and Manchester's **Whitworth Art Gallery.**

- **Lucien Freud (b. 1922).** Freud's portraits and marvelous nudes live in a depressing world of thick paint, fluid lines, and harsh light. The grandson of psychiatrist Sigmund Freud, the artist has pieces in London, Liverpool, and Manchester's **Whitworth Art Gallery.**

- **David Hockney (b. 1937).** The closest thing to a British Andy Warhol, Hockney employs a less pop-arty style than the famous American—though Hockney does reference modern technologies and culture—and is much more playful with artistic traditions. His work resides in London and Liverpool.

- **Damien Hirst (b. 1965).** The guy who pickles cows, Hirst is a celebrity/artist whose work sets out to shock. He's a winner of Britain's Turner Prize, and his work is prominent in the collection of Charles Saatchi, whose Saatchi Gallery in London displays his holdings.

2 Architecture 101

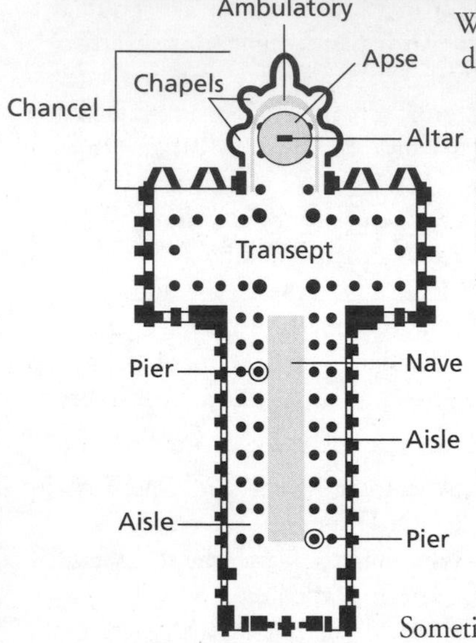

Church Floor Plan

While each architectural era has its distinctive features, there are some elements, floor plans, and terms common to many. This is particularly true of churches, large numbers of which were built in Europe from the Middle Ages through the 18th century.

From the Norman period on, most **churches** consist either of a single wide **aisle** or a wide central **nave** flanked by two narrower aisles. The aisles are separated from the nave by a row of **columns,** or square stacks of masonry called **piers,** connected by **arches.** Sometimes—especially in the medieval Norman and Gothic eras—there is a second level to the nave, above these arches (and hence above the low roof over the aisles) punctuated by windows called a **clerestory.**

This main nave/aisle assemblage is usually crossed by a perpendicular corridor called a **transept** near the far, east end of the church so that the floor plan looks like a **Latin Cross** (shaped like a crucifix). The shorter, east arm of the nave is called the **chancel;** it often houses the **altar** and stalls of the **choir.** Some churches use a **rood screen** (so called because it supports a *rood,* the Saxon word for *crucifixion*) to separate the nave from the chancel. If the far end of the chancel is rounded off, it is called an **apse.** An **ambulatory** is a curving corridor outside the altar and choir area, separating it from the ring of smaller chapels radiating off the chancel and apse.

Some churches, especially after the Renaissance when mathematical proportion became important, were built on a **Greek Cross** plan, with each axis the same length like a giant plus sign (+).

It's worth pointing out that very few buildings (especially churches) were built in only one particular style. Massive, expensive structures often took centuries to complete, during which time tastes would change and plans would be altered.

NORMAN (1066–1200)

Aside from a smattering of ancient sights—**pre-classical** stone circles as at Stonehenge and Avebury and **Roman** ruins such as the Bath spa and Hadrian's Wall—the oldest surviving architectural style in England dates to when the 1066 Norman Conquest brought the Romanesque era to Britain, where it flourished as the **Norman** style.

Churches in this style were large, with wide naves and aisles to accommodate the masses who came to hear Mass and worship at the altars of various saints. But to support the weight of all that masonry, the walls had to be thick and solid (meaning they could be pierced only by few and small windows) and rest on huge piers, giving Norman churches a dark, somber, mysterious, and often oppressive feeling.

IDENTIFIABLE FEATURES

- **Rounded arches.** These load-bearing architectural devices allowed the architects to open up wide naves and spaces, channeling all the weight of the stone walls and ceilings across the curves of the arches and down into the ground via the columns or pilasters.
- **Thick walls.**
- **Infrequent and small windows.**
- **Huge piers.** These load-bearing, vertical features resemble square stacks of masonry.
- **Chevrons.** These zigzagging decorations often surround a doorway or wrap around a column.

BEST EXAMPLES

- **White Tower, London (1078).** William the Conqueror's first building in Britain, White Tower is the central keep of the Tower of London. The fortress-thick walls and rounded archways are textbook Norman.

White Tower, London

- **Durham Cathedral (1093–1488).** The layout is Norman, save for the proto-Gothic, pointy rib vaulting along the nave. The massive piers are incised with chevrons.
- **Ely Cathedral (1083–1189).** The nave and south transept are perfectly Norman, though much of the rest of the interior is as Gothic as the exterior.

GOTHIC (1150–1550)

The French Gothic style invaded England in the late 12th century, trading rounded arches for pointy ones—an engineering discovery that freed church architecture from the heavy, thick walls of Norman structures and allowed ceilings to soar, walls to thin, and windows to proliferate.

Instead of dark, somber, relatively unadorned Norman interiors that forced the eyes of the faithful toward the altar where the priest stood droning on in unintelligible Latin, the Gothic interior enticed the churchgoers' gaze upward to high ceilings filled with light. While the priests conducted Mass in Latin, the peasants could "read" the Gothic comic books of stained-glass windows.

The squat, brooding exteriors of the Norman fortresses of God were replaced by graceful buttresses and soaring spires, which rose from town centers like beacons of religion.

The Gothic proper in Britain can be divided into three overlapping periods or styles: **Early English** (1150–1300), **Decorated** (1250–1370), and **Perpendicular** (1350–1550). While they all share some identifiable features (see the next section), others are characteristic of the individual periods.

Gothic style proved hard to kill in Britain. It would make comebacks in the 17th century as **Laudian Gothic** in some Oxford and Cambridge buildings, in the late 18th century as **rococo** or **Strawberry Hill Gotick** at Lacock Abbey, and in the 19th-century **Victorian Gothic Revival,** discussed later.

IDENTIFIABLE FEATURES

- **Pointed arches (all periods).** The most significant development of the Gothic era was the discovery that pointed arches could carry far more weight than rounded ones.
- **Cross vaults (all periods).** Instead of being flat, the square patch of ceiling between four columns arches up to a point in the center, creating four sail shapes, sort of like the underside of a pyramid. The "X" separating these four sails is often reinforced with ridges called **ribbing.** As the Gothic era progressed, four-sided

cross vaults became **fan vaults** (see below), and the spaces between the structural ribbing were spanned with decorative **tracery** (see below).

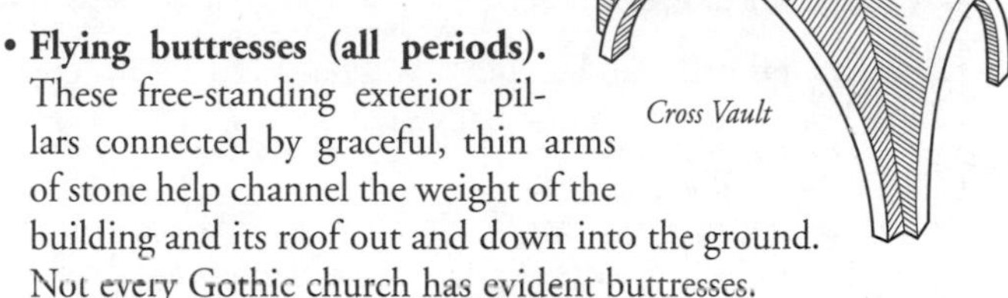

Cross Vault

- **Flying buttresses (all periods).** These free-standing exterior pillars connected by graceful, thin arms of stone help channel the weight of the building and its roof out and down into the ground. Not every Gothic church has evident buttresses.

- **Dogtooth molding (Early English).** Bands of a repeated decoration of four triangle-shaped petals are placed around a raised center.

- **Lancet windows (Early English).** Tall, thin, pointy windows, often in pairs or multiples, are all set into a larger, elliptical pointy arch.

- **Tracery (Decorated and Perpendicular).** These delicate, lacy spider webs of carved stone grace the pointy ends of windows and the acute lower intersections of **cross vaults** (see above).

- **Fan vaults (Perpendicular).** Lots of side-by-side, cone-shaped, concave vaults springing from the same point, fan vaults are usually covered in tracery (see above).

Fan Vault

- **An emphasis on horizontal and vertical lines (Perpendicular).** What defines the Perpendicular is its broad and rectilinear fashion, especially in the windows.

- **Mullioned, transomed windows (Perpendicular).** Perpendicular windows tend to be wide, under flattened arches, with their bulk divided into dozens of tiny pointed panes by **mullions** (vertical bars) and **transoms** (horizontal bars). This cage-like motif often carries over to the decoration on the walls as well.

- **Stained glass (all periods but more common later).** The multitude and size of Gothic windows allowed them to be filled with Bible stories and symbolism writ in the colorful patterns of stained glass. The use of stained glass was more common in the later Gothic periods.

- **Rose windows (all periods).** These huge circular windows, often appearing as the centerpieces of facades, are filled with elegant **tracery** (see above) and "petals" of stained glass.
- **Spires (all periods).** These pinnacles of masonry seem to defy gravity and reach toward heaven itself.
- **Gargoyles (all periods).** Disguised as wide-mouthed creatures or human heads, gargoyles are actually drain spouts.
- **Choir screen (all periods).** Serving as the inner wall of the ambulatory and outer wall of the choir section, the choir screen is often decorated with carvings or tombs.

BEST EXAMPLES

- **Early English: Salisbury Cathedral** (1220–65) is unique in Europe for the speed with which it was built and the uniformity of its architecture. (Even if the spire was added 100 years later, it was kept Early English.) The first to use pointy arches was **Wells Cathedral** (1180–1321), which has 300 statues on its original facade and some early stained glass.
- **Decorated:** The facade, nave, and chapter house of **York Minster** (1220–1480), which preserves the most medieval stained glass in Britain, are Decorated, though the chancel is Perpendicular and the transepts are Early English. **Exeter Cathedral** (1112–1206) has an elaborate Decorated facade and fantastic nave vaulting.
- **Perpendicular: King's College Chapel at Cambridge** (1446–1515) has England's most magnificent fan vaulting, along with some fine stained glass. **Henry VII's Chapel** (1503–19) in London's Westminster Abbey is textbook Perpendicular.

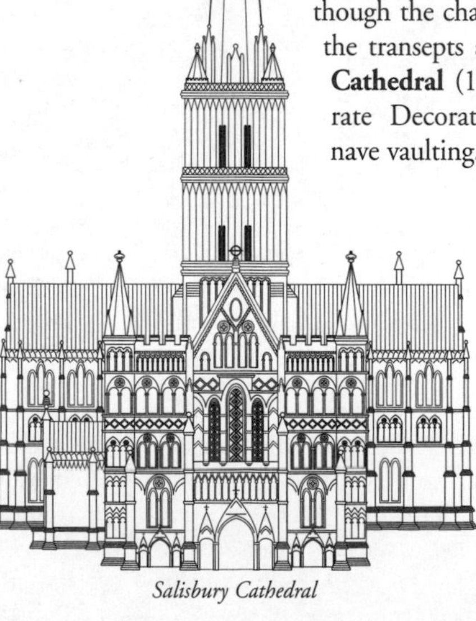
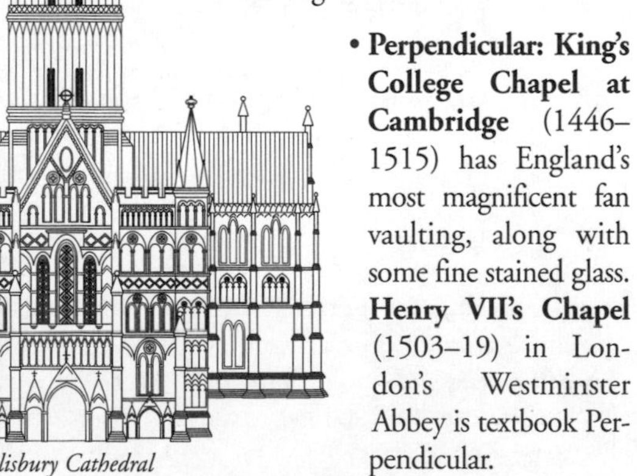

Salisbury Cathedral

RENAISSANCE (1550–1650)

While the Continent was experimenting with the Renaissance ideals of proportion, order, classical inspiration, and mathematical precision to create unified and balanced structures, England was still trundling along with the late **Tudor Gothic** Perpendicular style (the Tudor use of redbrick became a major feature of later Gothic revivals) in places such as Hampton Court Palace and Bath Abbey (great fan vaulting).

It wasn't until the Elizabethan era that the Brits turned to the **Renaissance** style sweeping the Continent. England's greatest Renaissance architect, **Inigo Jones** (1573–1652), brought back from his Italian travels a fevered imagination full of the exactingly classical theories of **Palladianism,** a style derived from the buildings and publications of **Andrea Palladio** (1508–80). However, most English architects of this time tempered the Renaissance style with a heavy dose of Gothic-like elements.

IDENTIFIABLE FEATURES

- **Sense of proportion.**
- **Reliance on symmetry.**
- **Use of classical orders.** This specifies three different column capitals: Corinthian, Ionic, and Doric.

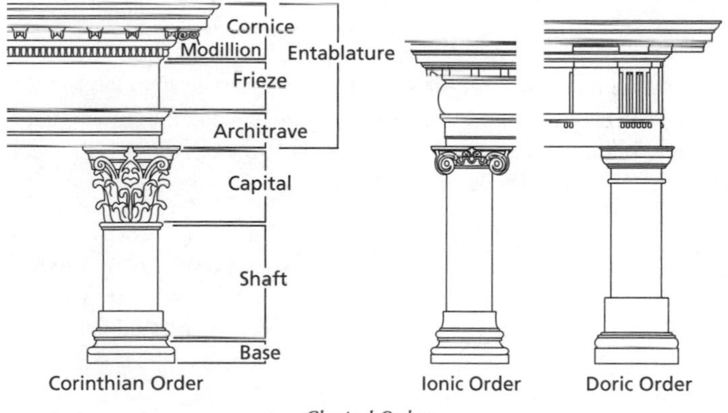

Classical Orders

BEST EXAMPLES

- **Robert Smythson (1535–1614).** This early Elizabethan architect was responsible for two of the greatest mansions of the period: **Hardwick Hall** (1590–97) in Derbyshire, virtually abandoned and therefore wonderfully preserved (if a bit dilapidated) in its

16th-century condition; and **Longleat House** (1559–80), an elegant Wiltshire manse with a park designed by Renaissance landscape architect and garden designer **Capability Brown.**

- **Inigo Jones (1573–1652).** Jones applied his theories of Palladianism to such edifices as **Queen's House** (1616–18 and 1629–35) in Greenwich; the **Queen's Chapel** (1623–25) in St. James's Palace and the **Banqueting House** (1619–22) in Whitehall, both in London; and the staterooms of Wiltshire's **Wilton House** (1603), where Shakespeare performed and D-Day was planned. Recently, London's **Shakespeare's Globe Theatre** dusted off one of his never-realized plans and used it to construct their new indoor theater annex.

BAROQUE (1650–1750)

England's greatest architect was **Christopher Wren** (1632–1723), a scientist and member of Parliament who got the job of rebuilding London after the Great Fire of 1666. He designed 53 replacement churches alone, plus the new St. Paul's Cathedral and numerous other projects. Other proponents of baroque architecture were **John Vanbrugh** (1664–1726) and his mentor and oft collaborator, **Nicholas Hawksmoor** (1661–1736), who sometimes worked in a more Palladian idiom.

IDENTIFIABLE FEATURES

- **Classical architecture rewritten with curves.** The baroque is similar to the Renaissance style, but many of the right angles and ruler-straight lines are exchanged for curves of complex geometry and an interplay of concave and convex surfaces. The overall effect is to lighten the appearance of structures and to add some movement of line.
- **Complex decoration.** Unlike the sometimes severe designs of the Renaissance and other classically inspired styles, the baroque was often playful and apt to festoon structures with decorations intended to liven things up.

BEST EXAMPLES

- **St. Paul's Cathedral, London (1676–1710).** This cathedral is the crowning achievement of both English baroque and of Christopher Wren himself. London's other main Wren attraction is the **Royal Naval College,** Greenwich (1696).

- **Queen's College, Sheldonian Theatre, and Radcliffe Camera, Oxford. Queen's College** is the only campus of Oxford constructed entirely in one style, and it includes a library by Hawksmoor. The **Sheldonian Theatre** (1664–69), an almost classically subdued rotunda showing little of later baroque exuberance, was Wren's first crack at architecture. Compare this to the more baroque **Radcliffe Camera** (1737–49), designed by James Gibbs (1662–1754), who influenced Thomas Jefferson.
- **Blenheim Palace, Woodstock (early 1700s).** John Vanbrugh's crowning achievement, Blenheim Palace is a British Versailles surrounded by perhaps the best of Capability Brown's gardens.
- **Castle Howard, Yorkshire (1699–1726).** Another masterpiece by the team of Nicholas Hawksmoor and then-neophyte John Vanbrugh, Castle Howard became famous as a backdrop to *Brideshead Revisited.*

NEOCLASSICAL & GREEK REVIVAL (1714–1837)

Many 18th-century architects cared little for the baroque period, and during the Georgian era (1714–1830) a restrained, simple **neoclassicism** reigned. It was balanced between a resurgence of the precepts of Palladianism (see "Renaissance" above) and an even more distilled vision of classical theory called **Greek revival.** This latter style was practiced by architects such as **James "Athenian" Stuart** (1713–88), who wrote a book on antiquities after a trip to Greece, and the somewhat less strict **John Soane** (1773–1837).

IDENTIFIABLE FEATURES

- **Mathematical proportion, symmetry, classical orders.** These classical ideals first rediscovered during the Renaissance are the hallmark of every classically styled era.
- **Crescents and circuses.** The Georgians were famous for these seamless curving rows of identical stone town houses with tall windows, each one simple yet elegant inside.
- **Open double-arm staircases.** This feature was a favorite of the neo-Palladians.

BEST EXAMPLES

- **Bath (1727–75).** Much of the city of Bath was made over in the 18th century, most famously by the father-and-son team of **John**

Royal Crescent, Bath

Woods, Sr. and Jr. (1704–54 and 1728–81, respectively). They were responsible, among others, for the **Royal Crescent** (1767–75), where you can visit one house's interior and even lodge in another.

- **John Soane's London sights.** The best Greek revival building by Soane in London is his own idiosyncratic house (1812–13), now **Sir John Soane's Museum.** Of his most famous commission, the **Bank of England** (1732–34) in Bartholomew Lane, only the facade survived a 20th-century restructuring.

- **British Museum, London (1823).** Not the most important example of Greek revival, the British Museum, by Robert and Sidney Smirke, is one that just about every visitor to England is bound to see.

VICTORIAN GOTHIC REVIVAL (1750–1900)

While neoclassicists were sticking to their guns in Bath, the early romantic movement swept up others with rosy visions of the past. This imaginary and fairy-tale version of the Middle Ages led to such creative developments as the pre-Raphaelite painters (see "The Romantics," earlier in this chapter) and Gothic revival architects, who really got a head of steam under their movement during the eclectic Victorian era.

Gothic "revival" is a bit misleading, as its practitioners usually applied their favorite Gothic features at random rather than faithfully re-created a whole structure. Aside from this eclecticism, you can separate the revivals from the originals by age (Victorian buildings are several hundred years younger and tend to be in considerably better shape) and size (the revivals are often much larger).

IDENTIFIABLE FEATURES

- **Mishmash of Gothic features.** Look at the features described under "Gothic," earlier in this chapter, and then imagine going on a shopping spree through them at random.

- **Eclecticism.** Few Victorians bothered with correctly rendering all the formal details of a particular Gothic era. They just wanted the overall effect to be pointy, busy with decorations, and terribly medieval.

- **Grand scale.** These buildings tend to be very, very large. This was usually accomplished by using Gothic style only on the surface, with newfangled industrial-age engineering underneath.

BEST EXAMPLES

- **Palace of Westminster (Houses of Parliament), London (1835–52).** Charles Barry (1795–1860) designed the wonderful British seat of government in a Gothic idiom that, more than most, sticks pretty faithfully to the old Perpendicular period's style. His clock tower, usually called "Big Ben" after its biggest bell, has become an icon of London itself.

Palace of Westminster, London

- **Albert Memorial, London (1863–72).** In 1861 Queen Victoria commissioned George Gilbert Scott (1811–78) to build this massive Gothic canopy to memorialize her beloved husband.
- **Natural History Museum, London (1873–81).** The Natural History Museum is a delightful marriage of imposing neo-Gothic clothing hiding an industrial-age steel-and-iron framework, courtesy of architect Alfred Waterhouse (1830–1905).

THE 20TH CENTURY

For the first half of the 20th century, England was too busy expanding into suburbs (in an architecturally uninteresting way) and fighting World Wars to pay much attention to architecture. After the Blitz during World War II, much of central London had to be rebuilt. Most of the new commercial buildings in the city held to a functional school of architecture aptly named Brutalism. It wasn't until the boom of the late 1970s and 1980s that **postmodern** architecture gave British architects a bold, new direction.

IDENTIFIABLE FEATURES

- **Skyscraper motif.** Glass and steel as high as you can stack it.
- **Reliance on historical details.** Like the Victorians, postmodernists recycled elements from architectural history, from classical to exotic.

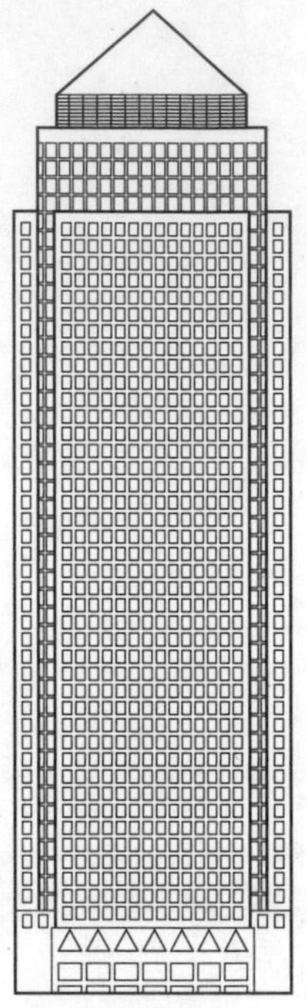

Canary Wharf Tower, London

BEST EXAMPLES

- **Lloyd's Building, London (1978–86).** Lloyd's is *the* British postmodern masterpiece by Richard Rogers (b. 1933), who had a hand in Paris's funky Centre Pompidou.
- **Canary Wharf Tower, London (1986).** Britain's tallest building, by César Pelli (b. 1926), is the postmodern centerpiece of the Canary Wharf office complex and commercial development.
- **Charing Cross, London (1991).** Whimsical designer Terry Farrell (b. 1938) capped the famous old train station with an enormous postmodern office-and-shopping complex in glass and pale stone.

Appendix C: Useful Toll-Free Numbers & Websites

AIRLINES

Aer Lingus
© 800/474-7424 in U.S.
© 01/886-8888 in Ireland
www.aerlingus.com

Air Canada
© 888/247-2262
www.aircanada.ca

Air France
© 800/237-2747 in U.S.
© 0820-820-820 in France
www.airfrance.com

Air New Zealand
© 800/262-1234 or -2468 in U.S.
© 800/663-5494 in Canada
© 0800/737-767 in New Zealand
www.airnewzealand.com

Alitalia
© 800/223-5730 in U.S.
© 8488-65641 in Italy
www.alitalia.it

American Airlines
✆ 800/433-7300
www.aa.com

BMI
No U.S. number
www.flybmi.com

British Airways
✆ 800/247-9297
✆ 0345/222-111 or 0845/77-333-77 in Britain
www.british-airways.com

Continental Airlines
✆ 800/525-0280
www.continental.com

Delta Air Lines
✆ 800/221-1212
www.delta.com

Easyjet
No U.S. number
www.easyjet.com

Iberia
✆ 800/772-4642 in U.S.
✆ 902/400-500 in Spain
www.iberia.com

KLM
✆ 800/374-7747 in U.S.
✆ 020/4-747-747 in Netherlands
www.klm.nl

Lufthansa
✆ 800/645-3880 in U.S.
✆ 49/(0)-180-5-8384267 in Germany
www.lufthansa.com

Northwest Airlines
✆ 800/225-2525
www.nwa.com

Olympic Airways
✆ 800/223-1226 in U.S.
✆ 80/111-44444 in Greece
www.olympic-airways.gr

Qantas
✆ 800/227-4500 in U.S.
✆ 612/9691-3636 in Australia
www.qantas.com

Ryanair
No U.S. number
www.ryanair.com

Scandinavian Airlines
✆ 800/221-2350 in U.S.
✆ 0070/727-727 in Sweden
✆ 70/10-20-00 in Denmark
✆ 358/(0)20-386-000 in Finland
✆ 815/200-400 in Norway
www.scandinavian.net

Swiss International Airlines
✆ 877/359-7947 in U.S.
✆ 0848/85-2000 in Switzerland
www.swiss.com

Turkish Airlines
✆ 800/874-8875 in U.S.; 212/339-9650 in New York, New Jersey, and Connecticut
✆ 90-212-663-63-00 in Turkey
www.flyturkish.com

United Airlines
✆ 800/241-6522
www.united.com

US Airways
✆ 800/428-4322
www.usairways.com

Virgin Atlantic Airways
✆ 800/862-8621 in continental U.S.
✆ 0293/747-747 in Britain
www.virgin-atlantic.com

CAR RENTAL AGENCIES

Alamo
© 800/327-9633
www.goalamo.com

Auto Europe
© 800/223-5555
www.autoeurope.com

Avis
© 800/331-1212 in continental U.S.
© 800/TRY-AVIS in Canada
www.avis.com

Budget
© 800/527-0700
www.budget.com

Hertz
© 800/654-3131
www.hertz.com

Kemwel Holiday Auto (KHA)
© 800/678-0678
www.kemwel.com

National
© 800/CAR-RENT
www.nationalcar.com

Sixt
No U.S. number
www.sixt-europe.com

Index

See also Accommodations and Restaurant indexes, below.

General Index

Accommodations

Restaurants

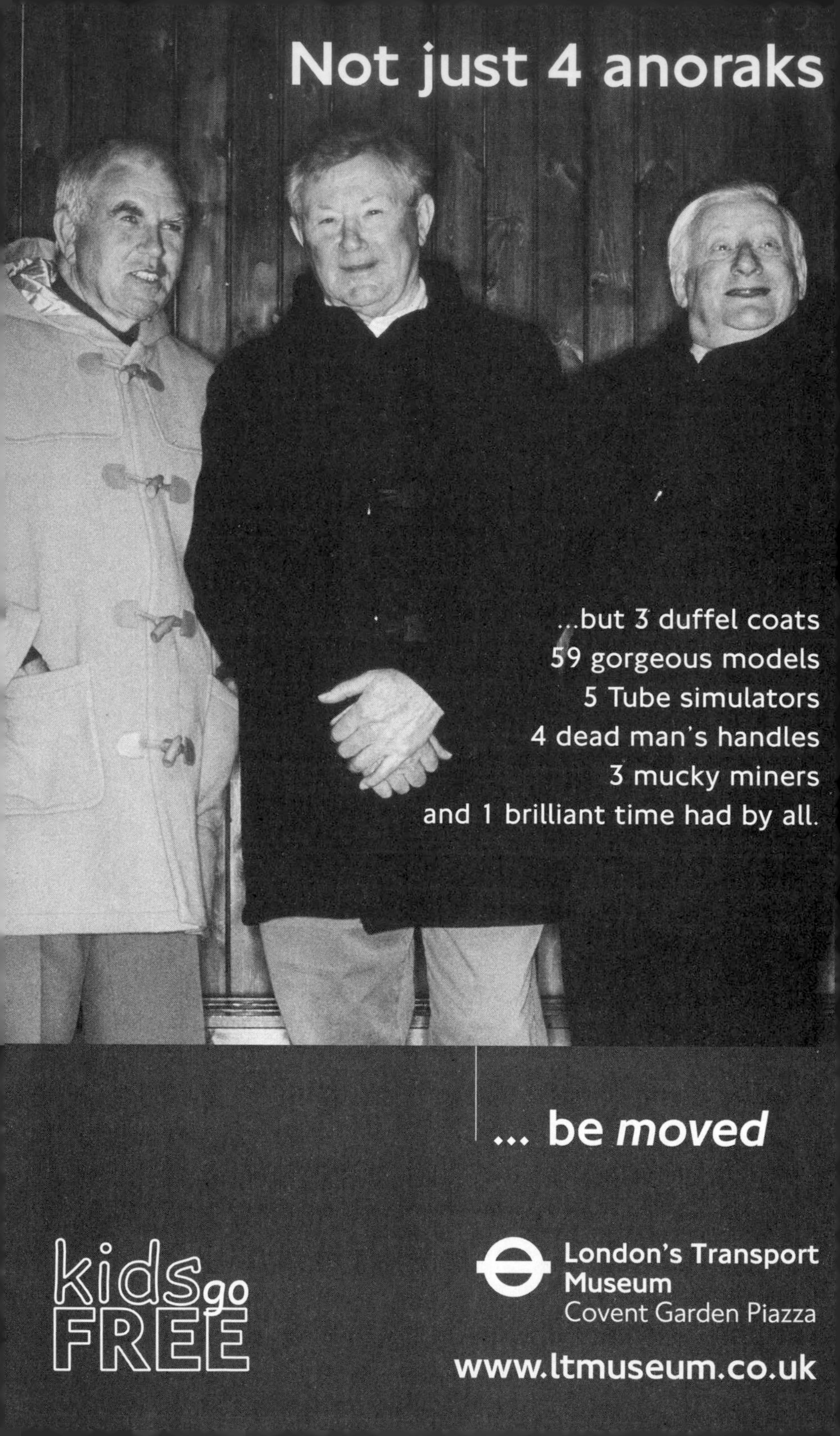

Frommer's® Complete Travel Guides

Alaska
Alaska Cruises & Ports of Call
Amsterdam
Argentina & Chile
Arizona
Atlanta
Australia
Austria
Bahamas
Barcelona, Madrid & Seville
Beijing
Belgium, Holland & Luxembourg
Bermuda
Boston
Brazil
British Columbia & the Canadian Rockies
Brussels & Bruges
Budapest & the Best of Hungary
California
Canada
Cancún, Cozumel & the Yucatán
Cape Cod, Nantucket & Martha's Vineyard
Caribbean
Caribbean Cruises & Ports of Call
Caribbean Ports of Call
Carolinas & Georgia
Chicago
China
Colorado
Costa Rica
Cuba
Denmark
Denver, Boulder & Colorado Springs
England
Europe
European Cruises & Ports of Call
Florida
France
Germany
Great Britain
Greece
Greek Islands
Hawaii
Hong Kong
Honolulu, Waikiki & Oahu
Ireland
Israel
Italy
Jamaica
Japan
Las Vegas
London
Los Angeles
Maryland & Delaware
Maui
Mexico
Montana & Wyoming
Montréal & Québec City
Munich & the Bavarian Alps
Nashville & Memphis
New England
New Mexico
New Orleans
New York City
New Zealand
Northern Italy
Norway
Nova Scotia, New Brunswick & Prince Edward Island
Oregon
Paris
Peru
Philadelphia & the Amish Country
Portugal
Prague & the Best of the Czech Republic
Provence & the Riviera
Puerto Rico
Rome
San Antonio & Austin
San Diego
San Francisco
Santa Fe, Taos & Albuquerque
Scandinavia
Scotland
Seattle & Portland
Shanghai
Sicily
Singapore & Malaysia
South Africa
South America
South Florida
South Pacific
Southeast Asia
Spain
Sweden
Switzerland
Texas
Thailand
Tokyo
Toronto
Tuscany & Umbria
USA
Utah
Vancouver & Victoria
Vermont, New Hampshire & Maine
Vienna & the Danube Valley
Virgin Islands
Virginia
Walt Disney World® & Orlando
Washington, D.C.
Washington State

Frommer's® Dollar-a-Day Guides

Australia from $50 a Day
California from $70 a Day
England from $75 a Day
Europe from $70 a Day
Florida from $70 a Day
Hawaii from $80 a Day
Ireland from $60 a Day
Italy from $70 a Day
London from $85 a Day
New York from $90 a Day
Paris from $80 a Day
San Francisco from $70 a Day
Washington, D.C. from $80 a Day
Portable London from $85 a Day
Portable New York City from $90 a Day

Frommer's® Portable Guides

Acapulco, Ixtapa & Zihuatanejo
Amsterdam
Aruba
Australia's Great Barrier Reef
Bahamas
Berlin
Big Island of Hawaii
Boston
California Wine Country
Cancún
Cayman Islands
Charleston
Chicago
Disneyland®
Dublin
Florence
Frankfurt
Hong Kong
Houston
Las Vegas
Las Vegas for Non-Gamblers
London
Los Angeles
Los Cabos & Baja
Maine Coast
Maui
Miami
Nantucket & Martha's Vineyard
New Orleans
New York City
Paris
Phoenix & Scottsdale
Portland
Puerto Rico
Puerto Vallarta, Manzanillo & Guadalajara
Rio de Janeiro
San Diego
San Francisco
Savannah
Seattle
Sydney
Tampa & St. Petersburg
Vancouver
Venice
Virgin Islands
Washington, D.C.

Frommer's® National Park Guides

Banff & Jasper
Family Vacations in the National Parks
Grand Canyon
National Parks of the American West
Rocky Mountain
Yellowstone & Grand Teton
Yosemite & Sequoia/Kings Canyon
Zion & Bryce Canyon

Frommer's® Memorable Walks

Chicago
London
New York
Paris
San Francisco

Frommer's® With Kids Guides

Chicago
Las Vegas
New York City
Ottawa
San Francisco
Toronto
Vancouver
Washington, D.C.

Suzy Gershman's Born to Shop Guides

Born to Shop: France
Born to Shop: Hong Kong, Shanghai & Beijing
Born to Shop: Italy
Born to Shop: London
Born to Shop: New York
Born to Shop: Paris

Frommer's® Irreverent Guides

Amsterdam
Boston
Chicago
Las Vegas
London
Los Angeles
Manhattan
New Orleans
Paris
Rome
San Francisco
Seattle & Portland
Vancouver
Walt Disney World®
Washington, D.C.

Frommer's® Best-Loved Driving Tours

Britain
California
Florida
France
Germany
Ireland
Italy
New England
Northern Italy
Scotland
Spain
Tuscany & Umbria

Hanging Out™ Guides

Hanging Out in England
Hanging Out in Europe
Hanging Out in France
Hanging Out in Ireland
Hanging Out in Italy
Hanging Out in Spain

The Unofficial Guides®

Bed & Breakfasts and Country Inns in:
- California
- Great Lakes States
- Mid-Atlantic
- New England
- Northwest
- Rockies
- Southeast
- Southwest

Best RV & Tent Campgrounds in:
- California & the West
- Florida & the Southeast
- Great Lakes States
- Mid-Atlantic
- Northeast
- Northwest & Central Plains
- Southwest & South Central Plains
- U.S.A.

Beyond Disney
Branson, Missouri
California with Kids
Central Italy
Chicago
Cruises
Disneyland®
Florida with Kids
Golf Vacations in the Eastern U.S.
Great Smoky & Blue Ridge Region
Inside Disney
Hawaii
Las Vegas
London
Maui
Mexio's Best Beach Resorts
Mid-Atlantic with Kids
Mini Las Vegas
Mini-Mickey
New England & New York with Kids
New Orleans
New York City
Paris
San Francisco
Skiing & Snowboarding in the West
Southeast with Kids
Walt Disney World®
Walt Disney World® for Grown-ups
Walt Disney World® with Kids
Washington, D.C.
World's Best Diving Vacations

Special-Interest Titles

Frommer's Adventure Guide to Australia & New Zealand
Frommer's Adventure Guide to Central America
Frommer's Adventure Guide to India & Pakistan
Frommer's Adventure Guide to South America
Frommer's Adventure Guide to Southeast Asia
Frommer's Adventure Guide to Southern Africa
Frommer's Britain's Best Bed & Breakfasts and Country Inns
Frommer's Caribbean Hideaways
Frommer's Exploring America by RV
Frommer's Fly Safe, Fly Smart
Frommer's France's Best Bed & Breakfasts and Country Inns
Frommer's Gay & Lesbian Europe
Frommer's Italy's Best Bed & Breakfasts and Country Inns
Frommer's Road Atlas Britain
Frommer's Road Atlas Europe
Frommer's Road Atlas France
The New York Times' Guide to Unforgettable Weekends
Places Rated Almanac
Retirement Places Rated
Rome Past & Present